Vital Statistics from Chittenango, New York Newspapers 1831–1854

PREPARED BY

Clara Metcalf Houck
HISTORIAN OF THE TOWN OF SULLIVAN,
MADISON COUNTY, NEW YORK

ASSISTED BY

RUTH MARSHALL, EVELYN PANEBIANCO,
AND
ANNE LENNOX, SULLIVAN TOWN CLERK

HERITAGE BOOKS
2020

HERITAGE BOOKS
AN IMPRINT OF HERITAGE BOOKS, INC.

Books, CDs, and more—Worldwide

For our listing of thousands of titles see our website
at
www.HeritageBooks.com

Published 2020 by
HERITAGE BOOKS, INC.
Publishing Division
5810 Ruatan Street
Berwyn Heights, Md. 20740

International Standard Book Number
Paperbound: 978-1-58549-830-7

TABLE OF CONTENTS

PREFACE

The first newspaper in Chittenango, NY, was the *Chittenango Herald* published by Isaac Lyon every Tuesday beginning March 1, 1831. It was composed of four sheets with most local items appearing in the center columns of pages two and three.

Beginning February 24, 1836, the paper was published on Wednesdays and continued publication until June 24, 1844. There may have been further publicaiton of the *Herald*, as in 1855, the *Madison Observer* which was published in Morrisville, reported that the editor, Mr. S. James Cobb had married.

The *Madison Democrat*, a "Free Soil" publication, was published for a brief period, 1846 and 1847. The editor was one Adam Sandford.

On December 13, 1848, Volume 1, No. 1 of the Chittenango Phenix commenced publication with J. P. Olmstead as editor and publisher. It continued through March 5, 1853.

The first edition of the *Democratic Gazette* appeared March 26, 1853. It was printed and published every Saturday by Walrath and Greenhow with its office opposite "Parry's Hotel" at a charge of $1.25 per year. On May 7, 1853 Greenhow turned sole publication over to George W. Walrath. After December 1853 it was published under the name *Chittenango Gazette*, and ceased publication with the January 7, 1854 edition.

The following newspapers have been abstracted for this compilation: *The Chittenango Herald*, *The Chittenango Republican*, *The Madison Democrat*, *Chittenango Phenix*, *Democratic Gazette*, and *The Chittenango Gazette*.

Microfilm copies of these newspapers are available at the Chittenango Station Middle School as well as the Town Historian at the Town of Sullivan offices in Chittenango Station, NY.

Clara Metcalf Houck

INTRODUCTION

The reader should keep in mind some of the peculiarities both in law and land divisions in New York State.

There are no "townships" in New York State as there are in states such as Pennsylvania, Ohio, Indiana, etc. The sub-divisions of counties in New York are called "towns" - never "townships" although they are much the same.

Also in New York there is yet another land sub-division which is a "village." Villages are generally incorporated entities with definitive borders and lie within the "town". Cities are of course only larger villages and are generally chartered by the state.

There are also "settlements" which are clusters of houses perhaps with a small grocery store and a watering trough. In years past many of these small settlements had a post office and perhaps a church. They were stopping places for the the traveller by horse and wagon to refresh himself. But now the high speed, mobile transportation methods, have bi-passed the little country store and the watering trough. And the little post office has been abolished in the process of centralization.

In using the records presented her, it is well for the reader to bear in mind that it was not until the close of the 19th century that New York required marriage licenses or recordation of births and deaths except for a few years in the 1840's. These latter records - if they exit - are generally located in the Town Clerk's Offices.

New York State also allowed marriages to be performed by Justice's of the Peace as well as ordained ministers/priests. The former are usually referred to in newspapers accounts as "Esquire" or abbreviataed as "Esq." However, not all "Esquires" were Justices of the Peace. Many were lawyers or highly respected members of a community

In using these newspaper abstracts, one may well be amazed by the numerous marriages between parties from different towns and from different counties inasmuch as transportation certainly was not what it is at the close of this twentieth century. I have concluded that many of these young people met one another through church functions or were introduced through correspondence with relatives. It was also rather common for young people to attend boarding schools some distance from there homes. One such notable school was the Cazenovia Seminary located in Cazenovia, NY.

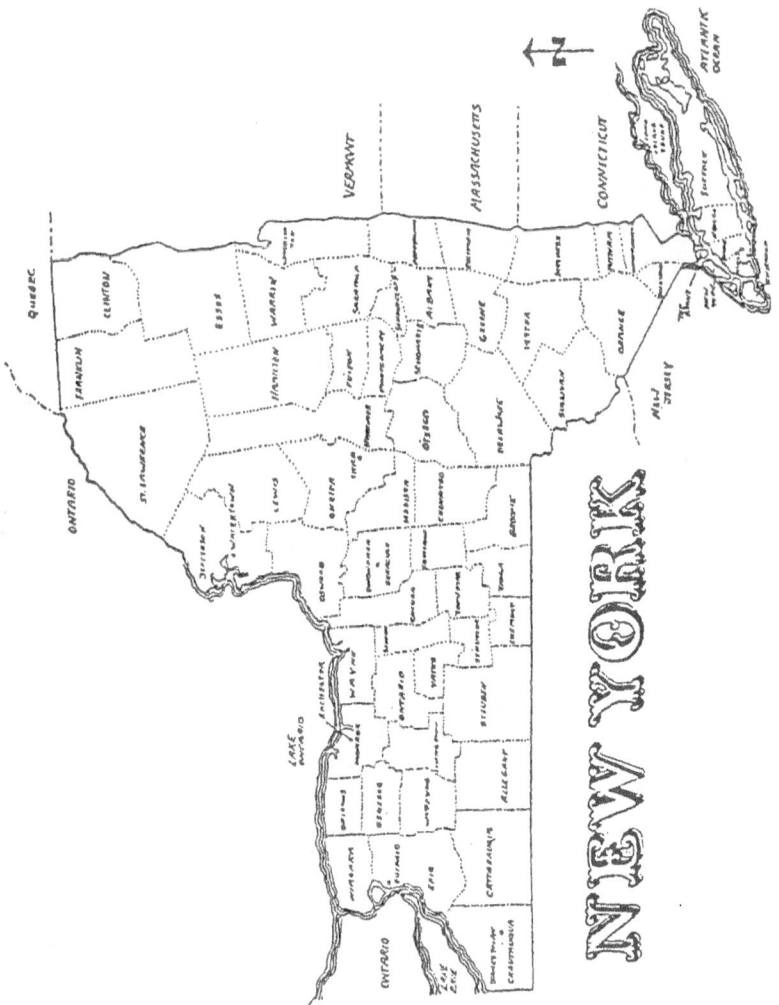

NEW YORK

GEOGRAPHICAL LOCATOR INDEX

Abbreviations: c = city; v. = village; co. = county; l= location, h.= hamlet; s. settlement; p.o = post office.

9

Clinton ....v. in t. of Kirkland, Oneida Co., NY
Clockville ....v. in town of Lenox, Madison Co., NY
Clyde......................v. in t. of Galen, Wayne Co., NY
Cohoes Falls................v. in Albany Co., NY
Conklin....................s. & t. in Broome Co., NY
Corning ....v. & t. in Stueben Co., NY
Cortland ....c. & c. seat of Cortland Co., NY
DeKalb ....v. & t. in St.Lawrence Co., NY
Delphi.....................v. in t. of Pompey, Onondaga Co., NY
Delta......................v. in Oneida Co., NY
Dryden ....v. & t. in Tompkins Co., NY
Durhamville................v. in t. of Lenox, Madison Co., NY
Eagle Village..............s. in t. of Manlius, Onondaga Co., NY
Earlville ....v. in t. of Hamilton, Madison Co, NY on the Chenango Co.
                           line.
East Avon ....v. in t. of Avon, Livingston Co., NY
East Hamilton ....s. in t. of Hamilton, Madison Co., NY
Eaton......................v. and t. in Madison Co., NY; sometimes called "Log City."
Eaton Centre...............same as a bove.
Edwardsville...............v. in t. of Morristown, St. Lawrence Co., NY
Elmira.....................c. in Chenango Co., NY
Fabius.....................v. and t. in Onondaga Co., NY
Fairfield ....v. & t. in Herkimer Co., NY
Fayetteville ....v.in t. of Manlius, Onondaga Co. NYorignally called orginally
                           called Manlius Square.
Fenner ....s. & t. in Madison Co., NY
Fenner Hill................l. in t. of Fenner. See above.
Flatbush...................v. & t. in Kings Co., NY
Fleming ....v. & t. in Cayuga Co., NY
Frankfort ....v. & t. in Herkimer Co., NY
Ft.Plain...................v. in t. of Minden, Montgomery Co., NY
Fulton.....................c. in t. of Volney Oswego Co., NY
Fyler's Settlement ....s. in t. of Sullivan, Madison Co., NY
Geneva.....................c. in t. of Seneca, Ontario Co., NY
Georgetown.................v. & t. in Madison Co., NY
Governeur ....v. & t. in St. Lawrence Co., NY
Granby ....t. in Oswego Co., NY
Granville...................v. & t. in Washington Co., NY
Greenbush..................v. & t. in Rensselear CoNY
Greene.....................v. & t. in Chenango Co., NY
Hamilton ....v. & t. in Madison Co., NY
Hanford's Landing..........s. in t. of Greece, Monroe Co., NY.
Hannibal ....v. & t. in Oswego Co., NY
Hartsville..................h. in t. of Manlius, Onondaga Co., NY
Haverstraw.................v. in Rockland Co., NY
Henrietta ....v. & t. in Monroe Co., NY
Herkimer ....v. & t. in Herkimer Co. NY

Hillsdale ....v. & t. in Columbia Co., NY
Holland Patent.............v. in t. of Trenton, Oneida Co., NY
Homer ....v. & t. in Cortland Co., NY
Ithaca ....c. in Tompkins CoNY
Jacksonville ....s. in t. of Lysander, Onondaga Co., NY
Jamesville ....v. in t. of Dewitt, Onondaga Co., NY
Jefferson....................v. in t. of Coxackie, Greene Co, NY ...also v. in t. in Schoharie
                              Co., NY
Jersey City................... c. in NJ
Johnstown.................Montgomery Co., NY (probably an error); a v. & t. in Fulton
                              Co., NY; also a s. in t. of Livingston, Columbia Co., NY
Jordan ....v. in t. of Elbridge, Onondaga Co., NY
Kinderhook ....v. & t. in Columbia, Co., NY
Kingsbury...................v. & t. in Washington Co., NY
Kingston......................v. & t. in Ulster Co., NY
Kirkland ....v. & t. in Oneida, Co., NY
Kirkville......................v. in t. of Manlius, Onondaga Co., NY
Knoxville....................s. in t. of Stockbridge, Madison Co., NY
L. I ....Long Island
Lafargeville ....v. in t. of Orleans, Jefferson Co., NY
Lakeport....................s. in t. of Sullivan, Madison Co., NY
Lansingburgh ....v. & t. in Rensselaer Co., NY
Lebanon ....v. & t. in Madison Co., NY
Lee ....v. & t. in Oneida Co. NY
Lee ....Onondaga Co., NY (this is an error). See above.
Lee Center..................v. in t. of Lee, Oneida Co., NY
Lenox.........................t. in Madison Co., NY
Lenox Furnace ....h. in t. of Lenox, Madison Co., NY
Lenox Hill ....l. in t. of Lenox, Madison Co., NY
Leonardsville...............v. in t. of Brookfield, Madison Co. NY
Leroy..........................v. & t. in Genesee Co. NY
Little Falls ....v. & t. in Herkimer Co., NY
Livingston ....t. in Columbia Co., NY
Madison ....t. & v. in Madison Co., NY
Manheim ....t. in Herkimer Co., NY
Manlius ....v. & t. in Onondaga Co., NY
Manlius Center.............s. in t. of Manlius, Onondaga Co., NY
Manlius Centre.............same as above
Manlius Square ....now Fayetteville, NYq.v.
Marshall ....t. in Oneida Co., NY
Matthew's Mills............s. in t. of Manlius, Onondaga Co., NY
McGrawville ....v. in t. of Cortlandville, Cortland Co., NY; also s. in Allegany
                              Co. NY
Mechanicville ....s. in t. of Sangerfield, Oneida Co., NY
Mentz..........................t. in Cayuga Co., NY
Milan..........................v. in t. of Locke, Cayuga Co. NY
Mobile.........................c. In AL

11

Montezuma...............s. in v. & t. in Cayuga Co.,NY
Morris......................t. in Otsego Co., NY
Morrisville...............v. in t. of Eaton, Madison Co., NY
Munnsville...............v. in t. of Stockbridge, Madison Co., NY
Nelson......................s. in t. of Nelson, Madison Co., NY
New Bedford.............prob. v. in MA
New Boston...............s. in t. of Sullivan, Madison Co., NY
New Hamburgh...........v. in t. of Poughkeepsie, Dutchess Co., NY
New Hartford.............t. & v. in Oneida Co., NY
New Haven................t. & v. in Oswego Co., NY
New Orleans..............c. in LA
New South Berlin......... v. in t. of South Berlin, Chenango Co., NY
New Woodstock.........v. in t. of Cazenovia, Madison Co., NY
New York.................largest c. in New York State
Newark....................t. & v. in Tioga Co., NY
Norwalk...................c. in Huron Co., OH
Norwich...................Oneida Co; this is an error; it is a t. & v. in Chenango Co., NY
Oneida Castle.............. v. in t. of Vernon, Oneida Co., NY
Oneida Depot.............now Oneida; v. in Madsion Co., NY
Oneida Lake..............h. in t. of Lenox, Madison Co., NY
Oneida Valley.............formerly called State Bridge, s. in town of Lenox, Madison Co.
Onondaga..................v. & t. in Onondaga Co., NY
Onondaga Hollow........l. in t. of Onondaga, Onondaga Co., NY
Oppenheim................v. & t. in Montgomery Co., NY
Oriskany Falls.............v. in t. of Augusta, Oneida Co., NY
Orville ....s. in t. of DeWitt, Onondaga Co.,NY; sometimes called Orville
                         Flat.
Oswego...................c. and t. of same name in Oswego Co., NY
Otego ....v. & t. in Otsego Co., NY
Otisco....................v. & t. in Onondaga Co., NY
Otselic ....v & t. in Chenango Co., NY
Owego ....v. & t. in Tioga Co., NY
Oxford...................v. & t. in Chenango Co., NY
Paris ....t. in Oneida Co., NY
Perryville................v. in t. of Fenner, Madison Co., NY
Peru.......................s. in t. of Elbridge, Onondaga Co., NY
Peterboro ....v. in t. of Smithfield, Madison Co., NY
Phoenix ....v. in t. of Schroeppel, Oswego Co., NY
Pittsfield ....v. & t. in Otsego Co., NY
Plainfield..................t. in Otsego Co., NY
Plattsburg.................v. & t. in Clinton Co., NY
Pompey....................v. & t. in Onondago Co., NY
Pompey Hill ....l. in t. of Pompey, Onondaga Co., NY
Portchester................v. in t. of Rye, Westchester Co., NY
Pouentine ....Probably a misprint for Palatine. q.v.
Pratts Hollow.............v. in t. of Eaton, Madison Co., NY
Pulaski....................v. in t. of Richland, Oswego Co., NY

Quality Hill.................l. in t. of Lenox, Madison Co., NY
Rensselaerville.............v. & t. in Albany Co., NY
Richland ....v. & t. in Oswego Co., NY
Rochester ....c. & co. seat of Monroe Co., NY
Rockton ....one time name of v. of Little Falls in t. of same name, Herkimer
                            Co., NY
Rome..........................c. & t. in Oneida Co., NY
Salina.........................v. in t. of same name, now within city limits of Syracuse,
                            Onondaga Co., NY
Salisbury.....................t. in Herkimer Co., NY
Sandy Creek................t. and v. in Oswego Co., NY - Oswego Co.,NY
Sangerfield ....v. & t. in Oneida Co., NY
Schenectady................c. and co. in NY State.
Schoharie ....v., t. & co. in New York State-
Schroeppel ....t. in Oswego Co., NY
Scott..........................v. & t. in Cortland Co. NY
Sempronius ....t. and p.o. in Cayuga Co., NY
Siloam ....s. in town of Smithfield, Madison Co., NY
Sing Sing....................v. in t. of Ossining, Westchester Co., NY; l. of infamous prison
                            of same name.
Skaneateles................. v. & t. in Onondaga Co., NY
Smithfield ....v. & t. in Madison Co., NY.
Solon..........................v. & t. in Cortland Co., NY
South New Berlin.........v. in t. of New Berlin, Chenango Co., NY
St.Johnsville ....v. & t. in Montgomery Co., NY
Stanford ....t. in Dutchess Co., NY
Stockbridge.................p. o. & t in Madison Co., NY
Stockbridge Hill ....l. in t. of Stockbridge, Madison Co.,NY
Stuyvesant...................p.o. & t. in Columbia Co., NY
Sullivan ....s. & t. in Madison Co., NY; s. also called Canaseraga
Sweden ....t. in Monroe Co., NY
Syracuse.....................c. and co. seat of Onondaga Co., NY
Troy ....c. in Rensselaer Co., NY
U.C ....Upper Canada
Union ....s. south of Cazenovia, Madison Co., NY
Union Village ....v. in t. of Greenwich, Washington Co., NY
Utica...........................c. in Oneida Co., NY
Van Buren...................v. & t. in Onondaga Co., NY
Vernon ....v. & t. in Oneida Co., NY
Verona ....v. & t. in Oneida Co., NY
Volney........................v. & t. in Oswego Co., NY
Walworth ....v. & t. in Wayne Co., NY
Wampsville..................v. in t. of Lenox & Madison Co. seat (NY)
Washington.................v. & t. in Dutchess Co., NY; also a co. in NY
Waterloo ....v. & t. in Seneca Co., NY
Watertown ....c. in Jefferson Co., NY
Watervliet....................v. & t. in Albany Co. NY

Westmoreland ....v. & t. in Oneida Co., NY
Wheeler.......................v. & t. in Stueben Co., NY
White Springs...............l. just s. of village of Chittenango in t. of Sullivan, Madison
                 Co., NY.
White Sulphur Springs. same as above - once site of noted health "spa".
Whitesboro..................v. in t. of Whitestown, Oneida Co., NY
Wolcott ....v. & t. in Wayne Co., NY
Woodstock.................in this instance probably New Woodstock q.v., as it was often
                 referred to only as "Woodstock."
Yates...........................v. & t. in Orleans Co. NY
Yates...........................Monroe Co. NY. This is an error. See above.
Yates...........................Co. in NY

** N. B.: Locations of the above places were taken from J. H. French, *Gazetteer of the State of New York*, 1860. Many of these small villages and settlements are not to be found on present day area maps and many no longer have post offices but are still known to "Old Timer" residents.

ABBREVIATIONS

ae	aged
A. M.	
c.	circa
CH	Chittenango Herald
CP.	Chittenango Phenix
c.	city
co.	county
d.	died
dau.	daughter
D. D.	Doctor of Divinity
DG	Democratic Gazette
Esq.	Esquire
Ft.	Fort
inst.	instant (this month)
Jun.	Junior
M. D.	Doctor of Medecine
mo(s)	month (s)
Rev.	Reverend
t.	town
U. C.	Upper Canada
ult.	ultimo (last month)
v.	village
W.C.	Western Canada
yr(s)	year(s)

Modern Post Office abbreviations used for the various states.

CHITTENANGO HERALD

CH - March 8, 1831. Married: At Smithfield, on the 1st inst., by Rev. Mr. Smith, Mr. Joseph Clary, of this village to Miss Louise Mallory, of the former place.

CH - March 22, 1931. Died: In this town, on Thursday night last, Mr. John Eickhart, in the 51st year of his age. (From Holland)

CH - April 5, 1831. Married: On the evening of the 3rd inst., by Rev. A. Yates, D. D., Mr. Amos F. Patrick, of Ohio, to Miss Jane E. Wells, of this town.

CH - April 5, 1831. Married: At Fenner, on Wednesday, the 30th ult., by Elder Samuel Gilbert, Mr. Albert Cole, Gospel Minister, of _____ Connecticut, to Miss Louisa M. Woodworth, of the above named town.

CH - May 10, 1831. Died: In this town on the 26th ult., Mrs. Dewitt, widow of the late John Dewitt.

CH - May 17, 1831. Married: At Lima, Livingston Co., on the 5th inst., by the Rev. Mr. Barnard, H. G. Warner,Esq., of this village, to Miss Sarah, dau. of Maj. Asahel Warner of the former place.

CH - May 17, 1831. Married: On Tuesday morning last, by the Rev. Dr. Yates, Mr. William W. Willard, to Miss Sarah Stokes, all of this village.

CH - May 17, 1831. Married: On the 5th inst., by the Rev. Mr. Pearce, Mr. Harry Benson, of this village, to Mrs. Deborah Manchester, of Madison.

CH - May 17, 1831. Married: On the 3rd inst., by J. French Esq., Mr. Peter Brower, to Miss Margaret M'Bride, all of this town.

CH - May 24, 1831. Married: On Sun. last, at [New] Woodstock, Mr. Sylvanus S. Haws to Miss Louisa Hunt, both of this village.

CH - May 24, 1831. Married: At Albany, on the 12th inst., by the Rev. Dr. Sprague, Mr. Eli Wellington, printer, to Miss Almira McCullen, both of Troy.

CH - May 31, 1831. Married: On Wednesday evening last, by Rev. A. Yates, D. D., Col. Albert T. Dunham, merchant of the firm of Parmalee & Dunham, to Elvira Ann, daughter of Col. Hezekiah Sage, all of this town.

CH - May 31, 1831. Married: On Thurs. evening last, at Pompey by Rev. Mr. Stockton, Mr. Geradus Clute, to Miss Mary Ann, daughter of Mr. Samuel Dunham, all of above place.

CH - May 31, 1831. Married: At Rensselaerville, on the 25th inst., by the Rev. Mr. Fuller, Mr. C. G. Palmer, senior editor of the *Schenectady Whig*, to Miss Clarine Amelia, daughter of Asa Colvard, Esq. of the former place.

CH - June 7, 1831. Married: At Canaseraga on Sunday, the 5th inst., by J. French, Esq., Mr. J. Crawford, to Maria, daughter of Mr. John Ransier, all of this place.

CH - June 14, 1831. Died: On the 11th inst., Mr. William Priest, aged about 50 years.

CH - Died: June 14, 1831: On the 12th inst., Mr. James Schuyler, aged about 70, a soldier of the Revolution.

CH - June 14, 1831. Died: On Sunday night last, widow of the late Jacob Schuyler, aged about 80 years.

CH - June 31, 1831. Married: On the 12th inst., by Jairus French, Mr. Benjamin Suits, to Miss Betsy Kennedy, all of this place.

CH - July 5, 1831. Married: At Chittenango on Wednesday evening last, by the Rev. Lewis Leonard of Cazenovia, Mr. Edward Sims, Merchant, to Miss Harriet C., daughter of Job Wells, Esq. of this town.

CH - August 2, 1831. Married: On Tuesday evening, the 26th ult. by Rev. William Johnson, Mr. Calvin H. Shapley of Nelson, to Miss Louisa Sutherland, of this place.

CH - August 2, 1831. Died: In this village on the 26th ult., a child of Dr. David Mitchell, aged twelve months and 17 days.

CH - August 9, 1831. Died: Suddenly in this town, on Thursday last, Mr. Abraham Webster, aged 80 years, a soldier of the Revolution. Mr. Webster, at the time of his death was in receipt of a pension for his services in the war for independence.

CH - August 9, 1831. Died: At his residence at Jersey City, on Saturday the 30th ult., Col. Richard Varick, at the advanced age of 79 years.

CH - August 16, 1831. Died: In Schenectady, on the 5th inst., after a lingering illness, Mr. George Richie, junior printer, in the 29th year of his age.

CH - August 30, 1831. Died: In this village on Saturday last, Richard Henry, youngest child of Mr. P. VanValkenburgh, aged about 3 months.

CH - September 13, 1831. Died: On Tuesday last, Mr. Robert Lyndsey, aged 38 years.

CH - September 13, 1831. Died: On Wednesday last, Mrs. Brown, wife of Jonas Brown, aged 49.

CH - September 13, 1831. Died: On Thursday last, Mrs. Mary Kennedy.

CH - September 13, 1831. Married: At Chittenango on Monday the 5th inst., by the Rev. Mr. Campbell, Mr. Isaac Knowles to Miss Charlotte Dickerson.

CH - September 13, 1831. Married: On wed. last, by the Rev. Dr. Yates, Mr. John Vosburgh, to Miss Mary Moss, both of this village.

CH - September 13, 1831. Married: In Perryville on Monday the 5th inst., by the Rev. Mr. Northrup, Mr. Benjamin Britt to Miss Catherine Farnham.

CH - September 13, 1831. Married: At Fenner, on Thursday last by the same, Mr. Aaron Cranson, of Lenox, to Miss Dianthe Flarding, of the former place.

CH - September 27, 1831. Died: On Saturday morning last Henry, youngest child of Mr. H. Perry, of this village, aged about two years.

CH - September 27, 1831. Died: In Fenner on the 17th inst. Mrs. Mary, wife of Harmanus VanVleck, Esq., in the 62nd year of her age.

CH - September 27, 1831. Died: At Van Buren, Onondaga Co. on the 14th inst. Miss Martha L. Willard, aged 19 years.

CH - September 27, 1831. Died: At Galway, Saratoga Co. of a pulmonary complaint, Mr. David Cligbee.

CH - October 18, 1831. Died: On Sunday the 9th inst., at Trenton, N. J. where he had been engaged for sometime previously in superintending the construction of canal locks, Mr. Abraham Walrath a much respected and worthy citizen of this village.

CH - October 18, 1831. Died: At Schenectady on Tuesday last, Mr. Patrick Dillon, formerly of this place.

CH - October 18, 1831. Died: In this village on Saturday last, Irene, infant daughter of Mr. Reuben Haight.

CH - October 25, 1831. Married: At Flatbush, L. I., by the Rev. Thomas Strong, Rev. William H. Campbell, pastor of the Reformed Dutch Church in this village to Miss Catherine Schoonmaker, of the former place.

CH - October 25, 1831. Married: On Tuesday last, by the Rev. Dr. Yates, Mr. Andrew VanVleck, to Miss Jane Evans, all of this place.

17

CH - October 25, 1831. Married: At Pompey on the 13th inst. Mr. Sylvester Ware of this village, to Miss Harriet Smith, of the former place.

CH - November 1, 1831. Married: In Smithfield on the 24th ult. Mr. Thomas Todd, to Miss Mary Ann Sweet, both of this village.

CH - November 1, 1831. Married: On th 25th ult., by the Rev. William Johnson, Mr. James Knowlin, to Miss Eve Bettinger, all of this town.

CH - November 1, 1831. Died: On Sunday morning last, Captain William Beebe, a resident of this town.

CH - November 8, 1831. Married: At Utica on Thursday evening last, by Rev. Mr. Aiken, Daniel B. Cady, Esq., Attorney and counsellor-at-law in this village, to Mary J. daughter of Dr. Jonas Fay, of the former place.

CH - December 20, 1831. Married: In this village on Thursday the 8th inst. Mr. John Kimball, of Manlius, to Miss Lucina Eaton, of the same place.

CH - January 10, 1832. Married: At Oswego, on the 5th inst. by Rev. Dr. Yates, Andrew J. Yates, Esq., to Miss Matilda H., daughter of the Honorable Rudolph Bunner, of that place.

CH - January 10, 1832. Married: In this village on Tuesday evening last, by the Rev. Mr. Campbell, Mr. John W. Taylor, of Eaton, to Miss Harriet VanValkenburgh, of this place.

CH - January 10, 1832. Married: On Thursday evening last, by the same, Mr. _____ West to Miss Catherine Ehle, all of this town.

CH - January 10, 1832. Married: A short time since by J. French, Esq., Mr. Thomas Knolan, to Miss Susan Fulford, both of Canaseraga.

CH - January 17, 1832. Married: In Sullivan on Thursday evening last, by the Rev. Mr. Willis, Capt. Jacob S. Lansing, to Miss Nancy P. Douglas, daughter of Col. Zebulon Douglas of the above named town.

CH - January 24, 1832. Married: In this village on the 18th inst., by the Rev. N. S. Smith, Mr. Ruhan Holmes, merchant of Lenox, to Miss Lucretia Smith of Sullivan.

CH - January 31, 1832. Married: In Lenox on the 25th inst. by the Rev. Ira M. Olds, Col. Daniel B. Moot, to Miss Eliza, daughter of Mr. John I. D. Nellis, all of this town.

CH - February 21, 1832. Married: At Canastota on the 9th inst. by the Rev. Mr. Olds, Capt. Warren Clark, to Miss Eunice Dorman, all of Lenox.

CH - February 21, 1832. Died: on Wednesday last, Miss Emily Swift, daughter of Mr. Elisha Swift, of this town, aged eighteen years.

CH - February 28, 1832. Married: In this village, on the 22nd inst. by the Rev. W. H. Campbell, Mr. Royal Fox, of Perryville, to Miss Betsey Baldwin, of the same place.

Ch - February 28, 1832. Married: On the evening of the 22nd inst. by J. French, Esq., Mr. Dennis Foot, to Miss Betsey Conrad, all of this town.

CH - February 28, 1832. Died: On Friday morning last, Mrs. Shaver, wife of Nicholas Shaver aged 34 (?) years.

CH - March 13, 1832. Married: On Wednesday evening last, Mr. John Anguish, to Miss Sarah Ann Young, all of this town.

CH - March 13, 1832. Died: In the town of Manlius on Saturday last, Mr. Christian Fink, aged 33 years.

CH - April 3, 1832. Married: On the 1st inst. by Jairus French, Mr. Henry Phillips, to Miss Abigail Conrad, all of this town.

CH - April 3, 1832. Married: On the 29th ult., by the Rev. E. Ransom, Harmanus VanVleck, Esq. of Fenner, to Mrs. _____ Thompson, of Verona.

CH - April 3, 1832. Died: At Lenox, on the 2nd inst. Mrs. Deborah Clark, wife of Mr. Oliver Clark, in the 53rd year of her age.

CH - April 3, 1832. Died: On the 29th ult. the only son of Mr. John Eddy, in the 2nd year of his age.

CH - April 17, 1832. Died: In this town, on the 12th inst. Mrs. Mary Lee, in the 33rd year of her age.

CH - May 1, 1832. Married: In Morrisville on the 10th inst. by Rev. Mr. Lord, Rev. Nathaniel S. Smith of this village, to Miss Susan H. B. Lord, daughter of the Rev. J. Lord and late instructress in Mr. Whittlesey's Seminary, Utica.

CH - May 1, 1832. Married: At Perryville, on the 23rd inst. by Rev. Mr., Northrup, Mr. Thomas J. Whiting, to Miss Harriet Baldwin, all of this town.

CH - May 1, 1832. Died: On Wednesday last, Mrs. Symphronia Shaver, in the 91st year of her age.

CH - May 22, 1832. Married: In Schenectady on Thursday the 10th inst. by Rev. P. A. Prod, Dr. Vernor Cuyler, of Albany, to Miss Caroline, daughter of Isaac Riggs, Esq.

CH - May 22, 1832. Died: In Cazenovia on Wednesday last in the 64th year of his age, Mr. Eliakim Roberts.

CH - May 22, 1832. Died: At Washington on the 14th inst. the Hon. Jonathan Hunt, member of Congress from Vermont.

CH - May 29th, 1832. Married: In this town on Wed. the 23rd inst., Mr. David Ehle to Miss Caroline Maria Cropsey.

CH - May 29, 1832. Married: On Thursday evening last, by the Rev. Dr. Yates, Mr. Thomas Southward to Miss Grace Powlsland, both lately from England, but now of this town.

CH - June 5, 1832. Died: At Perryville on the 27th inst., Mr. Othniel Brainard, in the 77th year of his age. Mr. Brainard fought for the liberty of his country during our Revolutionary struggle.

CH - June 12, 1832. Married: At Cazenovia on the 10th inst. by Elder Peck, Mr. Stephen M. Grenolds to Miss Martha Schuyler, both of this village.

CH - June 12, 1832. Married: In this village on Wed. last by the Rev. Dr. Yates, Mr. Jacob Decker to Miss Mary Ann Bain, both of Lenox.

CH - June 12, 1832. Married: On Thursday last by the Rev. Mr. Smith, Mr. Amos Atkins, to Miss Sally Ferand, all of this village.

CH - June 12, 1832. Notice: Thomas Roddis, resident of Chittenango, advertises for information about John Markram and Thomas Raddis, who emigrated to this country about three years since from Keyston, Huntingdon (England).

CH - July 10, 1832. Married: On the 3rd inst. by Rev. W. H. Campbell, Mr. Charles Knowles to Miss Magaretta Dewey, all of this town.

CH - July 31, 1832. Married: In this village on the 29th inst. by J. French, Esq., Mr. William H. Myers to Miss Mary Olcott, both of Cazenovia.

CH - July 31, 1832. Died: In this village on the 29th inst., a child of Mr. William Ramsey aged 15 months.

CH - July 31, 1832. Died: On Sunday afternoon last (29th) two daughters of Mr. Luther Woodworth of Fenner, killed by lightning (one aged 15, the other aged 5); 3 others were knocked down (all in the house) and one was so injured that "Life is despaired of". Communicated by U. S. Avery, Post Master.

CH - August 7, 1832. Died: Suddenly in this town on Sunday last, while engaged in binding wheat in the harvest field, Mr. John J. Smith, aged about 40 years (apoplexy).

CH - August 14, 1832. Married: In Sullivan on the 8th inst. by J. French, Mr. Silas Fyler, Junr. to Miss Lydia M. Eggleston, both of that place.

CH - August 14, 1832. Married: In Perryville on the 9th inst. by Rev. B. Northrup, Mr. Johnson Bliss to Miss Eliza Blakeslee, all of that place.

CH - August 14, 1832. Died: In this village, on Sunday morning last, of paralysis, Mrs. Caroline Grant, consort of Capt. George Grant of this village, in the 38th year of her age.

CH - August 14, 1832. Died: In Perryville, on the 5th inst. of a lingering illness, Mrs. Zilpha Lansing, wife of Peter Lansing, in the 50th year of her age.

CH - August 21, 1832. Married: On Sunday last, by Rev. William H. Campbell, Mr. Augustus G. Jewell to Miss Maria, daughter of Mr. Isaac Collier, all of this town.

CH - August 28, 1832. Died: In this town, on Saturday last in the 81st year of his age, Mr. Rufus Willard.

CH - September 4, 1832. Died: On the 3rd inst., Mr. John Grove, in the 60th year of his age, an old and respectable inhabitant of this town. Funeral at the home of Mr. J. Bellinger.

CH - September 11, 1832. Married: On Thursday the 6th inst. by Rev. John Grey, citizen of the world, Mr. Harry Lansing, of Auburn, to Miss Minerva Bond of Sullivan.

CH - September 18, 1832. Died: On Tuesday morning last, Mr. Charles Knowles of this town, in the 27th year of his age.

CH - September 18, 1832. Died: In this town on the 16th inst. Mrs. Mercy Willard, in the 71st year of her age.

CH - September 25, 1832. Married: On the 23rd inst. Mr. Isaac Bull, to Miss Jane E. Bull, both of this town.

CH - October 2, 1832. Married: In Perryville, on the 27th inst. by Rev. B. Northrup, Mr. Sergeant Britt to Miss Mabel Judd, both of this place.

CH - October 2, 1832. Died: At Perryville on the 17th inst. at the residence of her son-in-law, Rev. B. Northrup, Mrs. Hannah Breck, in the 72nd year of her age.

CH - October 9, 1832. Married: In Lenox on the 3rd inst. by the Rev. Edward A. Fraser, Mr. Harry Clark to Miss Nancy A., daughter of Maj. Joseph Bruce, all of that place.

CH - October 9, 1832. Died: On Friday last, an infant child of Mr. Newman Ware, of this village.

CH - October 9, 1832. Married: In this village, on the 7th by the Rev. William Johnson, Mr. Josiah Snell to Miss Phebe Stearns.

CH - October 16, 1832. Married: On Tuesday evening last, by Rev. William Johnson, Mr. Joseph Bingham, to Miss Eliza Quackenbush, all of this town.

CH - October 16, 1832. Married: At Delphi, on the 8th inst. by Elder Smitzen, Mr. A. P. Boardman, of Cazenovia to Miss S. M. Hawkins of Delphi.

CH - October 16, 1832. Married: In the town of Paris, Oneida County on the 9th inst. by Rev. _____ Smith, Mr. Martin A. Hubbard of Fenner, to Miss Emily Potter of the former place.

CH - October 16, 1832. Died: In this village on Thursday last, Mr. Solomon C. Holbrook, aged about 40 years.

CH - October 30, 1832. Married: At Sullivan on the 28th inst. by J. French, Esq., Mr. John Fink, to Miss Alice Parkhurst, all of this town.

CH - November 13, 1832. Died: On Wednesday the 7th inst. in this town, Mrs. Philena VanValkenburgh, wife of Mr. P. VanValkenburgh, in the 29th year of her age. Buried in Harrington Cemetery.

CH - November 20, 1832. Died: At Canastota on the 8th inst. Mrs. Almira Fay, consort of Mr. Nahum Fay, aged 23 years.

CH - December 4, 1832. Died: In this village, on Friday last, in the 50th year of his age, Mr. Jonas Holmes, a native of Yorkshire, England.

CH - December 4, 1832. Died: In Fenner, on the 16th inst., Mr. Smedley Hubbard, in the 22nd year of his age (Poem of lament says "buried 2 wives and one daughter).

CH - December 11, 1832. Married: At Perryville, on the 29th ult. by the Rev. B. Northrup, Peter Lansing, to the widow Mabel Blakeslee.

CH - December 11, 1832. Married: At Lenox on the 22nd ult. by the Rev. Mr. Spaulding, Mr. Nathan Lamb, to Miss Lovice, daughter of Mr. Elisha Palmer.

CH - December 11, 1832. Died: At Watervleit, Albany Co., on the 2nd inst. Miss Harriet, daughter of Isaac Fonda, aged 19 years.

CH - December 25, 1832. Married: At Sullivan on the 16th inst. by J. French, Esq., Mr. Elijah Hamilton, to Miss Eliza Worden.

CH - January 1, 1833. Married: On the 27th ult. in Chittenango, Mr. Sylvester Hills, of Manlius to Miss Hannah Sutherland of this town.

CH - January 1, 1833. Married: On the 27th inst., Mr. Enoch W. Earl of Canastota to Miss Dolly Ransier of this place.

CH - January 8, 1833. Married: On the evening of the 6th inst. by the Rev. H. Snyder, Mr. William Nelson, to Miss Jane Morrell, both of this place.

CH - January 15, 1833. Married: In Waterloo on the 16th inst. by the Rev. Dr. Mason, Dr. H. B. Bush of Fayetteville, to Miss Marietta Tubbs of the former place.

CH - January 22, 1833. Married: On Thursday evening last, by J. French, Esq., Mr. Henry V. Lathrop, to Miss Rachel Ransier, all of this village.

CH - January 22, 1833. Married: At New Boston, on Sunday evening last, by Rev. H. Snyder, Mr. Sidney N. Soper, to Rosannah Wood, both of that place.

CH - February 5, 1833. Died: At Fulton, Oswego Co., on the 1st inst. in a fit of apoplexy, Capt. Justus Durkey. (Funeral at Perryville Episcopal Church) Masonic member.

CH - February 12, 1833. Married: At Canastota, on Tuesday the 12th inst. by Rev. E. A. Frasier, Mr. E. H. Barton of the firm of Gregory & Barton, to Miss Angenett Crocker, all of the same place.

CH - March 12, 1833. Married: In Sullivan on the 10th inst. by J. French, Esq., Mr. Daniel Walter, to Miss Polly Walts, all of this town.

CH - March 12, 1833. Married: At Sullivan on the 21st ult. by the Rev. Yates, Henry Palmer, M. D. of Manlius to Harriet, daughter of Capt. Asa Cady of the former place.

CH - March 12, 1833. Died: Suddenly at Canaseraga in this town, on the 9th inst. of apoplexy, Mr. Michael Walter of Manlius, Onondaga Co., aged 59 years.

CH - March 19, 1833. Married: On the 17th inst. by Rev. Mr. Paddock, Mr. James Woolaver to Miss Eliza Ratnier, all of this town.

CH - April 2, 1833. Married: on the 30th ult., by Rev. Wm. Johnson, Mr. William Hood to Miss Rhoda, dau. of Richard Knollin, all of this town.

CH - April 23, 1833. Married: At Canastota on Sunday last, Mr. John J. Miers to Miss Harriett Elmira Williams of Cazenovia.

CH - May 7, 1833. Married: At Herkimer on the 7th inst. Mr. William T. Abercrombie to Miss Mary Lounsbury of that place.

CH - May 7, 1833: Died: On the 29th ult. a child of Mr. James Dewitt, of this village, aged about 3 years.

CH - May 14, 1833. Married: At Delphi, on the 7th inst. by Elder Smitzer, Mr. S. L. Barrett of Cazenovia to Miss Eliza Shankland, of the former place.

CH - May 14, 1833. Married: In this village on Thursday last, by Rev. H. S. Snyder, Mr. Henry D. June of Manlius to Miss Ann Burlinghame of this place.

CH - May 14, 1833. Married: On Wednesday last, by the Rev. A. Yates, D. D., Mr. George Powesland to Miss Mary Easterbrook, all of this village.

CH - May 14, 1833. Married: On the 12th inst. by J. French Esq., Mr. John Stephens, to Miss Clara Ann Myers all of this village.

CH - May 14, 1833. Married: On the 11th inst. by the Rev. E. Doolittle, Mr. Charles Wilson to Miss Polly Quackenbush, all of this town.

CH - May 14, 1833. Married: At Mobile, Alabama on the 4th ult., Dr. Christopher Y. Fonda, formerly of the City of Schenectady, to Mrs. E. McKensey of the former place.

CH - May 21, 1833. Married: At Cazenovia on Thursday evening last, by Rev. Mr. Leonard, Nathan T. Williams, Esq. cashier of the Madison County Bank, to Margaret L., daughter of Mr. John Williams.

CH - May 21, 1833. Died: On Sunday last in the 3rd year of her age, Anna, a child of Mr. James VanVoast of this village.

CH - May 28, 1833. Married: In Union Village, Washington County, on the 14th inst. by the Rev. Edward Barber, Wendell Lansing, editor of the *Banner*, to Miss Eliza, daughter of John Harrington, Esq. of Easton.

CH - June 11, 1833. Died: Yesterday morning in this town, Mrs. Mary Ann, wife of Jacob Moulter.

CH - June 18, 1833. Died: On Sunday last in this village, Mr. George Follet, aged 36 years.

CH - July 9, 1833. Died: At Canaseraga, on Saturday last, Miss Sally Beebe, aged 27 after a lingering illness.

CH - July 16, 1833. Died: In this town, on the 7th inst., Maj. Argalus Cady, aged 53 years.

CH - July 23, 1833. Married: On Thursday last, by Rev. D. Yates, Mr. Albert Mabee of Manlius to Miss Maria Ehle, eldest daughter of Mr. Henry Ehle of this town.

CH - July 23, 1833. Married: On the 10th inst. by Rev. Mr. Foot, Maj. Benjamin F. Bruce to Miss Eliza Ann, daughter of Dr. Nathaniel Hall of Lenox.

CH - July 30, 1833. Died: In this village on the 23rd inst. Maria Cummings aged 17 months, 10 days, daughter of Hiram Cummings (eulogy and acrostick).

CH - July 30, 1833. Died: On Wednesday last in this village Joseph Blackwood, aged 36.

CH - July 30, 1833. Died: On the 23rd inst. a child of Mr. Brownell about 3 years of age.

CH - August 6, 1833. Married: On Friday last, by Rev. Mr. Davis of Utica, Mr. David Price to Miss Eliza Rowland, both of this village.

CH - August 6, 1833. Died: Suddenly in this town, on the 5th inst. at the residence of Col. Zebulon Douglass, Mrs. Polly G. Douglass, his wife, aged 61 years (apoplexy).

CH - September 3, 1833. Married: On the 2nd inst. by J. French, Esq., Mr. Hamilton R. Fairman to Miss Celestia Warren.

CH - September 3, 1833. Married: On the 26th ult. by the same, Mr. Lymon Smith, to Miss Eveline Christman, all of this town.

CH - September 17, 1833. Married: At Schenectady on the 3rd inst. by Rev. J. VanVechten, Mr. David M. Lyon of Salisbury, Herkimer County, to Miss Deborah Peck of the former place.

CH - September 24, 1833. Married in this village, on the 18th inst. by Rev. B. Paddock, Mr. Simeon Pennock of Perryville, to Miss Rebecca Dickinson of Chittenango.

CH - September 24, 1833. Married: In this town on the 19th inst. by J. French, Esq. Mr. George Chawgo to Miss Polly Christman.

CH - September 24, 1833. Died: At his residence in this town after a short but painful illness, Mr. Leonard Dockstader, aged 63 years.

CH - September 24, 1833. Died: In this town on Friday morning last, Mrs. Hannah Allen, aged 70 years.

CH - September 24, 1833. Died: At Oppenheim, Montgomery County on the 16th inst., Edward Yates, Esq. of Schenectady in the 31st year of his age.

CH - October 8, 1833. Married: In this town on the 3rd inst. by Rev. Dr. Yates, Mr. Rodney Case to Miss Celistia Joy, all of this town.

CH - October 8, 1833. Married: At Sempronius, Cayuga County, on the 11th ult. by Matthias Lane, Esq. Mr. Christopher Ellison, to Miss Esther Maria Fowler of the former place.

CH - October 15, 1833. Died: On Sunday morning last, Charles Monroe, son of Mr. M. Parmelee of this village, aged 3 years, 9 months.

CH - October 15, 1833. Died: In this village on Sunday last, Mr. Joseph Miller, aged about 50 years.

CH - October 22, 1833. Died: At his residence in Fenner, on the 10th inst., Col. Arnold Ballou, aged 61 years 6 months.

CH - November 5, 1833. Married: In New Brunswick, N. J. on the 29th ult. Mr. Lee Wells, formerly of this village, to Miss Jane VanHorn.

CH - November 5, 1833. Married: In the same place at the same date, Robert Riddle, Esq. to Miss Phoebe Sunderland, both formerly of this village.

CH - November 5, 1833. Married: At Rio Janeiro, August 29th Robert G. Yates, son of V. N. Yates of Albany, to Jane Amelia, youngest daughter of the late Caleb Coffin of New York.

CH - November 19, 1833. Married: In Sullivan on the 6th inst. by the Rev. Mr. Slingerland, Mr. John Charles Everson, to Miss Harriet Almida, daughter of Mr. John G. Crapsey.

CH - November 19, 1833. Died: On Wednesday last, of apoplexy, Mrs. Catherine, wife of Mr. David Owens of this village.

CH - December 10, 1833. Died: In this village on the 5th inst. Amanda M. Wells, daughter of Job Wells Esq. in the 17th year of her age, and on the 8th, Polly Wells her mother, in the 53rd year of her age.

CH - December 10, 1833. Died: On Saturday evening last, Mrs. L. Morrell, wife of Mr. Stephen Morrell aged 60 years.

CH - December 17, 1833. Married: On the 11th inst. by Rev. Mr. Powell, Mr. George Williams to Miss Sarah Williams all of this village.

CH - December 17, 1833. Died: On board the ship *Niagara* on the 4th inst. on his passage from Charleston to New York, Mr. Edward Kirkland, son of General Kirkland of Utica.

CH - December 21, 1833. Married: At Syracuse, on the 26th inst. by Rev. Mr. Adams, Mr. Samuel F. Green, to Miss Harriet, daughter of Mr. Peter McDougall, all of this place.

CH - December 21, 1833. Died: In this town on the 20th inst., Harriet a child of Mr. Anson Hoger, aged 3 years.

CH - January 7, 1834. Died: At Canaseraga on the 26th ult. Mr. Derias Beecher, aged 63 years.

CH - January 28, 1834. Married: At Cazenovia, on the 24th inst., by Mr. Leonard, Capt. Burnett Schuyler of Chittenango, to Mrs.Margaret Phillips of Eagle Village.

Ch - January 28, 1834: Died: In this village, on Sunday last, Mrs. Margaret Reynolds, wife of Richard Reynolds, aged 50 yrs.

CH - February 4, 1834. Married: At Syracuse on the 28th inst. by Rev. Mr. Allen, Mr. Obadiah Tibbits to Miss Editha House, all of this town.

CH - February 11, 1834. Married: In Wayne County, on the 30th of January, by Rev. Mr. Jones, Capt. Oliver Clark, of Lenox, Madison Co., to Miss Polly Thomas of Rose.

CH - February 11, 1834. Married: At Schenectady on Tuesday the 4th inst. by Rev. Mr. Bacchus, Mr. John T. St. John to Miss Rachel, daughter of Mr. Mattaniah Lyon, all of that city.

CH - February 11, 1834. Died: In Tollin (Tolland?), Conn. on the 20th ult. Mr. Oliver Grant, aged 30.

CH - February 25, 1834. Married: In Lenox, on Tuesday, the 18th inst., by the Rev. Mr. Cooper, Mr. John A. Messinger, merchant, to Miss Elizabeth Ann, daughter of Andrew W. VanAlstine, all of that place.

CH - February 25, 1834. Died: In Lexington, Georgia, on the 30th ult., Mrs. Anne Alida wife of John D. Watkins, Esq., and daughter of Hon. Joseph C. Yates, of Schenectady, aged 27 years.

CH - March 4, 1834. Died: In this village, on the 19th ult., an infant son of Mr. John Evans.

CH - March 4, 1834. Died: On the same day, Mary, daughter of Mr. R. Howell, aged 4 years.

CH - March 4, 1834. Died: On Thursday last, in the 46th year of his age, Mr. Joseph Christman.

CH - March 4, 1834. Died: In Sullivan, on the 24th ult., of pulmonary consumption, Mrs. Eliza, wife of Mr. Isaac Beebe, aged 33 years.

CH - March 11, 1834. Died: In this village, on Tuesday, the 6th inst., Harriet, youngest daughter of Ebenezer O. and Mary Ann Grosvenor, aged 3 months and 13 days.

CH - March 18, 1834. Died: In this town, on the 13th inst., Adam Walter, aged 82.

CH - March 18, 1834. Died: On the 15th, George Soper, aged 17 years.

CH - March 25, 1834. Married: In Sullivan, on the 23rd inst. by Jairus French, Esq., Mr. William Holmes to Miss Hannah Snell.

CH - March 25, 1834. Married: On the same day, by the same, Mr. Ira Holmes to Miss Polly Conrod.

CH - March 25, 1834. Died: In Canastota, Madison Co., New York on Monday the 17th inst., Mr. Henry F. Spencer, in the 24th year of his age.

CH - April 8, 1834. Married: On Thursday last, by Rev. L. Myrick, Mr. Cornelius Coakley, of Kirkville, to Miss Charlotte Livingston, of this village.

CH - April 8, 1834. Married: On Sunday, the 6th inst., by Rev. Mr. Bort, Mr. S. M. S. Denton, to Miss Hannah A. Cady, both of this town.

CH - April 8, 1834. Died: On the 1st inst., in the town of Cazenovia, Mr. Frederick I. Snell, aged 56 years.

CH - April 8, 1834. Died: On the 5th inst., in the town of Cazenovia, Mr. James Kellogg, in the 45th year of his age.

CH - April 29, 1834. Married: On the 23rd inst., by the Rev. Dr. Yates, Mr. Peter VanVolkenburgh, of this place, to Miss Loania J. Barnes, of Brookfield, Massachusetts.

CH - April 29, 1834. Married: On Thursday evening last by Rev. E. Slingerland, Mr. Oliver K. Swift of Canaseraga, to Miss Irene, eldest daughter of Col. George Ehle, of this village.

CH - May 13, 1834. Died: In this village, on Friday last, of a lingering consumption, Dr. John N. Husted, aged 24 years.

CH - May 13, 1834. Died: On the 9th in this village, Mr. Wilkerson Eggleston, aged 42.

CH - June 24, 1834. Married: In Sullivan, on Thursday morning last, by Rev. F. L. North, Mr. Hiram Brown, merchant, to Miss Angeline Beach, all of the above town.

CH - June 24, 1834. Married: In New Haven, Connecticut on the 5th inst., by Rev. Dr. Croswell, Mr. E. M. Attwater, merchant of this village, to Miss Elizabeth, daughter of A. Budington, Esq., of the former place.

CH - July 15, 1834. Died: On the 7th inst. Sarah Antonett, daughter of Mr. Elijah Stern, of this village, aged 2 years and one month.

CH - July 22, 1834. Married: On Thursday last, by Rev. E. Slingerland, Mr. Ezra Bond, to Miss Charlotte Olcott, all of this place.

CH - July 29, 1834. Died: In Lenox, on 23rd inst. Mr. John Beebe, aged about 55 years. (Note-apoplexy).

CH - Aug 5, 1834. Died: In Lenox, on the 28th ult., Mrs. Mary Dalrympal, aged 85 years.

CH - August 12, 1834. Married: In Lenox, on the 7th inst., by the Rev. Mr. Allen, Mr. Cornelius Hoffman, to Miss Betsey Jackson, all of that town.

CH - August 12, 1834. Married: At Durhamville on the 7th inst., by John Otis, Esq., Mr. A. J. Mayo, of this village, to Miss Eliza Brown, of the former place.

CH - August 12, 1834. Died: In this village, on the 9th inst. Electa, daughter of Mr. Henry Perry, aged 13 months.

CH - August 12, 1834. Died: At Bridgeport, in this town, on the 3rd inst., Mrs. Mary Ann Hickok, wife of Harris Hickok, Esq.

CH - August 12, 1834. Died: In this village, on the 5th inst., Mary, daughter of Mr. David Whitney, aged 11 years.

CH - August 26, 1834. Married: In this village, on the 24th inst., by Rev. James T. Hough, Mr. Peter Cox, to Miss Hannah Holmes.

CH - August 26, 1834. Married: In this village, by Rev. E. Slingerland, on the 21st inst., Mr. Joseph Young, to Miss Sarah Jane Stillwell, both of Orville.

CH - September 2, 1834. Died: In this village, on Wednesday, August 27th after a long and painful illness, Col. Jelles E. Fonda, of Schenectady, at the age of 75. (Paragraph follows concerning him.)

CH - September 9, 1834. Died: On Friday last, Homer W., son of Mr. Moses Parmalee, aged 2 years and one month.

CH - October 7, 1834. Married: In this village, on the 2nd inst., by the Rev. Dr. Yates, Mr. John Chaugo, of St. Johnsville, Montgomery Co. (New York), to Miss Catharine Moyer, of this place.

CH - October 7, 1834. Married: At Perryville, on the 24th ult., by the Rev. B. Northrup, Mr. Hiram Ehle, to Miss Almira, youngest daughter of Mr. Noah Blakeslee.

CH - October 7, 1834. Married: At Cazenovia, on Saturday last, by J. French, Esq., Mr. James Wright, of Kirkville, to Miss Maria Ayres, of the former place.

CH - October 7, 1834. Married: In Wampsville, on the 2nd inst., by the Rev. Mr. Cooper, Mr. James W. Owens, to Miss Mehala Corson, both of Canastota.

CH - October 14, 1834. Married: At Syracuse, on the 11th inst. by Rev. L. Leonard, Rev. Oreb Montague, of Fabius, to Miss Cornelia L., daughter of Deacon Henry Chamberlain, of the former place.

CH - October 28, 1834. Died: On Sunday, the 25th inst., at the residence of the Rev. Andrew Yates, D. D. of this place, William Austin, infant son of A. J. Yates, Esq. of Oswego, aged 6 months.

CH - November 4, 1834. Married: At New Hartford, on the 22nd October, by the Rev. Mr. Coe, Asahel Beckwith of Chittenango, to Miss Harriet A. Seymour, of the former place.

CH - November 18, 1834. Married: In this village, on the 11th inst. by J. French, Esq., Mr. Jacob Dennis, to Miss Mary Bowen, both of Manlius.

CH - November 18, 1834. Married: On the 13th inst. by the same, Mr. Rodolphus E. Knight, to Miss Sally Baltsley, both of Fayetteville.

CH - November 18, 1834. Died: At Lee, Onondaga Co., on the 5th inst., Mr. Horace Sexton.

CH - November 25, 1834. Married: In Sullivan, on the 23rd inst., by Jairus French, Esq., Mr. Jacob English, to Miss Harriet Elizabeth Curtis, all of the same town.

CH - November 25, 1834. Married: In Sullivan on the 19th inst., by Rev. Mr. Atwell, Mr. James Case, to Miss Sophia Eaton, both of the same town.

CH - December 2, 1834. Died: In this village, on Friday last, Clark, youngest child of Dr. S. Fuller, aged one year and 10 months.

CH - December 2, 1834. Died: On Friday last, Mrs. Abigail Tobey, aged 85 years.

CH - December 2, 1834. Died: On Tuesday last, Thomas Dickerson, aged 54 years.

CH - December 2, 1834. Died: Last evening, Mrs. Betsey, wife of Franklin Moore, aged 25.

CH - December 16, 1834. Married: In this town, on Thursday evening last, by J. French, Esq., Mr. John W. Shaver, to Mrs. Margaret Porter.

CH - December 16, 1834. Married: On the 27th ult. by Elder Beckwith, Mr. Mills P. Brush, to Miss Lydia Ray, both of Fenner.

CH - December 16, 1834. Died: At Manlius, on the morning of Friday, the 11th inst., John Browning, a native of Devonshire (England), aged 47.

CH - December 23, 1834. Died: In this village on Friday last, Mrs. Eliza Thomas, a native of Wales, aged 45 years.

CH - December 30, 1834. Died: In this town, on Friday last, Mrs. James Peck, daughter of John Knowles, Esq., aged 35.

CH - January 6, 1835. Died: On Thursday last, at Verona, Oneida Co., in the 45th year of her age, Mrs. Sarah Jones, wife of Edward Jones, a native of Wales.

CH - January 20, 1835. Died: In this village, on Tuesday last, Mr. Reuben Hawley, aged 45 years.

CH - January 20, 1835. Died: On Thursday last, at an advanced age, the widow of Charles Freeman.

CH - January 20, 1835. Died: On Tuesday last, Mrs. Mahala Holmes, aged 57 years.

CH - February 3, 1835. Married: In this village, on Wednesday evening last, by Rev. A. Yates, D.D., Mr. Alonzo Bishop, to Mrs. Catherine Walrath, all of this place.

CH - February 3, 1835. Married: At New Brunswick, NJ by the Rev. Mr. Jones, Job Wells, Esq. of this village, to Mrs. Abigail Van Northwick, of the former place.

CH - February 10, 1835. Died: In this town, on Wednesday last, of delirium tremens, Mr. Ethan Benson, aged 35 years.

CH - February 17, 1835. Died: In this village, on Wednesday last, Mr. Silas Sutherland, in the 63rd year of his age.

CH - February 24, 1835. Married: In this town on the 17th inst., by J. French, Esq., Mr. William Ray, to Miss Polly Daharsh.

CH - February 24, 1835. Married: In this village, on the 18th, by Rev. J. T. Hough, Mr. William Hill, to Mary Ann C. Sherman, both of Verona, Oneida Co.

CH - February 24, 1835. Married: In Cazenovia, on the 10th inst. by Rev. E. S. Barrows, Mr. Charles M. Tibbals, to Miss Delia Lyman, daughter of Dr. Isaac Lyman, all of that village.

CH - February 24, 1835. Married: At the same time and place [as above], by the same, Mr. L. Burdette Brown, of Buffalo, to Miss Adaline Whipple, of Cazenovia.

CH - March 3, 1835. Married: In this town, on the 26th ult., by Jairus French, Esq., Mr. Nicholas Bettinger, to Miss Ann Storms, all of Sullivan.

CH - March 3, 1835. Died: In this town, on Thursday last, Miss Eliza Douglass daughter of Col. Zebulon Douglass, aged 19 years.

CH - March 3, 1835. Died: On the 23rd ult. at the city of Toronto, U. C., Alexander McDonnell, Esq. of Greenfield, member of the Provincial Parliament, and Sheriff of the Ottawa District.

CH - March 24, 1835. Died: In this village, on Wednesday last, Melinda, daughter of Mr. George T. Perry, aged about six years.

CH - March 31, 1835. Married: In Manlius, on Wednesday last, by A. Nims, Esq., Mr. Elijah Anguish, of Sullivan, to Miss Nancy Thompson, of the former town.

CH - March 31, 1835. Died: On Friday the 27th inst., in the 56th year of his age, at his residence in Cazenovia, Perry G. Childs, Esq. (Had been State Senator. Born in Pittsfield, Massachusetts. Resided in state for over 30 years.)

CH - April 14, 1835. Married: At Granview (Illinois), on the 3rd July last, Dr. Gallio K. Willard, formerly of Chittenango, New York to Miss Eleanor D., daughter of the Rev. John Smith, of the former place.

CH - April 14, 1835. Died: In this town, on Sunday last, Mrs. Amanda Nickerson aged 19.

CH - May 12, 1835. Married: In this town, on Wednesday last, by Rev. S. R. Smith, of Clinton, Rev. Jesse Bushnell, of Ft. Plain, to Miss Adelia, daughter of Mr. Levi Spaulding, of Canasaraga.

CH - May 19, 1835. Married: On Sunday last, at the Episcopalian Church in Fayetteville by Rev. B. Northrup, Mr. Francis Taylor, to Miss Elizabeth Williams, both of this village.

CH - May 19, 1835. Married: In Sullivan, on Sunday last, by J. French, Esq., Mr. John Curtis, to Miss Ann Truax.

CH - May 19, 1835. Died: In this village, on the 11th inst., Adam Conradt, aged 84 years.

CH - June 9, 1835. Married: At Georgetown, on the 7th inst., by the Rev. Mr. Corey, Mr. Oliver C. Petty, to Miss Mary A. Smith, both of Cazenovia.

CH - June 9, 1835. Died: At Frankfort, on Friday morning last, Dr. Jonas Fay, of Utica, aged 59 years. (Additional information concerning the accident on the canal, which led to his death.)

CH - June 16, 1835. Married: At Fayetteville, on the 9th inst., by A. Neely, Esq., Mr. Fayette Harris, to Miss Margery Forbes, both of Clockville.

CH - June 16, 1835. Died: In the town of Manlius, on the 9th inst., Mr. Melza Colton, aged 55 years.

CH - June 23, 1835. Married: In this village on the 17th inst. by J. French, Esq., Mr. John Rowland, Jr. to Miss Jemima Howell.

CH - June 30, 1835. Married: In this village, on Thursday evening last, by Rev. C. G. Sommers, of New York, Mr. James Cole, to Miss Ann Ehle, daughter of Col. George Ehle.

CH - June 30, 1835. Married: In Vernon, on Wednesday morning the 24th inst., by the Rev. Mr. Hough, J. Whipple Jenkins, Esq. to Miss E. Jennette Tuttle.

CH - June 30, 1835. Died: In this town, at the residence of her father, Mr. Richard VanValkenburgh, Mrs. Harriet, wife of John W. Taylor, of Eaton, aged 23 years, one month. The funeral service at the Dutch Church, this morning at 11 o'clock.

CH - June 30, 1835. Died: On Friday last, in this town, Anna daughter of Mr. Isaac Bettinger, aged 1 year, 8 months.

CH - August 4, 1835. Married: At Canaseraga on the 29th ult. by J. French, Esq., Mr. Eli A. Ellis, of Manlius, to Miss Myra Mead, of Canaseraga. Also, Mr. Lucius Gilbert of Canaseraga, to Miss Elizabeth Randall, of Augusta, Oneida Co.

CH - August 4, 1835. Died: In this town, on Thursday last, Mr. Edward Lincoln (son of Leonard), aged 17 years. (Buried in Harrington Cemetery.)

CH - August 11, 1835. Married: In this village, on the 8th inst., by J. French, Esq., Mr. John Fults, to Miss Maranda Warner, both of Manlius Centre.

CH - August 11, 1835. Died: At Ernestown (U.C.) on the 22nd ult., Mrs. Sophia Slingerland, wife of Mr. Jacob Slingerland, formerly of this village. She was a native of Schoharie Co.

CH - August 25, 1835. Married: At Perryville, on the 18th inst. by J. Whipple, Jr., Esq., Mr. Joseph Sweetland of Sandy Creek, to Miss Vashti Doty, of Cazenovia.

CH - August 25, 1835. Married: At Manlius, on the 24th inst., by Rev. Mr. Hollister, Mr. Sidney Stanton, to Miss Fanny Perkins, both of Cazenovia.

CH - September 1, 1835. Married: In Chittenango, on the 27th ult., by J. French, Esq., Mr. Philip Buckley, to Miss Amelia Taylor, all of the above place.

CH - September 8, 1835. Married: In this town, on the 5th inst., by J. French, Esq., Mr. Elisha Reynolds, of Pompey, to Miss Amanda Priest, of Sullivan.

CH - September 15, 1835. Died: In this town on Friday last, September 11th, a child of Mr. John I. Walrath, aged 3 months.

(From Pittsfield, Massachusetts, Sunday)
CH - September 15, 1835. Died: At the Seminary for young ladies in this town, September 6th, Catherine Anne, daughter of Peter I. Hoes, Esq., of Kinderhook, New York, aged 16 years.

CH - September 29, 1835. Married: In this town, on the 17th inst., by Rev. J. Bushnel, Mr. Gardiner Bond, to Miss Almira Mower.

CH - September 29, 1835. Married: On the 19th, by J. French, Esq., Mr. Martin VanAlstine, to Mrs. Nancy _____.

CH - October 6, 1835. Married: In this village, on the 3rd inst. by Rev. John C. F. Hoes, Mr. John S. Willard, to Miss Eleanor Billington.

CH - October 6, 1835. Died: In Manlius, on Friday last, Asa Nims, Esq., aged 51 years.

CH - October 13, 1835. Died: In Lenox, on the 2nd inst., Mr. Benjamin F. Clover, aged 22 years.

CH - October 20, 1835. Married: In this town, on the 13th inst., by the Rev. John C. F. Hoes, Mr. Jeremiah Gates, Jr., to Miss Emeline Doxtator.

CH - October 20, 1835. Married: In this village, on the 15th inst., by J. French, Esq., Mr. Henry DeLong, Jr. to Miss Betsey Worden, both of Manlius.

CH - October 20, 1835. Married: Also, at the same time and place [as above], Mr. James DeLong, of Dewitt, to Miss Catharine Christman, of Lenox.

CH - October 27, 1835. Married: In this village, on the 23rd inst., by Rev. Mr. Gregg, Mr. Mathew Tague, to Mrs. Mary Browning, all of this place.

CH - October 27, 1835. Married: At Wampsville, on the 22nd inst. by the Rev. Mr. Cooper, of Lenox, Mr. Jacob Ostrander, to Miss Catherine Smith, both of Wampsville.

CH - November 3, 1835. Married: In Sullivan, on the 23rd ult., by J. French Esq., Mr. William Henry Crownhart, to Miss Esther Hopkins.

CH - November 3, 1835. Married: On the 30th ult., by J. French, Esq., Mr. Archibald Wilkes to Mrs. Margaret Austin.

CH - November 3, 1835. Married: In Bronson (Ohio), on the 1st ult., by the Rev. E. Conger, Mr. Horace F. Huntington, of Norwalk, to Miss Amelia Webb, of the former place.

CH - November 10, 1835. Died: On Thursday last, in this village, Mrs. Jerusha Sutherland, in the 80th year of her age.

CH - November 17, 1835. Married: On Wednesday the 4th inst. at Granville, Washington County, New York by the Rev. Mr. Bellamy, of Manlius, Mr. Alfred Bellamy, of the firm of J. & A. Bellamy, of this village, to Miss Eliza A. Oliphant, daughter of R. W. Oliphant, Esq., of Granville.

CH - November 24, 1835. Died: In Cazenovia, on the 20th inst., Mr. William Love, a soldier of the Revolution, aged 93.

CH - December 8, 1835. Died: At Jersey City, on the 1st inst., of typhus fever, Mr. Theodore Wells, son of Job Wells, Esq., of this village, aged 17 years.

CH - December 8, 1835. Died: At Haverstraw, Rockland County, on the 26th inst., Mr. Silas G. Sutherland, printer, aged 19 years, formerly of this village.

CH - December 15, 1835. Died: In this town, on Tues. last, Mrs. Hannah Westerman, aged 55 yrs.

CH - December 15, 1835: Died: On Friday last, Mr. Henry Hood, age 22 yrs.

CH - December 15, 1835: Died: On the same day [as above], Mrs. Polly Ray.

CH - December 22, 1835. Married: At Sullivan, December 17th by J. French, Esq., Mr. John Campbell of Manlius, to Miss Amy Maria Haight, of Sullivan.

CH - December 22, 1835. Died: At Jamesville, Onondaga County, on Sunday the 13th inst., Mrs. S. Angeline Day, wife of Rev. Norris Day, formerly of East-Hampton, Massachusetts, age 26.

CH - December 29, 1835. Died: In Johnstown, Montgomery County, on the 21st inst. in the 22nd year of her age, Mrs. Catherine Chawgo, daughter of Capt. Daniel Moyer, formerly of this village.

CH - January 5, 1836. Married: On the 10th ult., by the Rev. Mr. Goodell, Mr. Benjamin F. Hunt, of this town, to Miss Mariam Hall of Lenox.

CH - January 12, 1836. Married: On Wednesday, the 6th inst. by the Rev. Mr. Cooper, of Wampsville, Mr. David Fowler, of Lenox, to Miss Susan Spring, of Smithfield.

CH - January 19, 1836. Died: In this town, on Monday, the 11th inst., a child of Mr. David TenEyck.

CH - January 19, 1836. Died: On Wednesday, a child of Mr. Charles H. Cook, aged 3 years.

CH - January 19, 1836. Died: On the same day, Mr. Jehial Button, aged 18. The cause of his death was a fracture of the skull from the falling of a tree.

CH - January 19, 1836. Died: On Saturday, Mrs. Helena Willard, aged 20.

CH - January 25, 1836. Married: At Perryville, on the 14th inst., by Elder Skinner, Mr. Charles D. Cruttenden, to Miss Melinda Monroe, eldest daughter of Jesse Monroe.

CH - February 2, 1836. Married: In Sullivan, on the 24th January by Jairus French, Esq., Mr. Lucien Meeker, to Miss Minerva Blodget, all of said town.

CH - February 2, 1836. Married: On the 28th by the same, Mr. William Dewitt, to Miss Mary Ann Snell, all of Sullivan.

CH - February 2, 1836. Married: In Hamilton, on the 20th ult., by the Rev. Mr. Knapp, Mr. Daniel Griffin, to Miss Sophie Haight, both of Fayetteville.

CH - February 9, 1836. Married: In Fenner, on the 28th ult., by Elder Paddock, Mr. Sylvanus Watson, of Perryville, to Miss Laura Hill, of the former place.

CH - February 16, 1836. Married: In Manlius, on the 11th inst., by Elder Paddock, Mr. Silas Bender, to Miss Eliza Ann Quackenbush, of the former place.

CH - February 24, 1836. Married: In Sullivan, on the 19th inst., by J. French, Esq., Mr. Joseph Woliver, to Miss Rebecca Davis.

CH - March 16, 1836. Married: In this village, on the 9th inst., by Jairus French, Esq., Mr. Antrim Williams, to Miss Elizabeth Osborn, both of Dewitt.

CH - March 16, 1836. Died: In Manlius, on the 7th inst., after a protracted and painful illness, Nicholas P. Randall, Esq., aged 57, an eminent counsellor at law.

CH - March 23, 1836. Died: In this town, a widow named Susan Thirkell, aged about 41 years. She had visited a place in Niagara County to see her brother in that quarter, and found on her arrival there that he had moved to Michigan. On her return to her home at Herkimer, on foot, she was taken sick in this place on the 1st inst., and died on the 16th. She stated that she had a family at Herkimer, composed of her mother, named Susan Austin, and 2 children, expecting her return to them.

CH - April 6, 1836. Married: On the 25th ult., by the Rev. Mr. House of Cazenovia, Mr. Luther G. Woodworth, to Miss Harriet L. Downer, both of Fenner.

CH - April 20, 1836. Married: At Fayetteville, on the 24th of March last, by Albert Neely, Esq., Mr. Daniel VanDeWorker of Chittenango, to Miss Serena daughter of Mr. David Moulter of Manlius.

CH - April 20, 1836. Died: In this village on Thursday last, Mrs. Mary Ann, wife of Henry Dewey, aged 19 years.

CH - May 18, 1836. Married: In this village the 11th inst., by Rev. John C. F. Hoes, Mr. Cyrus Cappenter of Dewitt to Miss Sophia Williams of Manlius.

CH - May 18, 1836. Married: At Cazenovia on the 17th ult., by Jairus French, Esq., Mr. Eleazor Rice to Miss Amanda Hutchinson.

CH - May 25, 1836. Married: In Manlius on Sunday last, Mr. Christopher Dewitt to Maureen Wentworth.

CH - June 1, 1836. Married: On Monday, the 23rd ult. at Kingsbury, Washington County, by Rev. N. Fox, Mr. Julius Bellamy, of the firm of J. & A. Bellamy of this village, to Miss Sarah J. Barney, daughter of Throop Barney, Esq. of the former place.

CH - June 16, 1836. Married: In Fayetteville on the 8th inst. by Rev. A. Smith, Mr. Curtis Sterne, to Miss Mary Ann Dewey, all of that place.

CH - June 16, 1836. Married: At West Troy on the 25th ult. by the Rev. Mr. Wood, Mr. James Dygart of this place to Miss Catherine Lansing of the former place.

CH - July 13, 1836. Died: At his residence in this place, on the 10th inst., after a short illness, the Hon. John B. Yates, in the 53rd year of his age.

CH - July 13, 1836. Married: In this town, on the 8th inst. by J. French, Esq., Mr. Porter Lee to Miss Catherine Sickles.

CH - July 13, 1836. Died: In this village, on Monday last, an infant daughter of Mr. P. VanValkenburgh.

CH - July 2, 1836. Died: In this village on Friday last, Edward, infant son of H. Cummings, Esq., aged four months.

CH - July 27, 1836. Died: On Wednesday last in Mauch Chunck, Northhampton County, Pennsylvania, Mr. David M. Wells, aged 22 years (killed by explosion on Lehigh Canal). He was the son of Job Wells (More details in August 2 issue of paper.).

CH - August 10, 1836. Died: At his residence in Perryville, on Wednesday the 3rd inst., after a short illness, Mr. Oren S. Avery, in the 42nd year of his age. (Left a wife, 2 sons, and an aged widowed mother.)

CH - August 17, 1836. Died: At the residence of his father, in Salisbury, Connecticut on the 7th inst in the 34th year of his age, Chester Averill, A. M., professor of Chemistry and Language in Union College.

CH - September 7, 1836. Married: In Cazenovia on the 1st inst., Mr. George W. Robinson of Cleveland, Oswego County, to Miss Electa Schuyler of the former place.

CH - September 7, 1836. Married: At Pompey Hill on Tuesday morning by Rev. Mr. Gridley, Mr. Dean Knowlton of Cazenovia, to Miss Merrilla Wood of the former place.

CH - September 21, 1836. Married: On the 15th inst., in the village of Cortland by the Rev. Joseph I. Foot, the Rev. John C. F. Hoes, of this place, to Miss Lucy Maria, eldest daughter of Gen. Roswell Randall.

CH - September 21, 1836. Died: On Saturday last in this town, Mr. Martin DeLine.

CH - October 5, 1836. Married: In Sullivan, on the 28th ult., by the Rev. E. S. Barrows, of Cazenovia, Mr. Abram Davis of Fenner, to Miss Mercy Cushing of Sullivan.

CH - October 5, 1836. Married: In Fenner, on the 27th ult., by Elder H. C. Skinner, Mr. Calvin Davis, to Miss Pamelia Keeler, all of that town.

CH - October 5, 1836. Married: In Sullivan, on the 11th of September by Jairus French, Esq., Mr. Charles O. Barnard to Miss Lany Daharsh.

CH - October 12, 1836. Died: In Sullivan, on the 6th inst., Mr. Nason Cass, aged 48 years.

CH - October 19, 1836. Married: In this village, on the 13th inst. by Rev. Mr. Gregg, Mr. James F. Gould of St. Simons, Georgia, to Miss Charlotte Ann, daughter of Gen. T. Livingston, of this place.

CH - October 26, 1836. Married: In Sullivan on the 18th inst. by J. French, Esq., Mr. Orrin Smith to Miss Martha Welton, both of Pompey.

CH - October 26, 1836. Married: At Onondaga on the 11th inst. by the Rev. Mr. Taylor of Salina, the Rev. Abner Morse of Portage, Indiana, to Miss Hannah Peck of the former place.

CH - October 26, 1836. Died: In Morrisville, on the 14th inst., Mrs. Elvira Granger, wife of Otis P. Granger, Esq., aged 27 years.

CH - November 9, 1836. Died: In this town on the 1st inst., after a long and painful illness, which she bore with Christian fortitude, wife of James Warren, aged 38 years.

CH - November 23, 1836. Married: At Milan, Cayuga County, on the 20th inst., Mr. Lester Stone, of Cazenovia, to Miss Mary Clark of the former place.

CH - December 14, 1836. Married: At Fayetteville, on the 12th inst., by A. Neely, Esq., Mr. Nicholas Gidley to Miss Mary Rook, both of Chittenango.

CH - December 28, 1836. Died: On the 12th inst., two children of Mr. Nathaniel Vail, New Boston, aged 8 and 10 years, were accidently drowned by falling through the ice on the canal at that place. They were found on the following day clasped in each other's arms.

CH - January 4, 1837. Married: In this town, on the 29th ult. by the Rev. Jesse Pound, of Manlius, Mr. Daniel Gates to Miss Lany Ehle, daughter of Mr. Henry Ehle.

CH - January 11, 1837. Married: In the Baptist Church at Cazenovia on Thursday morning last, by the Rev. O. Montague, Mr. George R. Parmalee to Miss Jane, daughter of Capt. John Hearsey, all of that place.

CH - January 17, 1837. Married: In this village on Wednesday evening last, by J. French, Esq., Mr. John Pickup to Miss Ann Hager, both of Clockville.

CH - January 25, 1837. Married: In this town on the 23rd inst. by J. French, Esq., Mr. Caleb Pack, to Miss Mary C. Brower, all of Sullivan.

CH - January 25, 1837. Died: At Canaseraga on the 20th inst., Mr. Alpheus French, aged 60 years.

CH - February 8, 1837. Died: In this town Friday morning last., of paralysis, Mrs. Sophia Riddle, wife of Thomas Riddle, Esq., aged 34 years.

CH - February 8, 1837. Died: At Bloomington, Illinois on the 19th January, Mr. William Bates, recently a merchant in Cazenovia, aged 39 years.

CH - February 29, 1837. Married: On Thursday the 23rd inst., by J. Whipple, Esq., Mr. John S. Willard, to Miss Mariah Clark, all of this place. [nb: There was no leap year in 1837.]

CH - February 29, 1837. Died: At his residence in Canastota, Madison County, New York on the 21st inst., Mr. John Wallace Mead, late of Greenwich, Connecticut in the 26th year of his age.

CH - February 29, 1837. Died: At the Isle of St. Croix, in the early part of January last, in the 60th year of his age, Montgomery Hunt, Esq., formerly cashier of the bank of Utica and for the last 2 years a resident of the city of New York.

CH - March 8, 1837. Married: In this village on the 5th inst. by J. French, Esq., Mr. Jerome B. Woodward of Fulton, Oswego County, to Miss Martha Miller of Manlius.

CH - March 8, 1837. Died: On Monday morning last, in the 47th year of her age, Mrs. Amanda H. Perry, wife of Mr. George T. Perry, of this village (next week's notice said died on Monday the 6th inst., in the 37th year of her age), leaving seven dependent children.

CH - March 8, 1837. Died: In Greenbush, Rensselaer County on the 6th inst. after a severe illness, Mr. John G. Yates, in the 47th year of his age, formerly a resident of this town.

CH - March 22, 1837. Died: Hon. Joseph C. Yates, late Governor of this State and eldest brother of the Hon. John B. Yates, deceased. He expired at his residence in Schenectady, on the 19th inst. about 2 o'clock P.M. at an advanced age.

CH - April 19, 1836. Died: Hon. Peter Smith, father of Gerrit Smith, Esq., of Peterboro. Died on the night of the 11th inst. of apoplexy, in the 69th year of his age.

CH - April 26, 1836. Married: At Fayettville on Wednesday last, by A. Neely, Esq., Mr. John Dewitt to Miss Laney Bellenger, both of this village.

CH - April 26, 1836. Died: In this town on the 14th inst., Mrs. Elizabeth Randall, wife of Jirah Randall, Esq.

CH - May 3, 1837. Married: In Manlius, Onondaga County on the 25th ult. by Esq. Huntley, Mr. James Moulter of Chittenango, to Caroline Thompson, of the former town.

CH - May 3, 1837. Married: In this village on the 30th ult. by the Rev. Oren Hyde, Mr. Horace M. Hovey, to Miss Caroline M. Grosvenor, daughter of Mr. E. O. Grosvenor of this village.

CH - May 3, 1837. Died: In this town on the 27th ult., Mr. David Beebe, aged 82 years.

CH - May 3, 1837. Died: On the 28th, a child of Mr. Milton Holmes, aged about 4 months.

CH - May 17, 1837. Married: At Cazenovia on Tuesday evening, May 12th by the Rev. E. N. Woolley, Mr. William S. Perkins, of the firm of Davenport & Perkins, to Miss Harriet, daughter of Mr. William Burton all of the above place.

CH - May 17, 1837. Married: In Sullivan, on Thursday last, by Jairus French, Esq., Mr. Sylvanus Storms, to Lucinda Ehle, all of said town.

CH - May 24, 1837. Died: In Schenectady on the 15th inst., after a lingering illness, Dr. Richard Fuller, aged 32 years.

CH - July 12, 1837. Married: In this village on the 7th inst. by Rev. E. A. Huntington, of Albany, Mr. Henry B. Burn, to Mrs. Dorothy Hewit, both of this town.

CH - July 26, 1837. Married: In this village on Thursday last by Rev. E. A. Huntington, Mr. Ely Bigelow, to Miss Mary Long, both of Pompey, Onondaga County.

CH - July 26, 1837. Died: In this town on Wednesday the 19th inst. Sidney Willett, aged 33? of Apoplexy following 2 slight shocks.

CH - August 2, 1837. Married: In this village on Thursday last by Jairus French, Esq., Mr. David Christopher of Perryville, to Miss Mary Morgan, of this place.

CH - August 2, 1837. Died: At New Woodstock, Madison County on the 20th ult., Mrs. Sarah A. Whiting, daughter of B. Babcock, Esq., Clinton, New York and consort of Mr. Joel Whiting principal of the New Woodstock Academy.

CH - August 9, 1837. Married: In this village, on the 29th ult. by Judge Warner, Mr. John Cushney of Syracuse, to Miss Mariet Weeks of the same place.

CH - August 9, 1837. Married: In Perryville, on the 23rd ult. by Elder Nicholson of Cazenovia, Mr. Thaddeus Stoddard, to Miss Abigail Avery, both of the former place.

CH - August 9, 1837. Died: In this town on the 24th ult., Angeline McKriles in the 15th year of her age, adopted daughter of H. Rightmyer, Esq.

CH - August 30, 1837. Married: At Oswego, on the 24th inst. by Rev. Mr. Nine, Mr. John Medcalf, of this town to Miss Asenath Richards of Virgil, Cortland County.

CH - August 30, 1837. Died: At his residence in this town on Wednesday the 23rd inst., Capt. Timothy Brown, aged 72 years.

CH - August 30, 1837. Died: At Manlius on the 26th inst. Mr. Correll H. Mills, aged 34 years. He has left a wife and four young children.

CH - September 6, 1837. Married: In Lenox on Wednesday last, by the Rev. Mr. Barrows, of Cazenovia, Mr. James Crouse of the firm of Crouse & Company, merhants of this village to Miss Laura Beecher, daughter of Sylvester Beecher, Esq., of Lenox.

CH - September 6, 1837. Married: In this town on the 31st ult. by Jairus French, Esq., Mr. Charles S. Hutchins to Miss Nancy Bitely all of Sullivan.

CH - October 4, 1837. Married: In this town on the 28th ult. by Rev. Mr. Bellamy of Manlius, Mr. George T. Perry, merchant of this village, to Miss Cornelia, daughter of Col. H. Sage.

CH - October 11, 1837. Married: In Fenner on the 5th inst. by the Rev. J. N. T. Tucker, Capt. Silas H. Covey, to Miss Adelia Ann Cornell, both of the above town.

CH - October 18, 1837. Married: In the town of Cazenovia on Thursday evening last, by the Rev. L. Myrick, Mr. Orrimell Russell of the firm of Russell & Walrath, tailors of this village, to Miss Martha A., daughter of Mr. Charles Parmelee, of the above named town.

CH - October 18, 1837. Married: In this town on the 16th inst. by J. French, Esq., Mr. Lorenzo Darling, to Mary Ann Guile, both of Dewitt, Onondaga County.

CH - October 25, 1837. Married: In Lenox on the 19th inst. by the Rev. Alvah Day, Dr. Edward Fuller of this village, to Miss Octavia, daughter of Col. Stephen Lee, of the former place.

CH - November 15, 1837. Married: At Fayetteville on the 8th inst. by the Rev. Orin Hyde, Mr. John Bates, of the firm of Sims and Bates, to Miss Cecelia Hubbell (died January 1838), of this town.

CH - November 15, 1837. Married: At the same time and place [as above], by the same, Mr. Damon Wells to Miss Sarah Cossett, both of this village.

CH - November 22, 1837. Married: In Manlius on Thursday last by C. Hibbert, Esq., Mr. Thomas Freeborn, of Cazenovia, to Miss Lane Mabie of Manlius.

CH - December 20, 1837. Married: In Fenner on Thursday last by Rev. Mr. Coryell of Cazenovia, Mr. Hiram Hall of Sullivan to Miss Maria Haight of Fenner.

CH - December 27, 1837. Married: In this town on Monday last by J. French, Esq., Mr. George Sterling of Elmira, Chenango County, to Miss Mary Ann Rogers of the former place. [Elmira is actually in Chemung Co., NY. ed.]

CH - December 27, 1837. Died: At Canastota on the 20th inst. of the inflammation in the head, Isaac Henry, only son of Isaac and Mary A. Quackenbush, aged 1 year, five months and three days.

CH - January 3, 1838. Married: In the town of Clay, Onondaga county on the 1st inst. by Elder Morgen, of Salina, Mr. Benjamin Hamlet, of Nelson, to Miss Mary Salisbury of the same place.

CH - January 3, 1838. Married: In this village on the 31st December by Jairus French, Esq., Mr. William M. Strong to Miss Ellen N. Comstock, both of Cazenovia.

CH - January 17, 1838. Died: In this town on Thursday last, of consumption in the 22nd year of her age, Mrs. Cecelia A., wife of Mr. John Bates of this village.

43

CH - January 17, 1838. Died: In the town of Cazenovia, on Thursday last, Mr. Archibald Bates, aged 76 years.

CH - January 17, 1838. Died: In this village on the 2nd inst. Mr. John J. Ransier, aged 72.

CH - January 24, 1838. Married: On the 4th inst. by the Rev. Mr. Tygart of Manlius, Mr. Horace B. Tucker of Perryville to Miss Abigail Norris of this town.

CH - January 24, 1838. Married: On Saturday last, Mr. Samuel Foat to Miss Jane Becker, both of this town.

CH - February 7, 1838. Married: In the town of Dewitt, Onondaga County, on the 25th ult. by the Rev. Mr. Taggart, Mr. James Rogers of Sullivan, to Miss Lydia A. Wright of the former place.

CH - February 7, 1838. Died: In this village on the 2nd inst., Horatio Gates, only son of Judge Warner, aged 19 and 1/2 months.

CH - February 14, 1838. Died: In this town on Monday evening last, in the 40th year of her age, Mrs. Charlotte. wife of Col. Samuel French.

CH - February 21, 1838. Married: In this town on the 15th inst. by Elder B. G. Paddock, Mr. John Collier, to Miss Mary Ann Walrath, both of this village.

CH - February 21, 1838. Married: On Sunday last by Rev. Mr. Tuttle, of Fayetteville, Mr. William H. Brown, to Miss Helen A. Reddish, both of this village.

CH - February 21, 1838. Married: At Morrisville, on Wednesday last by Elder Blakslee, Mr. William Knowlton, to Miss Nancy Cox of this village.

CH - February 21, 1838. Married: At the same time and place, by the same, Mr. Henry Brown, to Miss Maria Butler.

CH - February 21, 1838. Married: In this town on Wednesday last, Mr. Jacob Schuyler to Miss Delia Fairborn.

CH - February 21, 1838. Died: In Canastota on the 17th inst. of consumption, Mr. Horace D. Hitchcock, aged 37 years.

CH - February 21, 1838. Died: In this village on Sunday last, Nancy Fosdick, aged 14 years.

CH - February 28, 1838. Married: In Morrisville by the Rev. Mr. Willis, on the 20th inst., Mr. John Comstock to Miss Abbey Cossett.

CH - February 28, 1838. Died: In this village on the 22nd inst. of dropsey in the head, James C., son of Abram Ehle, in the 5th year of his age.

CH - February 28, 1838. Died: In this village on Monday last, an infant child of Mr. George D. Wheeler.

CH - March 14, 1838. Married: At Vernon on the 10th inst. by the Rev. H. P. Bogue, Mr. Benjamin L. Hood, of Lenox, to Miss Lucinda M. Toby of this village.

CH - March 14, 1838. Married: At Washington (Wisconsin Territory) on the 11th of February last, by the Rev. Mr. J. R. Barnes, John W. Taylor, Esq., Postmaster, (formerly of this village) to Miss Eliza A. Harrison of Syracuse, New York.

CH - March 14, 1838. Married: On Sunday last, Mr. Isaac Jones, to Miss Sally Stone, of this village.

CH - March 21, 1838. Married: In this village on the 14th inst., by Rev. J. Abel, Mr. Thompson Riddle of this village to Miss A. Selene Livermore, from Worcester, Mass.

CH - March 21, 1838. Married: On the 13th by J. French, Esq., Mr. Jacob Houghtailing, to Miss Lenay Conrad.

CH - April 4, 1838. Died: In this village on the 21st ult. of consumption, Emmaline Elizabeth, daughter of Norris and Emmaline Felt, aged two years.

CH - April 11, 1838. Married: In Clockville on Sunday the 8th inst. by the Rev. Mr. Randall, Mr. Asa Baldwin of Fenner, to Miss Louisa C. Button, formerly of Hamilton.

CH - April 11, 1838. Died: Suddenly in the town of Fenner on Sunday last, Mrs. Sally Osterhout, aged about 52. She was found a short distance from her home having, it is supposed, died in a fit.

CH - May 2, 1838. Married: In this town on the 29th ult. by Jairus French, Esq., Mr. Nathaniel West of Lenox, to Miss Emily Sherwin of this town.

CH - May 9, 1838. Married: In this village on Sunday evening last, by the Rev. J. Abell, Mr. Mandrack Rice, of Pompey, to Miss Diantha VanWie, of this place.

CH - May 16, 1838. Died: Suddenly, at Grand Rapids, Kent County, Michigan, on the 11th April, Mr. Benjamin F. Schuyler, aged 25, formerly of this village.

CH - May 23, 1838. Died: A child of Mr. Edward Roberts, aged about 15 months ... in this village on Monday last... thrown by horses and run over by wagon loaded with stone.

CH - May 30, 1838. Died: In this town, on the 20th inst., of a cancer, Mr. Richard Longshore, aged about 67.

CH - May 30, 1838. Died: In Utica, Commodore Melancthon T. Woolsey, U. S. Navy, aged about 60. He had been indisposed for several weeks past, from erysipelas, and then dropsey.

CH - June 6, 1838. Married: In Sullivan, on the 2nd inst., by J. French, Esq., Mr. Jonah Jones, of Utica, to Miss Catherine Owen, of this town.

CH - June 13, 1838. Died: In this town, on Monday last, of inflammation on the lungs, Harris Hickok, Esq., aged about 41.

CH - June 13, 1838. Died: Drowned, accidently, in the Chittenango Creek, on Friday last, Peter Kawhiss, an Indian of the Mohegan Tribe, long a resident of this town, aged 63.

CH - June 20, 1838. Married: In this town, on the 14th inst., by Elder Daggart, of Manlius, Captain Josiah Fink, to Miss Nancy Norris, both of this town.

CH - June 20, 1838. Died: In this town, on the 16th inst., Abigail, daughter of Edward and Abigail Davis, aged 18 (or 13) years.

CH - June 27, 1838. Note: "The mother of Judge Knowles of this village, now residing in Pittsfield, Massachusetts, rising 90 years of age, lately helped herself into a one-horse carriage and drove to church and back, a distance of several miles".

CH - July 11, 1838. Married: In this town, on the 4th inst. by the Rev. James Abell, Mr. Henry T. Hooker of Rochester, to Miss Mary B. Cobb, daughter of Mr. Henry J. Cobb, of this town.

CH - July 11, 1838. Married: At Trinity Church, in the village of Geneva, on Thursday the 21st ult. by the Rev. Pierre P. Irving, DR. Abel S. Baldwin (formerly of this county) to Miss Eliza Scott, all of that place.

CH - July 18, 1838. Wednesday. Married: At Manlius, on the 16th July inst., by the Rev. Mr. Bellamy, Col. Charles A. Spencer of Canastota, to Miss Mary Stillwell, daughter of S. Stillwell, of the former place.

CH - July 18, 1838. Died: In this town on the 14th inst., after an illness of 3 years, Mrs. Abigail Davis, wife of Mr. Edmund Davis, aged 62.

CH - July 18, 1838. Died: In this village, on the 10th, Mrs. Elizabeth Davis, wife of Mr. Henry Davis, aged 36.

CH - August 1, 1838. Died: At Canaseraga, in this town, on the 25th ult., Mr. Thomas French, aged 56.

CH - August 15, 1838. Married: At Cazenovia, on the evening of the 2nd instant, by the Rev. Mr. Barrows, Mr. E. C. Litchfield, to Miss Mary A., daughter of Jacob TenEyck, Esq., all of that place.

CH - August 15, 1838. Died: In the town of Cazenovia, on the 8th inst. of apoplexy, Mrs. Lucy B. Harrison, consort of Mr. William Harrison, in the 50th year of her age.

CH - August 13, 1838. Auction sale: By John Brower, "Near Bolivar" (farm and household goods) "as I am about to leave this part of the country for the West".

CH - August 22, 1838. Personal adv.: Jacob Lower offers property for sale, indicates trouble with his "old friend" George Ehle.

CH - September 19, 1838. Married: In this village, on the 17th inst., by the Rev. Z. Paddock, Mr. John W. Haight, of Auburn, to Miss Julia A. Comstock, of this village.

CH - September 19, 1838. Died: In this village, on Wednesday the 12th inst., after a short and painful illness, Miss Mary Ann Campbell, daughter of Mr. Adam I. Campbell, aged 31.

CH - October 3, 1838. Died: In this town, on Wednesday morning last, Mr. Thomas West, aged about 59. His death was caused by injuries received by an accidental fall from the upper story of A. P. Downers store house, while engaged in taking in grain. He was taken up insensible and lived but 2 or 3 days.

CH - October 3, 1838. Died: In the city of Houston, Texas, on the 15th August last, Major John K. Allen, formerly a resident of Chittenango, in the 28th year of his age. Major Allen removed to Texas in 1832.

CH - October 31, 1838. Died: Suddenly at the residence of her grandfather, Mr. A. Hotchkiss, in this town, on the 28th inst., Sarah Maria Kent, aged 5 years, daughter of Mr. James Kent, of Walworth, Wayne County.

CH - November 28, 1838. Died: At Niles, Michigan, on the 7th inst., Mr. Titus B. Willard, aged 58.

CH - December 5, 1838. Married: In this village on Sunday evening last, by the Rev. James Abell, Mr. John Bates, of the firm of Sims and Bates, merchants, to Miss Charlotte Ehle, daughter of Col. George Ehle, all of this village.

CH - December 5, 1838. Died: On the 22nd of August last, at the town of LeRoy, Calhoun County, Michigan, of bilious fever, Mr. Sanford Burdick, formerly of this town.

CH - December 5, 1838. Married: In this village on Sunday evening last, by the Rev. James Abell, Mr. John Bates, of the firm of Sims and Bates, merchants, to Miss Charlotte Ehle, daughter of Col. George Ehle, all of this village.

CH - December 12, 1838. Married: On the 9th inst., by J. French, Esq., Mr. James Reels, of Manlius, to Miss Maria Truax, of Sullivan.

CH - December 12, 1838. Died: In the town of Cazenovia, on Sunday last, Mr. Charles Parmelee, a soldier of the Revolution, aged 85.

CH - December 12, 1838. Auction sale: All the interest of Guy Davis in his premises in Chittenango.

CH - December 19, 1838. Died: Long poem "To the memory of Miss Mary Elizabeth Wilcox", who died at Oxford, Chenango County, New York, July 31st, aged 18 years.

CH - December 19, 1838. Died: In this village, on Saturday night last, a child of Mr. M. Morange, aged about one year.

CH - January 2, 1839. Married: In New York, on the 27th ult. at South Baptist Church, Mr. David White How, to Miss Mary Elizabeth Yates, eldest daughter of the Rev. Charles G. Sommers, all of that city.

CH - January 2, 1839. Died: In this village, on Saturday last of dropsey in the head, Elizabeth G. Perry, daughter of Capt. George T. Perry, aged eleven years and six months.

CH - January 2, 1839. Died: A tribute to Neils VonSchoultz, who was executed at Kingston, December 8, 1838.

CH - January 9, 1839. Married: At Fayetteville, on the 25th ult., Mr. James Shaver, to Miss Julia Ann North, both of this town.

CH - January 16, 1839. Died: In this village on Thurs. morning last, Mr. Richard Holmes, aged 30 yrs.

CH - January 30, 1839. Married: At Perryville, on the 1st of January inst. by the Rev. Z. Paddock, Mr. George Brainard, to Miss Maria H. Blood.

CH - January 30, 1839. Married: At the same place [as above], on Sunday the 27th inst. by Rev. W. Webber, Mr. William H. Dewing, to Miss Polly E. Morris, all of Perryville.

CH - February 13, 1839. Married: In Sullivan, on Monday evening last, by the Rev. James Abell, of Chittenango, Mr. Daniel Denton, of Churchville, Monroe County, to Miss Maria Cady, of Sullivan.

CH - February 13, 1839. Married: In Sullivan, on the 10th inst., by J. French, Esq., Mr. Leonard Rogers, to Miss Sally Ann Ryon, all of that town.

CH - February 13, 1839. Married: At New York, on Tuesday the 5th inst. by the Rev. C. G. Sommers, Mr. Edward Scribner, to Miss Elizabeth Gertrude, eldest daughter of Allen Brown, Esq., all of that city.

CH - February 20, 1839. Married: At Canandaigua, on the 31st ult., Jesse Kilborn, Esq., of Cazenovia, to Miss Content Clark, of the former place.

CH - February 20, 1839. Died: In Fenner, on Sunday night last, Harmanus VanVleck, Esq., aged about 70 years.

CH - February 27, 1839. Married: At Fayetteville, on Saturday evening last, by Elder Fippen, Mr. Orwin R. Norton, to Miss Ann Sammon, both of this village.

CH - March 6, 1839. Married: In this town on the 27th ult., by J. French, Esq., Mr. Peter Daharsh, to Miss Mary Ann Bell.

CH - March 13, 1839. Married: At Perryville, the present month, by Rev. B. Paddock, Mr. James Warren, of Sullivan, to Miss Ann Mitchell.

CH - March 13, 1839. Married: In Sullivan, Mr. William W. Hill, to Miss Laura Mitchell.

CH - March 13, 1839. Married: In Fenner, by Elder Randal, Mr. David Young, to Miss Catherine Onion, both of that town.

CH - March 20, 1839. Died: In Clockville, on Wednesday morning last, of apoplexy, Mr. Reuben Watson, aged 64.

CH - March 20, 1839. Died: In this village, on Saturday last, an infant child of Mr. John Vosburgh.

CH - April 10, 1839. Married: At Perryville on Thursday the 4th inst. by Silas Judd, Esq., Mr. Adams Bicauyea (Buyea?), to Miss Catherine Card, both of Lenox.

CH - April 24, 1839. Married: At Bolivar, on the 7th inst. by J. French, Esq., Mr. James Beeman, to Miss Caroline Case, all of this town.

CH - May 1, 1839. Died: In this village, on Saturday morning last, Mr. David Rowland, aged 21.

CH - May 1, 1839. Died: In [New?] Woodstock, on the 26th ult., Mr. David Ehle, son of Mr. John P. Ehle, of this town, aged 29.

CH - May 1, 1839. Married: At Binghamton, on the 14th ult., by J. Wait, Jr. Esq., Mr. Alphus Finch, Jr. of Conklin, to Miss P. Jane Waterman, of Binghamton.

CH - May 8, 1839. Married: In this village, on Thursday last, by the Rev. Mr. Clark of Cazenovia, Mr. Charles M. Manvill, of Towanta [Towanda?], Pennsylvania, to Miss Mary A. Knowles, daughter of John Knowles, Esq. of this village.

CH - May 8, 1839. Married: In this village, on the 2nd inst., by J. French, Esq., Mr. John Russell, to Miss Sarah Woodford, both of Lenox.

CH - May 8, 1839. Died: In this village, on Monday last, in the 27th year of her age, Mrs. Mary Ann Suits, wife of Mr. Benjamin Suits. (Corrected next week to read Mr. Joseph Suits.)

CH - May 29, 1839. Died: In this village, on Monday morning last, of apoplexy, Mrs. Sally Knowles, wife of John Knowles, Esq., in the 67th year of her age.

CH - May 29, 1839. Died: In Canaseraga, on Wednesday last, Miss Jane, daughter of Mr. J. Chapman, age 18.

CH - May 29, 1839. Died: At the same place [as above], on Monday last, Mrs. Matilda Beecher, aged 64.

CH - June 5, 1839. Died: In this village, yesterday morning, Joseph C. son of Mr. B. Mecomber, aged 8 years.

CH - June 12, 1839. Died: At the residence of Col. S. Lee, in this town on Thursday last, William L., son of Dr. E. Fuller, aged 5 months.

CH - June 19, 1839. Died: In this village, on Saturday last, Mr. Zachariah Sickles, aged 92, a soldier of the Revolution.

CH - June 19, 1839. Died: At Canasaraga, on the 15th inst. of dropsey in the chest, Samuel French, son of the late Thomas French, age 16.

CH - June 19, 1839. Died: In this town, on the 18th inst., Mrs. Eliza Ann Hutchins, consort of Mr. L. Hutchins, and daughter of Mr. Jacob Fink, aged 19.

CH - June 19, 1839. Died: In Schenectady, yesterday morning, Jeremiah Fuller, Esq., aged about 80, one of the oldest and most respected inhabitants of that city.

CH - June 26, 1839. Died: At Cohoes Falls, on the 24th inst., Mr. Edward L. Jones, in the 21st year of his age, formerly of this village.

CH - July 10, 1839. Married: At her father's residence in Lenox, Madison County, New York, on the 2nd inst., by the Rev. Mr. Van Santvoord, Israel S. Spencer, Esq. of Canastota, attorney at Law, to Mary Jane, daughter of N. S. Roberts, Esq. civil engineer.

CH - July 10, 1839. Married: In this village, on the 3rd inst. by the Rev. J. Abell, Mr. Edward B. Hadley, of Syracuse, to Miss Mary Lowndsbury of Onondaga Hollow.

CH - July 10, 1839. Married: On the 5th inst., by the same, Mr. James N. Lumbard, of Cazenovia, to Miss Rebecca M. Lawton, of Fenner.

CH - July 10, 1839. Married: In Fenner, on the 4th inst. by the Rev. A. Parker, Mr. Harrison Robins, to Miss Jane Mills, all of the above town.

CH - July 24, 1839. Died: Suddenly, in this village, on Thursday night last, Mr. Harvey Barrett, aged 45.

CH - August 7, 1839. Married: On Tuesday morning, the 30th ult. at Schenectady, by the Rev. Dr. VanVechten, Rev. E. A. Huntington, of Albany, to Anna E., eldest daughter of Rev. Dr. VanVechten.

CH - August 7, 1839. Married: At the same time and place [as above], Professor Edward Savage, of Union College, to Sarah, 2nd daughter of the Rev. Dr. VanVechten.

CH - August 7, 1839. Died: At Hanford's Landing, Monroe County, on the 22nd ult., Daniel B. Harrington, in the 39th year of his age, formerly of this place.

CH - August 14, 1839. Died: Suddenly, in this town, on Friday last, Mr. Aaron Thrasher, aged about 50 [illegible].

CH - August 14, 1839. Died: In this town, on Thursday morning last, Mrs. Lydia Beebe, consort of the late David Beebe, Esq, in the 76th year of her age.

CH - August 14, 1839. Died: In Lenox, on Friday last, Mr. Franklin Doolittle, aged about 30.

CH - August 21, 1839. Auction sale: Erastus Hulbert, [at] "Fyler's Settlement", "going west".

CH - August 28, 1839. Married: In this town, on Thursday last, by Jairus French, Esq., Christopher Johnson to Phebe Landers.

CH - August 28, 1839. Died: In Hartsville, Onondaga County on Monday last, Mrs. Maria Thompson, wife of Pardon Thompson, aged 32.

CH - September 25, 1839. Married: In this village, on the 18th inst., by the Rev. J. Abel, Mr. Joseph G. Schryver, of Waterloo, Seneca County, to Miss Lucy Knowles, daughter of John Knowles, Esq. of this village.

CH - September 25, 1839. Died: In this village, on Wednesday night last, Mr. Edwin Vibbard, aged about 20.

CH - October 2, 1839. Married: In this village, on Thursday evening last, by Elder Paddock, of Cazenovia, Mr. Adrian V. Boardman, of the firm of VanValkenburgh and Boardman, merchant-tailors, to Miss Betsey Shaver of this village.

CH - October 2, 1839. Married: At the same time, by the same, Mr. Jonas A. Munroe, to Miss Betsey Tibbits, both of this village.

CH - October 2, 1839. Married: In this village on Thursday last, by the Rev. J. Abell, Mr. Jared Black, of Smithfield, to Miss Betsey Daharsh, of this village.

CH - October 2, 1839. Married: In Smithfield, on the 23rd ult. by Elder Jones, Ezra Mathewson, to Fanny Jane Warren, both of that town.

CH - October 2, 1839. Married: In this town on the 1st inst. by J. French, Esq., James Bowman to Miss Lucia Maria Palmeter.

CH - October 2, 1839. Died: In this town, on Saturday last, of a cancer in the breast, Catherine, wife of Mr. John G. Crapsey, aged 46 years.

CH - October 2, 1839. Died: In this town, on Tuesday the 24th ult., Mr. Elisha Hall, aged about 70, one of the earliest settlers of this part of the country.

CH - October 2, 1839. Died: At Washington, Wisconsin Territory, on the 11th September, in the 22nd year of her age, Eliza, wife of John W. Taylor, Esq., formerly of this place.

CH - October 9, 1839. Married: In this town on the 2nd inst. by the Rev. E. S. Barrows, of Cazenovia, Mr. George W. Hyatt, of Nelson, to Miss Emily, daughter of Enos Cushing, Esq. of this town.

CH - October 9, 1839. Died: In Wampsville, on the 6th inst., Mr. Joseph H. Jewell, aged 18 years.

CH - October 18, 1839. Died: In this village, on the 10th inst., in the 54th year of her age, Mrs. Dolly VanWie, wife of Mr. Henry VanWie.

CH - October 23, 1839. Died: In this village, on Sunday last, Mrs. Mary Sunderlin, aged 37 years.

CH - October 30, 1839. Married: Wednesday in Lenox, on the 24th inst., by the Rev. A. T. Mason, of Clockville, Mr. Myron H. Bronson, of Smithfield, to Miss Emeline Fort, of the former place.

CH - October 30, 1839. Died: In Mobile, on the 23rd ult. of yellow fever, William Tell Jones, formerly a resident of Chittenango.

CH - November 13, 1839. Married: In this town, on the 6th inst., by Elder Clark, of Cazenovia, Mr. Erastus Standard of Yates, Monroe County, New York to Miss Zevia Knowles, daughter of Mr. James Knowles, of this town.

CH - November 20, 1839. Died: In this village, this morning, after a short illness, Mr. Peter Brooks, aged about 35.

CH - December 18, 1839. Died: In this village, on Tuesday last, of consumption, Miss Jane Owens, daughter of Mr. David Owens, aged 23 years.

CH - December 18, 1839. Died: In this town, on the 17th, Mrs. Doxtader, consort of the late Mr. Leonard Doxtader.

CH - January 8, 1840. Married: At Fayetteville, on the 1st inst., by the Rev. J. Smitzel, Mr. John D. Madge to Miss Joanna D. Browning, both of this village.

CH - January 8, 1840. Married: In Nelson, on the 1st inst., by the Rev. Elder Aaron Parker, of Fenner, Mr. Hiram W. Taylor, of Smithfield, to Miss Lovicy C. Chapman, of the former place.

CH - January 22, 1840. Married: In this town, on the 16th, by the Rev. Mr. Clark, of Cazenovia, Mr. John Pettes, of Towanda, Bedford County, Pennsylvania, to Miss Sarah F. Knowles, daughter of J. Knowles Jr., Esq. of this town.

CH - January 22, 1840. Died: In this village, on Monday last, Mr. Ephraim Clark, aged about 80 years . . . he was from Windsor, Vermont, and was on his way to Waterloo and Clyde to visit his children.

CH - March 11, 1840, Wednesday. Married: In New Woodstock, February 13th, Spencer Mitchel, of Perryville, to Matilda L. Dryer of the former place.

CH - April 1, 1840. Married: In Lenox, on the 25th ult. by the Rev. A. P. Mason, Mr. William Munroe, of New Boston, to Miss Elmira, daughter of Silas Sayles, Esq. of Lenox.

CH - April 15, 1840. Married: In Schenectady on the 9th inst. by the Rev. A. Yates, D. D., John R. Stuyvesant, Esq. of Edgewood, Hyde Park, and Miss Mary A. Yates, of that city.

CH - April 22, 1840. Died: In this town, at 3 o'clock this morning, Mr. John P. Ehle, aged 65 years.

CH - April 29, 1840. Married: In this village, on Sunday last, by the Rev. Mr. Abell, Mr. Edward Jones to Miss Rebecca Mills, all of this village.

CH - May 6, 1840. Married: On Wednesday evening, April 29, by the Rev. Mr. Tuttle, at the residence of John McViccar, Esq., Rev. Charles Jones, of LaFargeville, Jefferson County, to Miss Calcina P. Gardner, of Fayetteville, Onondaga County.

CH - May 6, 1840. Died: At Canastota, very suddenly, on the 14th ult., in the 20th year of her age, Mary Jane, wife of Israel S. Spencer, Esq., and daughter of Nathan S. Roberts, of Lenox.

CH - May 13, 1840. Died: On the 22nd ult. at North Easton, Massachusetts of consumption, Miss Lucy M. Sanger, aged 24 years, eldest daughter of Joseph Sanger, Esq. of this village.

CH - May 20, 1840. Died: At Wheeler, Steuben County, on the 13th of May, Mrs. Mary, wife of Conrad Overhizer, in the 85th year of her age (poem).

CH - July 1, 1840. Married: In Fayetteville, on Sunday last, by the Rev. M. Hase, Mr. Patrick Curtis, of this village, to Miss Thirza Browning, of the former place.

CH - July 1, 1840. Married: In Nelson, on the 24th inst., by the Rev. E. L. Wadsworth, Mr. Orlando Cushing, of Sullivan, to Miss Clara Hyatt, of the former place.

CH - July 1, 1840. Died: In this village on Saturday morning last, Mr. Aaron Kellogg, aged 78 years, an old and respected inhabitant of this town.

CH - July 8, 1840. Married: In this village, on Sunday last, by the Rev. Z. Barnes, Mr. William Shaver to Miss Ann Jones of this village.

CH - July 8, 1840. Married: In this village, on the 5th, by the Rev. Z. Barnes, Mr. David Sunderlin to Mrs. Sarah Horner, both of this village.

CH - July 15, 1840. Died: In this town, on Saturday last, Mr. William Starr, aged 56 years.

CH - July 22, 1840. Married: In East Avon, Livingston County, on Wednesday morning the 15th inst. by the Rev. C. Coats, Mr. George Steele, of the firm of Curtis and Steele, merchants of this village, to Miss Adelia E. Wright of the former place.

CH - July 22, 1840. Died: In this town, on Monday evening last, after a lingering illness, Mr. William Brown, aged about 33 years (of Canaseraga).

CH - July 22, 1840. Died: At Wheeler, Steuben County, on the 7th inst., Mr. Conrad Overhizer, in the 87th year of his age.

CH - July 29, 1840. Married: In Fayetteville, on Sunday last, by the Rev. Mr. Smizter, Mr. Richard Quackenbush, of Cicero, Onondaga County, to Miss Betsey Ehle, of this town.

CH - August 12, 1840. Died: In this town, on Thursday night last, Mrs. Eliza Deline, wife of Henry Deline.

CH - August 26, 1840. Died: In New Boston, on the 18th, Mr. Calvin Burr, aged 54 years.

CH - August 26, 1840. Died: In this town, on the 18th, Mr. Peter Myers, aged 54.

CH - August 26, 1840. Died: On the 25th inst., Helen Maria, infant daughter of Albro and Adeline Hall.

CH - August 26, 1840. Died: At Verona, Oneida County, on the 16th inst., Mr. Isaac Benedict, aged 21 years and 5 months.

CH - September 2, 1840. Died: In this town, on Wednesday last, a child of Mr. N. Lathrop.

CH - September 2, 1840. Died: On Thursday last, Miss C. Adams, aged 23 years.

CH - September 2, 1840. Died: Darwin Bartholomew of Cazenovia, drowned at Cazenovia, July 11 (poem).

CH - September 2, 1840. Died: Miss Sarah Stone, died at Skaneateles, August 3rd, aged 24 years.

CH - Septmeber 9, 1840. Married: In this town, on Wednesday evening last, by the Rev. Mr. Smitzer, of Cazenovia, Mr. Perry C. Weaver, to Miss Mary Jane, daughter of John Knowles, Jr., Esq. of this town.

CH - September 9, 1840. Died: In this town on the 5th, Jefferson Marble, aged 16 (killed by a falling tree).

CH - September 16, 1840. Died: On Saturday evening, in this village, at the residence of the Rev. J. Abell, after a short but distressing sickness, Miss Emily S., daughter of D. P. Bogue, Esq., of St. Albans, Vermont, aged 16 years. (attended Female Seminary, Utica)

CH - September 16, 1840. Died: At Fayetteville, Onondaga County, New York, on the 14th of September inst., Mary M. Palmer, daughter of Sandford B. Palmer, age 20 years; (2 brothers and 2 sisters survive).

CH - September 23, 1840. Died: In the town of Nelson, on Tuesday the 22nd inst., after a lingering illness, Jeremiah Whipple, Esq., aged 74.

CH - September 30, 1840. Married: In New Boston, on Wednesday last, by the Rev. James Abell, of Chittenango, Mr. Amos L. Story, of Syracuse, to Miss Laura A. Barr, of New Boston.

CH - September 30, 1840. Married: In Cazenovia, on Thursday evening last, by the Rev. Mr. Leonard, Mr. Leonard Williams, of this village, to Miss Sophia, daughter of Col. George Ehle, of the former place.

CH - October 7, 1840. Married: In the town of Fenner, on Sunday evening the 4th inst., by Silas Judd, Esq., Mr. Lewis L. Holmes to Miss Jane M. Barrett, both of Chittenango.

CH - October 7, 1840. Died: At Lenox on October 1 (Thursday last), Nancy P. Lansing, wife of Jacob, age 33 (2 stanza poem).

CH - October 14, 1840. Married: In this town, on the 9th inst., by J. French, Esq., Mr. Alfred B. Morgan to Miss Mary E. Skank.

CH - October 14, 1840. Died: At Amsterdam, Montgomery County, on the 12th inst. of bilious fever, Cornelia B., wife of Mr. George T. Perry, formerly of this village (obituary next week, see note on next page).

CH - October 14, 1840. Died: In this town of Peru, Onondaga County, on the 14th ult. of bilious fever, Mr. James Peckham. (He stated that his father lived in or near Perryville, Madison County.)

CH: - October 14, 1840. Married: At Albion, Orleans Co., on the 8 (?) inst., by the Rev. Gilbert Crawford, Gen. John B. Lee, to Miss Mary Jane Dayton, daughter of Herman V. Prentice, formerly of Lenox.

CH - October, 28, 1840. Died in this village, Monday last, Mrs. Elizabeth, wife of Mr. A. V. Boardman, age 21 yrs.

CH - November 4, 1840. Died in Schenectady, on Sat. eve last, after a lingering illness, Mrs. Margaret, wife of Mr. Mattaniah Lyon, of that place.

CH - November 11, 1840. Married at Clockville on the 8th inst. by Rev. Allen Murray, Mr. Solomon Webb to Miss Harriet Gilbert, daughter of William Gilbert, Esq., all of Lenox

CH - November 25, 1840. Married in Syracuse on the 11th inst. by Rev. J. W. Adams, Gen. Rensselaer Van Rensselear, of the Patriot Army, to Miss Mary Euphemia, only dau. of Maj. Samuel S. Forman of Syracuse.

CH - November 25, 1840. Died suddenly in this town, on Saturday evening last, Mr. Henry Doxtader, age 24 yrs.

CH - December 2, 1840: married in this town, on Thurs. evening, the 26th of November, by Rev. James Abell, Mr. Perez D. Harrington, to Miss Charlotte Riddle. Also at the same time, by the same, Mr. Benjamin Jenkins to Miss Frances Riddle, dau. of Robert Riddle, Esq., all of this town.

CH - December 9, 1840. Mr. Samuel Baldwin, age 22 yrs., found dead in his bed, on Sun. morning the 6th of Dec. in the house of Pardon Barnard, Esq. of Lenox (poisoned by carbonic acid gas from a dish of coals in his room.)

CH - December 23, 1840. Died in Kingston, Upper Canada, on the 11th of Dec., inst., at the residence ot Mr. H. Haight, after a protracted illness of five weeks, Mrs. Ann Livingston, aged 77 yrs.

CH - January 6, 1841. Married at Burnt Hills, Saratoga Co.[NY]. on the 31st ult., by the Rev. Mr. Greene, Mr. Benjamin H. Sage, to Miss Sarah M. Hollister all of that place. Also at the same time, Mr. Samuel Titus, Jun., to Miss Mary Hollister, all of that place.

CH- January 6, 1841. Died in this village, on the morning of the 4th inst., after a protracted illness of 8 weeks, Mrs. Rebecca Rogers, age 76 yrs.

CH - January 20, 1841. Married at the residence of her father in Lenox, on the evening of the 4th inst., by the Rev. Alanson P. Mason, Mr. Daniel Cady, of the firm of N. S. and D. Cady, Clockville, to Miss Fidelia W. Palmer, only dau. of A. H. Palmer, Esq.

CH - January 20, 1841. Died in Lenox, on the 5th inst., after a short illness, Mr. Asa Cranson, one of the Patriots of the Revolution, aged 80 yrs.

CH - January 27, 1841. Notice: John Evans advertised his wife, Susan, "eloped from my bed and board."

CH - February 3, 1841. Married in Lafayette, Onondaga Co., NY on Monday, 25th Jan., by Rev. Mr. McCarthy, Mr. Wellington E. Barnard, of this town, to Miss Louisa, dau. of Mr. Samuel A. Keene of the former place.

CH - February 3, 1841. Married in Clockville, on Wed. last, Mr. Joseph V. Wells of this town to Miss---Forbes of Lenox.

CH - February 3, 1841. Died at Fayetteville, Onondaga Co., NY on Sat., the 23rd ult., Mrs. Charlotte (formerly Charlotte Haight, of Chittenango), wife of Mr. Elms of that place, aged 36 yrs.

CH - February 10, 1841. Married in Brookfield on Thurs., the 4th inst., by Rev. J. Wells, Mr. Joshua Crumb of Plainfield, to Miss Grace Brown, of the former place. The groom was about 6 ft. in height and the bride a little more than half his stature.

CH - February 10, 1841. Died in Smithfield on Tues. morning, the 2nd inst., Mr. Czar Dikeman, aged about 55 yrs. He was found dead in his bed and is supposed to have died of a nightmare.

CH - February 10, 1841. Died in Perryville, on Friday the 5th, Miss Margaret Tuttle, daughter of Mr. John Tuttle, aged 23 yrs.

CH - February 10, 1841. Died at Lenox, MI, 28 Dec. 1840, Mansfield Harris, son of Mason Harris formerly of Madison Co., NY.

CH - February 17, 1841. Married in Fayetteville, on Wed., 10th inst., by Rev. M. Switzer, Mr. James Hatch, to Miss Charlotte Holbrook, both of this village.

CH - February 24, 1841. Died in this town in the 9th inst., of dropsey, Mr. Josiah Snell, aged 30 yrs.

CH - February 24, 1841. Died in this town on the 15th inst. of dropsey, Miss Mary Davis, daughter of Edmond Davis, aged 25 yrs.

CH - March 10, 1841. Married in this village, on Wed., last by Rev. J. Abell, Esq., Mr. Horace Heath, to Miss Mary Jane Wesley, both of this town.

CH - March 10, 1841. Married in Fayetteville, on the third inst., by the Rev. A. C. Tuttle, Mr. William H. Palmer, to Miss Sarah S. Warner, both of Lenox [Madison Co.]

CH - March 17, 1841. Married at the house of Salmon Wilcox, in Clockville, March 8th, 1841 by Isaac J. Forbes, Esq., Mr. Lewis Friedman, to Miss Caty Ann Ostrander.

CH - March 17, 1841. Died suddenly at Perryville, on Sat., the 13th inst., Miss Elizabeth Hill, daughter of Mr. Nathaniel Hill, aged 20 yrs.

CH - March 24, 1841. Married in Stockbridge, on the 10th inst. by the Rev. S. M. Bainbridge, Mr. Roswell Whitman, formerly of Lenox, to Miss Betsey Porter of the former place.

CH - March 24, 1841. Married in this village, on the 20th inst., by the Rev. M. O'Farrel, Mr. Enos Eggleston, to Mrs. Sally Wattles, all of this place.

CH - March 24, 1841. Died in Sullivan, on the 25th inst., Mr. Samuel Harper, aged 65 yrs. He said he had relations near Binghamton.

CH - April 7, 1841: Died in Augusta, Oneida Co., on the 3rd inst., Archibald Murray, aged 80 yrs.

CH - April 21. 1841. Married in Fayetteville, on Thurs. last, by Elder Switzer, Mr. Charles B. Bannister, to Miss Maria W. Lawrence, both of that place.

CH - April 21, 1841. Died in this town on the 13th inst., Mr. Silas Fyler, aged 58 yrs.

CH - May 5, 1841. Died in Fenner, on the 30th ult., Mr. David Baldwin, aged 74 yrs.

CH - May 5, 1841. Died, Polly Mitchell of Madison Co., on the canal boat, *Rodney* on May 2nd.

CH - May 5, 1841. Died in Perryville, on the 1st inst., Seth Holmes, aged 5 yrs.

CH - May 5, 1841. Died at Key West [FL], on the 12th of April, of consumption, Mr. Joseph S. Beecher, aged 22 yrs., only son of Sylvester Beecher, Esq., of Lenox in this county.

CH - May 26, 1841. Died in Canaseraga, on Wednesday, last, in the 17th year of her age, of consupmtion, Miss Mary Starr, eldest daughter of Seth Starr, Esq.

CH - June 2, 1841. Died at Key West [FL], on 12th of April, Joseph S. Beecher, only son of Hon. Sylvester Beecher...[additional obituary]. [Local legend has it that his body was returned home in a barrel of whiskey.]

CH - June 7, 1841 [Mon.]. Married in this town, on Thursday evening last, by Rev. Mr. Breese, Major Alvin Keller, to Miss Olive Ehle, daughter of Henry Ehle, Esq., all of this town.

CH - June 7, 1841. Married on Thursday evening last, in this town, by the Rev. D. M. D. O'Farrell, Mr. Adrian V. Boardman to Miss Lavenia Louer.

CH - June 16, 1841. Married in Lenox, on the 18th of May last, by Rev. Washington Kingsley, Mr. N. R. Chapman, Esq., to S. C. Evans.

CH - June 16, 1841. Married in Smithfield on the 26th ult., by Rev. Mr. Stanley, Mr. James Cowen to Miss Miranda Brown.

CH - June 16, 1841. Died in this town, June 3rd, in the 58th year of her age, Mrs. Edith Buttolph, wife of Mr. John Buttolph.

CH - June 16, 1841. Died in Lenox, on the 29th ult., Pardon Barnard, Esq., formerly sheriff of this county, in the 58th year of his age.

CH - June 16, 1841. Died in Clockville, on the 8th inst., Mrs. William Wilcox.

CH - June 16, 1841. Died on the 3th (?) of May last, at Knoxville, IL, Col. Harman Knox, formerly of Knoxville, Madison Co., age abt. 45 yrs.

CH - June 16, 1841. Died in Knoxville, on the 28th ult.(?), Miss Nancy Stuart, aged 29 yrs.

CH - June 16, 1841. Died in Morrisville, on the 28th ult., a daughter of Mr. N. Richmond, age 2 yrs.

CH - June 16, 1841. In the same place [as above], on the 29th [May?], Mrs. Oliva Brown.

CH - July 7, 1841. Died in this village, on Sun. morning last, Mrs. Margaret Bristol, age 88 yrs.

CH - July 7, 1841. Died in Lenox, on the 16th of June, Amelia, dau. of N. H. Palmer, aged 2 yrs.

CH - July 7, 1841. Died in Stockbridge, on the 21st [June?] Mr. William Porter, age 52 yrs.

CH - July 14, 1841. Married at Chittenango Falls, July 10, by Rev. J. Watson, Mr. Nicholas Easterbrook, of Manlius, to Miss Susanna Gidley, recently from England.

CH - July 28, 1841. Died on the 24th inst. at Chittenango, Madison Co., NY, after a short illness of eight hours, Sarah Catherine, only child of James Crouse, Esq. age 1 yr. and 6 mos.

CH - July 28, 1841. Died at Stonington, CT, on Tues, the 13th inst., Capt. Ebenezer Cobb.

CH - August 4, 1841. Died on Sat., the 31st ultimo, Mr. Clark Rodgers, formerly of this town, a blacksmith, committed suicide at his residence in the town of Fabius.

CH - August 11, 1841. Died on the 30th ult., at Lisbon, NH, Mary, wife of Fletcher J. Barron, Esq., in the 40th yr. of her age

CH - August 18, 1841. Died in this town on the 6th inst., Mrs. Sarah Warren, age 78 yrs.

CH - August 25, 1841. Married in this town on Tues., the 12th inst., by Rev. J. Abell, Mr. Andrew Luther, to Miss Susan Sickles, all of this town.

CH - September (1?), 1841. Died at Lake Court House, IN, August 7, Mrs. Harriet C. Palmer, wife of Henry D. Palmer, M. D., and dau. of Asa Cady of Sullivan, age 30 yrs.

CH - September 8, 1841. Died at Cohoes Falls, yesterday morning, Maj. Joseph W. Sage, son of Col. H. Sage of this town.

CH - September 8, 1841. Died in this town, on Friday, the 13th ult., Mrs. Hannah, wife of Mr. Chauncey Wright, age 36 yrs.

CH - September 22, 1841. Married at Matthew's Mills on the evening of the 12th inst., by the Rev. G. W. Thomson, Mr. Vespasian Adams, to Miss Sophia Delany.

CH - September 22, 1941. Died in Canaseraga, Thursday, last, on the 11th inst., Marcus Casler, age 75 yrs.

CH - September 29, 1841. Died at his residence in Morrisville, on Thurs., the 16th inst., Bennet Bicknell, Esq., in the 60th year of his age (a native of Mansfield, CT, settled in Morrisville in 1808. In 1812, he represented Madison in the Assembly; in 1814, the State Senate, etc. etc.).

CH - October 6, 1841. Married at the White Springs in this town by the Hon. H. G. Warner, Mr. Philo C. Weaver, of Frankfort, Herkimer Co., NY to Miss Robah C. Willard, daughter of Mr. Rufus Willard, of the former place.

CH - October 6, 1841. Married in Auburn on the 29th ult., by the Rev. D. A. Shepard, Mr. Almon Dwight, to Miss Mary L. Comstock, of the former place.

CH - October 6, 1941. Married on Thurs, the 30th ult., at Sweden, Monroe Co., NY, by Rev. A. Handy, of Chittenango, Mr. George C. Smith and Miss Matilda Cook, both of the former place.

CH - October 6, 1841. Died in New York [City], on the 28th ult., Mrs. Catharine, wife of Hon. Henry Yates, and mother of Charles Yates, Esq. of that city.

CH - October 6, 1841. Died in this town, on Sun. morning last, Mr. E. Sherwin, aged 61 yrs.

CH - October 13, 1841. Died in the village of New Salem,. Albany Co., NY, on Friday the 1st inst., Mrs. Margaret Stalker, consort of Alexander Stalker, deceased, age 66 yrs.

CH - October 20, 1841. Married in this town, on Wed. the 13th inst., by Rev. A. Handy, John W. Cady, Esq., of Johnstown, Fulton Co., NY, and Miss Marianne Hayes, of Rome, Oneida Co. NY.

CH - October 20, 1841. Married in the town of Cazenovia, on the 13th inst., by the Rev. Luther Myrick, Mr. Cyrus Whitcomb, to Miss Harriet E. Whipple, all of that town.

CH - November 3, 1841. Died in this village, on Thursday night last, of consumption, Mrs. Rachel, wife of Abner P. Downer, Esq., age 42 yrs.

CH - November 3, 1841. In New Boston, on Friday morning last, of inflamation of the lungs, Mr. Abram Lee, in the 61st year of his age; one of the oldest and most respectable inhaabitants of this town.

CH - November 10, 1841. Died in New York [City], on the 6th inst., after a lingering illness, Mr. John M. Todd, in the 42nd year of his age.

CH - November 17, 1841. Died in this village, on Monday morning last, Mary Olevia, dau. of Mr. Thomas French, in the 4th year of her age.

CH - November 17, 1841. Died on the 10th inst., William Wallace, son of Mr. James Rouse, aged 11 yrs.

CH - November 24. 1841. Married in this town on the 17th inst., by J. French, Esq., Mr. Harry Babcock of Earlville to Miss Margaret Becker of this town

CH - November 24, 1841. Married in this town on the 17th inst., by the Rev. Mr. Handy, Mr. Richard Dunn and Miss Lina Robinson.

CH - November 24, 1841. Died in Schenectady, on the 15th [inst.], Mr. Stephen Carter, formerly of Chittenango, aged about 30 yrs.

CH - December 1, 1841. Died in Fenner, on the 12th ult., Miss Lavinia Covey, dau. of Deac. Amos Covey, aged 17 yrs.

CH - December 1, 1841. Died in Lenox, on the 26th [ult.], Mr. Ephraim R. Reynolds, aged 24 yrs.

CH - December 8, 1841. Married on Thurs. last, at Syracuse, by Rev. Mr. Gregory, Mr. William H. Gale, to Miss Elizabeth Marks, dau. of Samuel Marks, of this village.

CH - December 22, 1841. Died on the 13th [inst], in the Glen and Yates allotment, on the Sacandaga River, Saratoga Co., NY, at the country seat of Miss Ann Yates, Alexander Macdonnell, Esq., of Glengarry, Canada, aged 41 yrs., nephew of the Hon. J. B. Yates, deceased.

CH - December 22, 1841. Died in Auburn, on the 4th inst., James Thompson, infant son of John W. and Julia A. Haight, aged 9 months.

CH - December 22, 1841. Married in Fenner on the 14th inst., by the Rev. Mr. White, of Clockville, Mr. Lester Tucker, of Smithfield, to Miss Lucy Cranson, of the former place.

CH - January 19, 1842. Died in Stuyvesant, on the 9th inst., in the 35th year of her age, Rebecca, wife of Richard Graves and dau. of the late Col. Daniel Warner of Canaan, and sister of Hon. H. G. Warner, of Chittenango.

CH - January 26, 1842. Died in this town, suddenly, on the 19th inst., Fidelia Delaney, eldest dau. of Mrs. James Peck, age 18 yrs.

CH - February 2, 1842. Died in this town, Jan. 27th, of consumption, Miss Sarah L. Beebe, only dau. of James and Alathea Beebe, age 17 yrs., 4 mos.. and 15 days;.Funeral at the Universalist Church in Sullivan. (Long eulogy published the following week.)

CH - February 16, 1842. Married in this town on the 15th, by Rev. A. Handy, Philip Wager, Jun. to Miss Phebe Anne Barnard, all of this town.

CH - February 23, 1842: Married at Skaneateles, on the 14th inst., by Rev. S. W. Brace, Mr. John G. Crapsey, of this town, to Miss Eliza Ann Olin, of the former place,

CH - March 2, 1842. Married on Thurs. last, Mr. Joseph S. Wager, to Miss Hannah Niffen.

CH - March 2, 1842. Married at Chittenango, on the 24th ult., by Rev. Thomas Houston, Mr. Albert VanSlyke, to Miss Elvira Riant, both of Dewitt, Onondaga Co., NY.

CH - March 9, 1842. Died at Bridgeport, of consumption, Mr. Isaac H. Edgerton, in the 54th year of his age.

CH - March 9, 1842. Died in this town on the 24th ult., of consumption, Mr. James Peck, age 52 yrs., one of the early settlers of this town.

CH - March 16, 1842. Died in Nelson on Friday last, Mr. Charles Burton, age 66 yrs.

CH - March 23, 1842. Married in this town, on the 20th inst., by J. French, Esq., Mr. Harvey W. Hall, to Miss Lucy J. Miller.

CH - March 23, 1842: Died in this village on Saturday last, Mrs. Charlotte, wife of James L. Hatch, aged 20 yrs.

CH - March 30, 1842. Died in Schenectady, on Mon. morning last, of consumption, Mrs. Henrietta, wife of Prof., J. A. Yates of Union College, age 33 yrs.

CH - April 6, 1842. Died on Sunday evening, the 27th ult., at Union College, Mrs. Henrietta M. Yates, wife of Rev. John Austin Yates, D. D., aged 33 yrs.

CH - April 13, 1842. Died in this village, on Fri. morning last, of consumption, Mr. Abraham DeLine, age 33 (or 38) yrs.

CH - April 27, 1842. Married in this town, on Tues. evening the 26th inst., by the Rev. James Abell, Mr. Luther Kelley, of Geneva, to Miss Jennette E. Sage, dau. of Col. H. Sage, of this town.

CH - April 27, 1842. Died in this town on the 22nd inst., Mrs. Ruth Clark, Wife of Thomas Clark, Esq., in the 65th yr. of her age

CH - May 11, 1842. Married in Oswego, on the 28th ult., by the Rev. R. W. Condit, Mr. Thomas S. Myrick, editor of the *Madison County Eagle*, To Miss Hannah B. Sprague, of Oswego.

CH - May 18, 1842. Married in Brookfield, MA on the 21st ult., by Rev. Moses Chase, Mr. Oliver S. Cooke, of the firm of Mariam & Cooke, book printers, to Miss Abby E. Barnes, all of that place.

CH - May 18, 1842. Married in Canastota, on the 24th of April, by Rev. Mr. Stokes, Mr. Asa Cranson of Lenox Hill, to Miss Olive Ward.

CH - May 18, 1842. Married on the 8th [May], the Rev. Mr. Pease, to Miss Ann Pinney, of Clockville.

CH - May 18, 1842. Married in Fenner on the 12th [May], by the Rev. L. Wright, of Clockville, Mr. William Onion, and Miss Eunice Shelly.

CH - May 18, 1842. Died on Lenox Hill, May 7th, Elizabeth, dau. of Mr. William Morrison, Jr., aged 11 yrs.

CH - May 25, 1842. Died in Perryville on Sun. last, of consumption, Mr. Thomas J. Whiting, age 37 yrs.

CH - May, 25, 1842. Died in this town on the 20th inst., William, son of Isaac and Nancy Garlock, age 3 yrs., 5 mos.

CH - May 25, 1842. Died on the 10th inst., Prof. Amos Eaton, of Troy, in the 66th year of his age.

CH - May 25, 1842. Died in Cazenovia, on the 14th inst., of cancer, Mr. Jesse Kilborn, in the 64th yr. of his age. He was from Litchfield, CT and settled in this town more than 35 yrs. ago.

CH - June 1, 1842. Died in this town, yesterday afternoon, [May 31] Col. Stephen Lee, aged 62 yrs.

CH - June 1, 1842. Died at Perryville, Madison Co., NY, May 22nd, Mr. Thomas J. Whiting, aged 37 yrs. Obituary follows: "Long a resident of Perryville; his wife died 2 yrs. ago; a brother survives."

CH - June 8, 1841. Married in Pautucket, RI, May 20th by Rev. Silas Spaulding, Mr. Oliver Clark of this town, to Miss Sarah Green of the former place.

CH - June 15, 1842 (Wed.). Married in this village Wed. last, by Rev. T. Houston, Mr. George Adams, to Miss Mary Ann Forbes, all of this village.

CH - June 29, 1842. Died in Moscow, Livingston Co., NY, on the 20th inst., Mrs. Helen M. Vanderkar, dau. of Thomas Livingston, formerly of this place.

CH - July 6, 1842. Died on Lenox Hill, the 20th of June, Mr. William Kasson, of delirium tremens, aged 28 yrs.

CH - July 13, 1842. Died in Auburn, on Tues., the 5th inst., Mary Comstock, wife of Mr. A. Dwight, in the 23rd year of her age. She was a member of the Methodist Church.

CH - July 27, 1842. Died on Lenox Hill on the 21st inst., of consumption, Mrs. Lovicy D., wife of Major N. B. Lamb, aged 27 years.

CH - July 27, 1842. Died at Wampsville, on the 23rd [July], a son of Mr. Lambert Burghardt, aged 10 years.

CH - August 3, 1842. Married at Cazenovia on the 14th instant, by Rev. Francis Hawley, Calvin Carpenter, Esq. and Miss Marietta S. Gridley, all of that village.

CH - August 3, 1842. Died in the village of Cazenovia, July 21st, after a long an lingering illness, Jane Hearsey, wife of G. R. Parmalee, aged 23 yrs., 11 mos. and 3 days.

CH - August 3, 1842. Died in Fenner, of consumption, in the 16th year of her age, Betsey Hall, dau. of Asabel and Chloe Hall.

CH - August 10, 1842. Married at Wampsville, on the 31st of July, by the Rev. Mr. Cooper, Mr. George Parkill, to Miss Electa Herrick, both of Clockville.

CH - August 10, 1842. Married in this town, on Thursday, the 23rd ult., George B. Greenwood to Ro[w]ena Crawford.

CH - August 10, 1842. Died in Fenner, Mr. Benjamin Woodworth, a patriot of the Revolution, aged 83 yrs. [A long obituary published in the Aug. 24th issue.]

CH - August 17, 1842. Married in Utica on the 8th inst. by the Rev. Dr. Potter, Eliphalet Nott, D. D., President of Union College, Schenectady, to Miss Urania E. Sheldon, Principal of the Utica Female Seminary.

CH - August 31, 1842. Died in Sullivan, Madison Co., NY, on Sat., the 27th of August, aged 54 yrs., Mrs. Polly Heath, consort of John Heath.

CH - September 7, 1842. Married at Chittenango, on the 4th inst. by Rev. T. Houston, Deacon David Smith, of Nelson to the widow Sylvia Warren of New Boston.

CH - September 14. 1842: Married in Morrisville on the 15th [Aug.?] Mr. Gerrit Sayles, to Miss Mara Garvey, both of Clockville.

CH - September 14, 1842. Died in this village, on Friday last, Edward Henry, son of Mr. A. Bellamy, age 2 yrs., 6 mos.

CH - September 14, 1841. Died in New Boston, in the 16th inst., Mr.George I. Monroe, aged about 53 yrs.

CH - September 28, 1842. Married in Van Buren, Onondaga Co., on the 15th(?) inst. by the Rev. Mr. Houghton, Mr. Asabel Clark, to Miss Betsey M. Peck, all of that town.

CH - September 28, 1842. Died in Smithfield, on the 10th inst., Mrs. Marshall, wife of Cyrennus Marshall, formerly of Stockbridge Hill, in this county, aged 45 yrs.

CH - October 5, 1842. Married in Camillus, on the 18th ult., by the Rev. Mr. Daggett, Mr. James Kinne, of Dewitt, to Miss Almira, youngest dau. of Esq. Hay of the former place.

CH - October 19, 1842. Married at Fenner on the 12th inst., by Rev. T. Houston, Abner P. Downer, Esq, of this village to Miss Harriet Hamblin, of the former town.

CH - October 19, 1842. Married at North Granville, Washington Co., NY, on Wednesday evening, Oct. 5, by Leonard Johnson, Mr. James Walrath, of the firm of Walrath & Bellamy, merchants of this village, to Miss Esther R., dau. of the late R. W. Oliphant, of the former place.

CH - October 19, 1842: Married in Lenox, on Sunday last, Mr. William Noyes, to Miss Harriet Holmes of Canaseraga.

CH - October 19, 1842. Married in Sullivan, on the 24th ult., Simon Fargo, to Jerusha Thompson, of that town.

CH - October 19, 1842. Married in this village, on the 17th inst., Richard McCoy to the widow Ransier.

CG - October 19, 1942. Died in Troy on the 9th inst., Jane, dau. of Mr. John G. Yates of Chittenango, age 18 yrs.

CH - October 19, 1842. Died in New Orleans, on the 19th ult., of yellow fever, Elisha W. Baker, printer, formerly of Cazenovia, aged 32 yrs.

CH - November 2, 1842. Died suddenly in Fenner on Monday last, Helen, daughter of Widow H. Barrett, of this village, aged 14 yrs.

CH - November 9, 1842. Married in Canastota, on Wednesday last, by the Rev. Mr. Wright, Col. Stephen G. Lamb to Miss Harriet Lewis, all of the town of Lenox.

CH - November 16, 1841. Married in this town, on the evening of the 15th inst., by the Rev. J. Abell, Miss Mary E. Sage, dau. of Col. H. Sage, to Mr. Augustus Frisbee, all of this town.

CH - November 23 1842. Married in this town, on the 20th, by the Rev. J. Abell, Mr. William Button, to Miss Polly Kelly, all of this town.

CH - November 30, 1842. Married in Smithfield, on the 16th Oct., by the Rev. S. M. Bainbridge, Mr. Royal L. Mason, to Miss Betsey Marshall.

CH - November 30. 1842: Married on Lenox Hill, on the 17th of Nov., by Rev. Lyman Wright, Mr. Thomas S. Streeter, to Miss Maria, daughter of Joshua J. Palmer. The parties are aged 14 and 18 yrs.

CH - November 30, 1842. Married in Clockville, on the 20th [Nov.], Mr. Truman Partidge, to Miss Clarissa Farley.

CH - Wednesday, December 7, 1842. Died in this town, on the 3rd inst., Mr. Electus Adams, aged 34 years, after a lingering illness.

CH - December 14, 1842. Married at Jamesville, on the 8th inst., by Rev. Mr. Cleveland, Mr. Philander Trowbridge, of Hartsville, to Miss R. H. Hadley of the former place.

CH - December 21, 1842. Died in this village, on the 13th inst., Miss Anna Maria Gidley, aged 28 yrs.

CH - December 21, 1842. Died in this town, on Wed. last, of consumption, Mr. Hiram Ehle, son of Peter P. Ehle, aged about 26 yrs.

CH - December 14, 1842. Died on Sunday last, Mr. --- Jennings.

CH - December 28, 1842. Married at Eagle Village, on the 22nd inst., by Rev. Mr. Knox, Mr. Andrew Anguish, of this town, to Miss Mary A. Skellenger, of the former place.

CH - December 28, 1842. Married in this village, on the 25th, by the Rev. James Abell, Mr. Elijah Moyer, to Miss Mary Bellinger, all of this village.

CH - Jan. 18, 1843. Married in this village, on Sunday last, by Rev. James Abell, Mr. Thomas Parks, of Waterloo, Seneca Co., NY, to Miss Charlotte Van Wie, of this village.

CH - January 18, 1843. Married in this town on the 12th inst., by Rev. James Abell, Mr. Henry Herrick, to Miss Fidelia Lee, all of this town.

CH - January 18, 1843. Married in the town of Cazenovia, on the 17th inst., by Rev. Mr. Clarke, Mr. Fordice Cowing, to Miss Betsey Jane Kellogg, of the former place.

CH - Jan. 18, 1843: Married in Fayetteville, on the 4th inst., by Rev. Mr. Hickok, Mr. Brown Sayres, of Manlius, to Miss Henrietta Eastwood, of this town.

CH - Jan. 18, 1843: Married in Cazenovia, on the 4th, by Rev. Mr. Redfield, H. N. Shapley, Esq., and Miss Jane Eliza, only daughter of Col. James Berthrong, all of that place.

CH - Jan. 18, 1843: Died at his residence in Cazenovia, on the 12th inst., Mr. Charles Parmelee aged 55 yrs.

CH - Jan. 25, 1843: Married in Niles, MI, in the 24th ult., by the Rev. Mr. Boughton, Mr. Benjamin Horned, to Miss Eliza P. Willard, dau. of Mr. Rufus Willard, of this town, all of the above place.

CH - July 5, 1843. Wed. A. M. Married in Fenner, May 21, by the Rev. T. Houston, Mr. John Heath, to Miss Catharine Lansing, both of Fenner.

CH - July 5, 1843. Married in this village May 31st by Rev. T. Houston, Mr. Thomas Teft to Miss Rachel Decolon of Chittenango.

CH - July 5, 1843. Married in the village on the 7th of May, by Rev. Mr. Blakeslee of Perryville, Mr. Robert Harrison, to Miss Mary A. Button, both of this village.

CH - July 5, 1843. Married on the 26th of March, at the Reformed Church in the village, by Rev. James Abell, Mr. James Drew, to Miss Phebe Sunderland, all of this village.

CH - July 5, 1843. Married in this village, on the 2nd of March, by Rev. James Abell, Mr. J. S. Harrington, of Utica, to Miss Henrietta Riddle, dau. of Robert Riddle, Esq., of this village.

CH - July 5, 1843. Married in this town, April 5, Rev. Mr. Blakeslee, Mr. John Sickles, to Miss Sarah Farnham, both of this town.

CH - July 5, 1843. Married at Canaseraga, April ---, by Rev. Mr. Blakeslee, Mr. Charles Severance, to Miss Sarah Wylie.

CH - July 5, 1843. Married at Mr. Balch's Hotel in this village, by Rev. Mr. Blakeslee, Mr. George Dewey, of Pompey, to Miss Helmer.

CH - July 5, 1843. Died in this village, on the lst of June, Mrs. Clementine, wife of Mr. Thomas French, age 43 yrs.

CH - July 5, 1843. Died in this town, on the 26th of May, at the residence of Aaron Kellogg, Esq, Mrs. Ruth Bartlett, aged 78 yrs.

CH - July 5, 1843. Died in this town on the 7th of June, Ruth, wife of Mr. F. Braithwaite, age 33 yrs.

CH - July 5, 1843. Died in this village on the 23rd of May, Mr. Orren E. Thompson, aged 28 yrs.

CH - July 5, 1843. Died in Fenner, on the 26th of April, Miss Susan Mills, aged 60 yrs.

CH - July 5, 1843. Died in this town on the 4th May, Mrs. Catharine, wife of Mr. Bicknell West, age 31 yrs.

CH - July 5, 1843. Died in this village, on the 6th of March, last, Eliza A., wife of Alfred Bellamy, and dau. of the late Robert W. Oliphant, Esq. of North Granville, NY, aged 27 yrs.; member of the Baptist Church of Chittenango.

CH - July 12, 1843. Died at Bridgeport, on the 26th ult., Mr. Moses Jennings, aged 40 yrs.

CH - July 12, 1843. Died at Oneonta, Otsego Co., NY, Mrs. Rachel, wife of J. T. St. John, of that place.

CH - July 26, 1843. Married in Lenox, on the 9th inst., by J. French, Esq., Mr. Ichabod Fink, of Van Buren, to Miss Elizabeth Brown of Sullivan.

CH - August 9, 1843. Married in Pulaski, Oswego Co., NY, on the 30th ult., Mr. Barclay Wooster, to Miss Elizabeth Tifft, of that place.

CH - August 9, 1843. Married in this village on Sun. evening last, by J. French, Esq., Mr. Jireh Baker, to Mrs Mary Warren, both of Syracuse.

CH - August 9, 1843. Died in this town, on the 1st instant, Mrs. Sarah Frederick, aged 91 yrs.

CH - August 23, 1843. Died at his residence in Morrisville, on Sun., the 13th inst., Andrew S. Sloan, Esq, formerly clerk of this county, aged 55 yrs.

CH - August 30, 1843. Married in Salina, on the 20th ult., by the Rev. Mr. Hays, Michael Moore, to Miss Julia Ann Carlon, both of this town.

CH - August 30, 1843. Died in this village, on the 17th inst., Mary E. Shaver, aged 12 years.

CH - September 13, 184. Married at Canaseraga, on the 10th inst., by Jarius French, Esq., Mr. Jacob S. Lansing, to Miss Amelia Douglass, both of that place.

CH - September 13, 1843. Married in this village, Sun. evening last, by Rev. T. Houston, Mr. Jason E. Hazard, to Miss Catherine Walrath, all of this village.

CH - September 13, 1843. Died at Canaseraga, on Fri. evening last, Mrs. Lucy Chapman, consort of Capt. John Chapman, of that village.

CH - September 20, 1843. Married in Morrisville, on the 6th inst., by Rev. Mr. Harrington, Mr. Edward Norton, one of the publishers of the *Madison Observer*, to Miss Almira Westfall, all of that place.

CH - September 20, 1843. Died at Sandstone, Jackson Co., MI, on the 1st inst., Rev. Luther Myrick, formerly of Cazenovia.

CH - October 11, 1843. Married in this village, on the 21st ult., by Rev. T. Houston, Mr. Alonzo Donalson, to Miss Maranda Rice, both of Pompey, Onondaga Co., NY

CH - October 11, 1843. Married in Siloam, on the 14th Sept., Mr. Harrington, to Miss Sarah J. Marshall.

CH - October 11, 1843. Married in Morrisville, on the 28th [ult.?], by the Rev. Mr. Putnam, Mr. Royal C. Sayles, to Miss Margaret Carpenter, both of Clockville; also at the same time and place, and by the same, Mr. Henry Herrick, to Miss Caroline Forbes, also of Clockville.

CH - October 11, 1843. Died in New York [City], on the 3rd inst., Mrs. Sarah L. Sommers, wife of Rev. C. G. Sommers, aged 45 yrs., 2 mos. and 3 days.

CH - October 11, 1843. Died at Clyde, NY on Wed., Oct. 4th of typhus fever, Mr. Julius Bellamy, formerly a merchant of this village, aged 34 yrs.

CH - October 11, 1843. Died in this town Friday last, Mr. Ransom Curtis, aged 41 yrs.

CH - October 11, 1843. Died in Lenox, on Monday last, Miss Salina, dau. of Mr. Norman Clarke, aged about 18 yrs.

CH - October 18, 1843. Married in this village, on Sunday evening last, by Rev. James Abell, Mr. Luke Brosseau, to Miss Jane Hood, all of this town.

CH - October 18, 1843. Died in Baltimore, Maryland, on the morning of the 11th inst., of consumption, Minerva S., wife of John H. Haskell, and daughter of the late Robert W. Oliphant, Esq., of North Granville, NY, aged 26 yrs.

CH - October 18, 1843. Died at Cazenovia, on the morning of the 2nd inst. of an "affection" of the brain, Nicholas Henry, Esq, in the 61st year of his age.

CH - October 18, 1843. Died in this town, on the 9th inst., Miss Celina, dau. of Norman Clark, aged 19 yrs.

CH - October 25, 1943. Died in Lenox, on the 16th [Oct.], John P. Webb, Esq.

CH - November 1, 1843. Married at Peterboro, on Wed. evening, the 18th inst., by Rev. Beriah Greene, Charles Dudley Miller, Cashier of the Madison County Bank, and Miss Elizabeth Smith, dau. of Gerrit Smith, of Peterboro.

CH - November 8, 1843. Married at Middletown, CT, on the 24th October last, by the Rev. E. E. Griswold, Chaucey [Chauncey?] Shaffer, Esq., attorney-at-law, in this village, and Maria R., daughter of Isaac Warner, Esq., of the former place.

CH - November 8, 1843. Married in this village, on Mon. evening last, by Rev. James Abell, Mr. James French, of Syracuse, to Miss Harriet Button, of this village.

CH - November 8, 1843. Married in this village, on Tuesday, the 7th, by Rev. James Abell, Mr. Joseph Matthews, to Miss Mary Ann Hood, all of this village.

CH - November 15, 1843. Married in Fayetteville, on Thursday last, by Rev. James Abell, Mr. Hezekiah Cass, of this town, and Miss Catharine Sayles, of Manlius.

CH - November 22, 1843. Died at Clyde, Wayne Co., NY, on the 4th ult., of billious fever, Br. Julius Bellamy, son of the venerable Dea. Jonathan Bellamy.

CH - November 22, 1843. Married at Canastota, on Wed. evening, the 15th inst., by Rev. Mr. Stanley, Mr. John N. Norton, to Miss Henrietta Quackenbush, all of Canastota.

CH - November 29, 1843. Married in this village, on Wed. last, by Rev. James Abell, Mr. Harvey E. Williams, of Batavia, to Miss Welthy Ann, daughter of Mr. J. G. Cropsey, of this town.

CH - December 6, 1843. Married at Canaseraga, on Sun. evening last, by Rev. James Abell, Thomas French, Esq. to Miss Olive Ann Lee, all of this town.

CH - December 6, 1843. Died in this village, on the 29th of Nov., Helen Elizabeth, only child of Jonas A. and Elizabeth Munroe, age 2 years, three months and fourteen days.

CH - December 13, 1843. Married in this town on the 7th inst., by Rev. James Abell, Mr. Oliver P. Willard, to Miss Phebe Ann Herrick, all of the town.

CH - December 13, 1843. Died in Hamilton, on the 30th ult., Mr. Ichabod Griggs, aged 48 yrs.

CH - December 27, 1843. Married in this town, on Sun. evening last, by Rev. William Morse, Mr. Horace Lincoln, to Miss Nancy Lavantia Campbell, all of this town.

CH - December 27, 1843. Died on Tuesday night, the 19th inst., Miss Jerusha Cobb, 2nd sister of Henry S. Cobb, Esq., both formerly of Norwich, CT.

CH - January 3, 1844. Died in this village, on the morning of the 27th ult., after a short illness, Sarah Ann, only daughter of John and Asenath Metcalf, age 3 years, seven months and seven days. A poem follows.

CH - January 24, 1844. Died in Canaseraga, on Sun. morning last, of consumption, William D. Starr, aged about 21 years, son of Seth Starr, Esq., of that place.

CH - January 24, 1844. Married in Chittenango, on Wednesday evening last, by Rev. James Abell, Mr. Marcus C. Walrath, to Miss Alvira Frederick, all of that place.

CH - January 24, 1844. Married at Perryville, on Monday evening last, by Rev. Daniel S. Morey, Mr. Thomas Dickinson, of Chittenango, and Miss Cynthia, daughter of A. Britt, Esq. of the former place.

CH - January 24, 1844. Married in Chittenango, on the 22nd inst., by Rev. T. Houston, Mr. C. B. Kellum, merchant of Albany, to Miss C. M. Tibbits, of Cazenovia.

CH - January 24, 1844. Married on the 21st inst., at Canastota, by Rev. William E. Fisk, Esq., M. Sanford Hubbard, to Miss Catharine Packard, all of the same place.

CH - January 24, 1844. Married in Chittenango, on the 18th inst., by Jairus French, Esq., Warren Randall, to Miss Catherine Betsinger, both of Clockville.

CH - January 31, 1844. Married in Fayetteville, on Thursday evening last, by the Rev. Mr Cleveland*, Mr. Darwin E. Hurd, of Canastota to Miss Angeline F., daughter of Frederick Pratt, Esq., of the former place. [* Rev. Cleveland was the father of President Grover Cleveland.]

CH - February 21, 1844. Married at Canastota, on Thursday evening last, by Rev. William W. Rand, Mr. William W. Kennedy, to Miss Elmira C., eldest daughter of Jonathan P. Phillips, Esq., all of that place.

CH - February 21, 1844. Married in Chittenango, on the 15th inst., by Rev. James Abell, Mr. James Nichols, of Lysander, Onondaga Co., and Miss Susan Rice of Pompey, Onondaga Co..

CH - February 21, 1844. Married in the same place, and on the same day as the above, by the same, Mr. Samuel Barton, of Vermont, and Miss Lydia Rice, of Pompey.

CH - February 21, 1844. Married in Manlius, on the 14th [inst.], by Rev. James Abell, Mr. Palmer Gardner, of Wisconsin, and Miss Margaret Williams, of the former place.

CH - February 21, 1844.: Married in Chittenango, on the 15th [inst], by J. French, Esq., Mr. James Easterbrook, of Manlius, to Miss Catharine Kasler, of Parrish, Oswego Co., NY.

CH - February 28, 1844, Married at Ogden, Monroe Co., NY, on the 15th inst., by Rev. Mr. Dunning, Mr. James Lyon, to Miss Caroline Cook, only daughter of Daniel Cook, Esq., all of that place.

CH - March 20, 1844. Died in this town, Thursday last, Mr. Thomas Clark, aged 69 years.

CH - March 20, 1844. Died in this town, on Saturday night last, Mrs. Catherine Ehle, aged 92 years.

CH - March 20, 1844. Died in the City of New York, on the 12th inst., Mary Anna, daughter of David White How, and gr. daughter of Rev. C. G. Sommers, aged 1 year, 6 months, 11 days.

CH - March 20, 1844. Died at Orange, Steuben Co., NY, in the 66th year of her age, Mrs. Abigail, wife of Mr. James Overhizer, and daughter of the late Mr. Conrad Overhizer, formerly of this place.

CH - March 20, 1844. Died in this village, Feb. 6th, Sarah Sophia, daughter of David and Sarah Sunderlin, aged 10 months.

CH - March 27, 1844. Married in Chittenango, on the 25th, by J. French, Esq., Henry Greenwood, to Miss Elizabeth Cornelia Hayward, of Lenox.

CH - April 3, 1844. Died on Thursday last, Miss Harriet Swift, at the State Lunatic Asylum on the 28th ult., aged 32 yrs., 6 mos., 6 days, daughter of Mr. Elisha Swift of this town.

CH - April 3, 1844. Died in Sullivan (Canaseraga), on the 20th of March, Mr. Josiah Piersons, eldest son of Anson and Clarissa Piersons, aged 21 yrs, 9 mos., 4 days.

CH - April 10, 1844. Married in Chittenango, on the 2nd inst., by Rev. T. Houston, Mr. Samuel Fisher, of Bloomfield, Ontario Co., NY, to Miss Ann L. White (?), of New Woodstock, Madison Co., NY.

CH - April 10, 1844. Died in Canaseraga on Tues. morning last, Jerome C., son of Jacob and Adelia Schuyler, aged 5 years, 2 months & 11 days.

CH - April 10, 1844. Died in Wayne Co., NY, on the 23rd ult., of consumption, Mr. David Beebe, formerly of this town, aged 35 years.

CH - April 17, 1844. Died in Cazenovia, on Thursday last, Hon. Barak Beckwith, formerly a judge of the County Court, aged about 62 years.

CH - May 1, 1844. Married at H. Judd's Hotel, in Chittenango, on the 23rd of April, by Rev. Mr. Houston, Mr. Warren Forbes, to Miss Mary Richards, both of Lenox.

CH - May 8, 1844. Died in this town, on Monday morning last, Peter Lansing Esq., aged about 60 years.

CH - May 15, 1844. Married in this village, on Sat. evening last, by Rev. Mr. Abell, Mr. Joseph Belmore, to Miss Sarah Ann Case, all of this village.

CH - May 15, 1844. Married in Syracuse, on the 8th (May), by Rev. Mr. Hayes, Patrick McNichols to Mrs. Ann Hennesy, both of this town.

CH - May 15, 1844. Married in Fenner, on the 8th (May), by Rev. L. Wright, of Clockville, Col. N. B. Lamb, of Lenox to Miss Elmira Roberts of Fenner.

CH - May 15, 1844. Died in Canastota, on the 6th inst., Mrs. Caroline Cotton, dau. of Capt. Oliver Clark, aged 25 years.

CH - May 15, 1844. Died on Lenox Hill, on the 9th (May), Mr. B. F. Randall, aged 27 years.

CH - May 15, 1844. Died in Fenner, on the 11th (May), Mrs. Alvah Roberts, aged about 50 years.

CH - May 22, 1844. Married on Lenox Hill, on the 11th inst., by Rev. L. H. Stanley, of Perryville, Mr. Gershom Ray, to Mrs. --- Mowers, both of the former town.

CH - May 29, 1844. Died in this village, on Sunday morning, the 26th last, of consumption, Mr. David Sunderlin, aged 44 years.

CH - May 29, 1844. Died in this village, on Sun. morning last, Antha, infant daughter of Mr. Ira Worden, age 14 months.

CH - May 29, 1844. Died in New Hartford, Oneida Co., NY, on the 22nd inst., Miss Ann Peabody, formerly of Chittenango.

CH - May 29, 1844. Died in Lenox, on the 21st [inst.], Earl Allen, son of Mr. R. Allen, aged 17 years.

CH - May 29, 1844. Died in Perryville, on the 23rd [inst.], and infant dau. of Mr. Harry Lansing, aged 3 months.

CH - May 29, 1844. Died on Lenox Hill, the same day [23rd inst.], of Scarlet Fever, an infant daughter of Alex Morrison, aged 5 years.

CH - June 12, 1844. Died in this town, on Monday last, Mrs. Adeline, wife of Mr. Albro Hall, aged 33 years.

CH - June 26, 1844. Married on Sunday evening last, in the   Universalist Church at Canaseraga, by the Rev. Dolphus Skinner of Utica, Mr. Henry Freeman, to Miss Julia Benson, all of this town.

CH - June 26, 1844. Died at Canaseraga, on Sunday the 16th inst., of the Scarlet Fever, William Henry, youngest child of Ebenezer and Maria Hazeltine, aged 3 years and 9 months.

THE MADISON DEMOCRAT

MD - March 4, 1846. Married on the 19th ult., by Rev. William Clarke, Mr. George Grover, of Cazenovia to Miss Melinda Kinkaid, of Cicero.

MD - March 4, 1846. Died in Cazenovia, on the 21st ult., Mrs. Elizabeth Abell, widow of the late Jabez Abell, age 83 yrs.

MD - March 4, 1846. Died at Jefferson, on the 6th ult., Mr. G. N. Kenedy, of Sullivan, Madison Co., in the 24th year of his age. He came to Geneva in August last, in the company of Mr. Clark, where he was engaged in taking daguerreotype likenesses. On his way to Corning on the morning of February 2nd, was taken sick and died in Jefferson. His remains were sent to Madison County.

MD - March 11, 1846. Married in this village on the 10th inst., by Rev. James Abell, Emerson Stone, of Lenox, to Miss Diana Ward, also of Lenox.

MD - March 11, 1846. Married at Fenner, on the 25th ult., by Rev. Mr. Rand, Mr. John Peters, of Fayetteville, to Miss Jane Douglass, Esq. [sic], of Fenner.

MD - March 11, 1846. Died at Morrisville, on the 26th ult., Mr. Heman Towsley, age 46 yrs.

MD - March 11, 1846. Died at Delphi, Onondaga Co., NY, February 26th, Marietta G., daughter of Dr. M. M. and Lucy Marsh, age 4 mos.

MD - March 11, 1846. Died at Clockville, on the 20th ult., Mrs. Sylvia Finney, wife of John Finney, aged 36 yrs.

MD - March 11, 1846. Died at Clockville, February 24th, Elmer W., only child of B. Franklin and Huldah W. Chapman, age 1 year, 9 months.

MD - March 11, 1846. Died at Cazenovia, on the 21st ult., Martha, wife of Nicholas Welch, in her 84th year.

MD - March 18, 1846. Married at Dewitt, Onondaga Co., on the eve of the 11th inst., by Rev. James Abell, J. Walrath, Esq., to Miss Margaretta Higley of the former place.

MD - March 18, 1846. Married in this village, on the 1st inst., by J. French, Esq., Mr. David H. Siver to Miss Honola S. Botsford, both of Cicero.

MD - March 18, 1846: MURDER AT FLEMING! Near Auburn, Mr. John G. Van Nest, wife and two year old child stabbed to death. Mrs. Wykoff, mother-in-law and Mr. Cornelius Van Arsdale, wounded. Murderer was 5' 6", thick set and either a Negro or disguised as a black man.

MD - March 25, 1846. Died on the 21st inst., Miss Betsey Emery, of Monroe , ME, hung herself with a skein of yarn.

MD - March 25, 1846. Married at Chillicothe, OH on the 3rd inst., by Rev. Mr. Howe, Mr. Charles B. Johnson (?), of Milwaukie [sic], Wisconsin Territory, to Miss Irena Wilcox, of Clockville, Madison Co.

MD - April 1, 1846. To be sold at public auction, the Inn now kept by Harley Judd, of the village of Chittenango, land in the town of Sullivan, on the 14th of May: Lot #37 in Oneida Reservation, beginning at the N. E. corner of Lot #36.

MD - April 8, 1846. Married in Cazenovia, on the 19th ult., by Rev. Mr. Hawley, Mr. Allen Holbert, of Solon, to Miss Harriet M. Parmelee, of Cazenovia.

MD - April 8, 1846. Died in this village, on the morning of the 5th inst., Mrs. Rachel Harrington, in her 69th year. She was one of the early settlers of this place.

MD - April 8, 1846. Died in this village, February 13th, Sophia Jane, only daughter of John and Asenath Metcalf, age 9 mos., 16 days.

MD - April 8, 1846. Died at Galena, IL, March 1st, Mrs. Sarah, wife of H. C. Park, and daughter of Capt. John Wilson, formerly of this village. Her sickness was protracted and severe.

MD - April 8, 1846. Notice of meeting of the Chittenango Band, at the Band Room on the morning of the 7th inst.

MD - April 15, 1846. Married in Rome, on the 12th inst., by Rev. H. Mattison, Alfred Sandford, of this village, to Miss Susan Hayden, of the former place.

MD - April 22, 1846. Married in Fenner, on the 19th inst., by the Rev. J. B. Pixley, Mr. Franklin Woodworth, to Miss Fidelia Stafford, all of that town.

MD - April 22, 1846. Married at New Orleans, March 2nd, by Rev. Dr. Scott, Mr. Ebenezer Colfax, of that city, to Miss Helen Louisa Sherman, formerly of Rome, NY.

MD - April 22, 1846. Died in Fenner, on the 18th inst., Mrs. Nancy Bradley, wife of Elisha Bradley, and dau. of Mr. Benjamin Robbins, of that town.

MD - April 29, 1846. Married in Clockville, on the 19th inst., by Rev. A. A. Graley, Mr. A. B. Stewart, of Oriskany Falls, to Miss Elizabeth M. Northrup, of the former place.

MD - April 29, 1846.. Married on the 19th inst., by Rev. Mr. Shute, Mr. H. C. Wilson, of State Bridge, Madison Co., to Miss Adelia Sweet, of the same place.

MD - April 29, 1846. Married in Rome, on the 21st inst., by Rev. G. S. Boardman, Mr. Bradford C. Dean, to Miss Hannah Trip, all of that place.

MD - April 29, 1846. Died in Canaseraga, at the residence of her son, Col. Samuel French, Mrs. Nancy Phillips, in her 77th year. Mrs. P. became a resident of that village 41 years ago next June. There remain only four who were contemporaries with her in the first settlement of the place. She leaves seven children, 39 grand-children and 3 great grand-children.

MD - April 29, 1846. Died in Sullivan, Madison Co., NY, at the home of Mr. C. Schoonmaker, on Sunday morning, 5 April, Mr. Joseph Hamilton, age 52 yrs. He was born in this state and trained by pious parents; resided mostly at Plattsburg where he married and had five children; four years ago his wife and three children died; two years since his remaining two children died. He came to the dwelling of Mr. Schoonmaker, on the morning of the 13th of March, which he never left. He came destitute, friendless and shivering.

MD - May 6, 1846. Married at Sullivan, April 30th, by J. French, Esq., Mr. Charles Augustus March, of Lenox, to Miss Mary Lower, of Sullivan

MD - May 13, 1846. Married at Oneida Castle, on the 29th ult., Timothy Albert, son of Hon. Timothy Jenkins, age 1 year, 19 days.

MD - May 13, 1846. Married in Cazenovia, on the 5th inst., by Rev. William Clarke, Mr. George Hackley, to Miss Mary Anne Clarke, all of Cazenovia.

MD - June 3, 1846. Married in Canastota, on the 26th ult., by the Rev. L. E. Swan, Mr. Samuel Calkins, of Troy, to Miss Julia A. Marsh, of the former place.

MD - June 10, 1846. Married in Sullivan by Rev. John Smitzer, Mr. Allen Scovill, of Pompey, to Miss Susan E. Hotchkiss, of the former place.

MD - June 17, 1846. Sheriff's Sale: land of Aaron Edwards, being a part of Lot #76 in the N. W. part of Oneida Reservation, on the south bank of Oneida Lake.

MD - June 24, 1846. Married at Phelps, Ontario Co., NY, on the 31st ult., by Rev. J. H. Stebbins, Mr. Henry M. Shute, of this village, to Miss Julia A. Van Winkle, of the former place.

MD - June 24, 1846: Married in Hamilton on the 2nd inst., by Rev. N. Kendrick, D. D., Professor in Madison University, the Rev. A. Judson, D. D., of Maulain, Burmah, to Miss Emily Chubbuck, daughter of Mr. Charles Chubbuck, of the former place.

MD - June 24, 1846. Died in this village, on Monday, 22nd inst., an infant son of William Velasko, Esq.

MD - July 1, 1846. Sheriff's Sale: land of Henry and Hannah Hotchkiss, in the town of Sullivan. Lot no. not given...border stated.

MD - July 8, 1846. Married at Ft. Plain, on the 22nd ult., by Rev. G. A. Lintner, Mr. Heman D. Ward, of Lenox, to Miss Jane A. Webster, of the former place.

MD - July 8, 1846. Married in Norwich, Chenango Co., NY, on the 24th ult., by the Rev. John Duncan, Mr. Ezra B. Barnett, of Morrisville, to Miss Emeline Packer, of the former place.

MD - July 8, 1846. Died in Kingston, Ulster Co., NY, on the 12th ult., after a protracted illness, Louisa Antoinette, youngest daughter of Rev. John C. F. and Lucy Maria Hoes, age 1 year 2 mos. 17 days.

MD - July 8, 1846. Died in Eaton, Madison Co., on the 22nd ult, Mr. Vashti Mosely, aged 59 years.

MD - July 8, 1846. Died in Albany, on the 29th ult., (on his way to visit friends), Matthias Bruen, Esq., of Perth Amboy, NJ.

MD - July 15, 1846. Married in Lebanon, on the 2nd inst., by Rev. A. L. Brooks, Mr. Vaulkert Lamphere, of Eaton, to Miss Frances M. Durfee, of the former place.

MD - July 15, 1846. Died in Hamilton, on the 29th ult., Mr. S. Wilcox, in his 45th year.

MD - July 15, 1846. Sheriff's Sale: land of Peter Fonda; George W. Cone; Hiram S. Wilson; William H. Stevens - land granted to Aaron Lane & Derick Lane, 4 Dec., 1806, known as Lot #63 in the N. W. part of the Oneida Reservation.

MD - July 22, 1846. Married on Thursday, the 9th inst., by Rev. Charles Jerome of Salina, George Henry Jerome, Esq., of St. Louis, MO, to Charlotte Julia, dau. of the late Eleazer Dana, of Oswego, [NY].

MD - July 29, 1846. William Littlebrandt, of Clay, committed suicide by taking poison on Thursday the 9th and died on Sunday the 12th.

MD - July 29, 1846. Died in Lenox, on the 22nd inst., Wiliam Clark, son of Mr. Oliver Clark, age 24 yrs.

MD - August 5, 1846. A company of volunteers from Chenango [Co.], under the command of Capt. K. H. Dimmick, are on their way to join Col. Stevenson's California expedition.

MD - August 12, 1846. Married in this village, on the 2nd inst., By J. French, Esq., Mr. Elijah Rouse, to Miss Nancy Betsinger, both of Lenox.

MD - August 12, 1846. Died in Fenner, on the 27th ult., Mr. Alpheus Twist,. [No age given.]

MD - August 12, 1846. Died in Fenner, on Wed., the 29th ult., Mrs. Sybil Town, relict of Mr. Daniel Town.

MD - August 19, 1846. Married at Fayetteville, on the 9th inst., by the Rev. Mr. Wright, Mr. Asa Town, of Fenner, to Miss Jane Harmon, of Lenox.

MD - September 2, 1846. Married in Fenner, on the 25th ult., by Rev. J. Watson, Mr. Alfred Burroughs, of South Port, WI, to Miss Adelia Ann Persons, of the former place.

MD - September 2, 1846. Died in Cazenovia, on the 23rd ult., Esther A., only dau. of Edmund and Caroline Knowlton, in her 23rd year.

MD - September 2, 1846. Died in Lenox, on the 25th of August, Capt. Martin Lamb, age 65 yrs. He was an early settler of Lenox; born in MA; removed to New Hartford, Oneida Co. this state with his father when 12 years old, where he remained until 1805. He then removed to the farm where he died of cancer of the lip. He left a wife, to whom he was married 42 years and left 11 children.

MD - September 2, 1846. Sale at Public Auction at the Inn of Abel Wood, Chittenango, 1 Sept. 1846: the N. E. corner of Lot #22 in Varick's Location, deeded by John Chapman to Appleton Barnes, 3/4 acre; 1/2 acre to Anson Cranson; 1 1/4 acre to Chauncey and Philo Soper; 1/4 acre to Sylvester Clark; 1/2 acre to John Mitchell; 1/2 acre to Elizabeth Shippey, etc.

MD - September 16, 1846. Married in Smithfield, on the 10th ult., by Rev. S. Wells, Mr. Lester Tucker, of Fenner, to Miss Eunice Homes, of Stonington, CT.

MD - September 16, 1846. Married in Cazenovia,. on the 6th inst., by Rev. William Clarke, Mr. Elihu Laird, of Fenner, to Miss Mary Clay of Cazenovia.

MD - September 16, 1846. Died in this village, on the 10th inst., Mr. Jonas A. Monroe, aged 31 years.

MD - September 16, 1846. Died in Nelson, on the 1st inst., after a short illness, Mary, dau. of Mr. Willis Humphrey, in her 13th year.

MD - September 16, 1846. Died in Cazenovia, on the 7th inst., Austin Lyon, aged 28 years.

MD - September 16, 1846. Died in Syracuse, on Friday, evening, the 4th inst., Harriet, dau. of John Fleming, Esq., aged 3 yrs.

MD - September 23, 1846. Married in Fenner, on the 17th inst., by Rev. Mr. Davenport, Mr. Calvin Davis, to Miss Susan Weed, dau. of Mr. Silas Weed, all of that town.

MD - September 23, 1846. Married on the evening of the 18th, by Rev. James Abell, Mr. William H. Cress, of Cazenovia, to Miss Mary Jane Myers, of Sullivan.

MD - September 23, 1846. Died in Stockbridge, on the 12th inst., Ward L., only son of Hervey and Martha Gaston, aged 2 yrs. 4 mos. 23 days.

MD - September 23, 1846. Died in Morrisville, on the 2nd inst., Mr. Conway Lewis, aged 55 years.

MD - September 30, 1846.. Married in Grace Church, New York City, on the 24th inst., by Rev. Charles G. Sommers, Mr. Stephen J. Brinckerhoff, of the former place, to Mrs. Mary E. Yates, of this village.

MD - September 30, 1846. Married in Hamilton, on the 17th inst., by Rev. N. Kendrick, D. D., Linus M. Peck, A. M., of Cazenovia, to Miss Cordelia C., only dau. of Nathaniel Kendrick, D. D. of the former place.

MD - October 7, 1846. Bill for foreclosure of mortgage: James Crouse and Laura M. his wife vs. Lorenzo D. Williams and Harman Scott.

MD - October 14, 1846. Married at the Lincklaen House, in Cazenovia on the 3rd inst., by Rev. Mr. Frichett, Mr. John Travis to Miss Caroline, dau. of Hon. S. Seeber, of Lenox.

MD - October 14, 1846. Married at New Bedford, on the 1st, by Rev. Ephraim Peabody, of Boston, Mr. N. P. Willis, Esq., of NY to Cornelia, dau. of the Hon. Joseph Grinnell, M.C.

MD - October 14, 1846. Died at Kirkville, on the 27th ult., Mr. John N. Patten, of Camillus, Onondaga Co, aged 21 yrs. Funeral services on the 30th ult.

MD - October 21, 1846. Married in this village on the 19th inst., by Rev, L. E. Swan, Mr. T. J. Tefft, of New Haven, Oswego Co., to Miss Harriet M., dau. of J. B. Plank, Esq., of this village.

MD - October 21, 1846. Married in Manlius, on the 15th inst., by Rev. John Smitzer, Mr. Thaddeus Heath, of Sullivan, to Miss Marietta A. Cook, of Manlius.

MD - October 21, 1846. Died at Fenner, October 15th, Mr. Jacob Barrett, a Soldier of the Revolution, in his 86th year.

MD - October 28, 1846. Married on the 18th inst., by Rev. J. J. Marsh, Mr. George Plumb, to Miss Mary Bushnell, dau. of Ira Bushnell, all of Oneida Lake, NY

MD - October 28, 1846. Married at Canastota, on the 6th inst., by Rev. W. Stickney, Mr. Hamilton Cotton, to Miss Mary Adams, dau. of Capt. Frederick Adams, all of Lenox.

MD - October 28, 1846. Died at Canastota, on the night of the 26th inst., Laura Jane, only dau. of Daniel and Jane Crouse, aged 9 years.

MD - October 28, 1846. Died at Cicero, Onondaga Co., on the evening of the 13th inst., of apoplexy, Mrs. Mary, wife of Deacon Peter Colyer, in her 66th year.

MD - November 4, 1846. Died in Verona, Oneida Co., NY, on the 31st ult., of spasmodic rheumatism, Mr. Bruster Abell, in his 66th year.

MD - November 4, 1846. Died at Clockville, September 22, Sarah Ann Keeney, in her 15th year.

MD - November 18, 1846. Catharine Cahale, who resided with Hiram Perry in the town of Pompey, committed suicide November 16th, by hanging herself in the woodshed. Cause supposed to be a disappointment in love.

MD - November 18, 1846. Married at Immanuel Church, Little Falls, on the 3rd inst., by Rev. Edward Livermore, Mr. George Ashley, to Miss Helen M. Livingston, dau. of H. Nolton, Esq., of that place.

MD - November 18, 1846. Died in Manlius, on Thursday, the 12th inst., Harriet, wife of Mr. John Van Scharck, in her 27th year.

MD - November 25, 1846. Married on the 11th inst., by Rev. William Clarke, Mr. John Knowles and Miss Catherine Monk, all of Cazenovia.

MD - November 25, 1846. Died in Hamilton, on the 4th inst., Charles A., son of Samuel and Flavia White of Pulmonary Consumption, ae 21 yrs.

MD - December 2, 1846. Notice: "State Bridge", Madison Co., shall hereafter be called "Oneida Valley", both village and Post Office.

MD - December 2, 1846. Died in this village, on Sun. the 29th ult., very suddenly, Fanny Maria, only daughter of Alfred and Maria Bellamy, aged 7 mos.

MD - December, 2, 1846. Died at his residence in this town on the 25th ult., Mr. Leonard Lincklaen, in his 75th year.

MD - December 16, 1846. A little son of Mr. John Montrose, Jr., of Canastota, aged about 3 yrs., was run over by a sleigh in front of his father's door.

MD - December 16, 1846. Married in Smithfield, on the 2nd inst., by Rev. Mr. Schofield, of Hamilton, Mr. John Douglass, of this village, to Miss Cordelia L. Johnson, of the former place.

MD - January 6, 1847. Married in Sullivan, on the 30th ult., by Rev. O. Hesler, Mr. Henry A. Merrill, to Miss Marion, dau., of Rev. F. Walrath, of the same place.

MD - January 6, 1847. Married at Eaton village, on the 23rd ult., by Rev. O. Brown, Mr. Edward P. Morse and Miss Sarah P. Storrs.

MD - January 6, 1847. Married at Morrisville, on Christmas eve, by Rev. L. Davis, Mr. C. H. Randall and Miss Jane A. Hale, both of Oneida Depot. Married at the same place and time, Mr. W. D. Twogood, of Oneida Depot, to Miss Eliza Forbes, of Clockville.

MD - January 6. 1847. Died in this village, on the 29th ult., William L., infant son of Luke and Jane A. Brosseau.

MD - January 13, 1747. Married at the residence of J. V. H. Clark, Esq., in Manlius, by Rev. J. C. Rudd, D. D., Delos Lake, of Utica, to Sarah Helen Clark of this town.

MD - Jan 13, 1847. Married in this village, on the 31st ult., by Rev. O. Hesler, Mr. George Kilts, of Manheim, Herkimer Co., to Miss Catharine Clock, of this place.

MD - Jan. 13, 1847. Married in Manlius, on the 24th ult., by Rev. David Pise, Mr. S. Gasquoine, to Miss Helen M. Dunbar.

MD - January 20, 1847. Married in this village, on the 13th inst., by Rev. James Abell, Mr. William H. Walrath to Miss Margaret Elizabeth, eldest daughter of John G. Yates, Esq.

MD - January 20, 1847. Died in this village, on the 13th inst., at the residence of his step-father, George Grant, Esq., Ebenezer Grant in his 27th year.

MD - January 27, 1847. Married in this village, on the evening of the 21st inst., by Rev. O. Hesler, Mr. Charles Tuttle, of Perryville, to Miss M. A. DeWitt, of this place; married on the same evening by the same, Mr. P. Bettinger to Miss Maria Quick, all of this place.

MD - February 3, 1847. Died in this town, on the 29th ult., of Consumption, Mary, wife, of Mr. Isaac Cook, in her 26th year.

MD - February 10, 1847. Married at the Eagle Tavern in Hamilton, on the 2nd inst., by Rev. A. Scofield, Giles S. Cranston, of Peterboro, to Miss Mary C. Bligh, of Clockville.

MD - February 10, 1847. Died in this town, on the evening of the 3rd inst., of dropsy, Mrs. Belinda, wife of Deacon Albro Hall, in her 30th year.

MD - February 17, 1847. Married in this village, on Thursday, Feb, 11th, by Rev. O Hesler, James Hood, to Miss Catharine Ehle, both of this place.

MD February 24, 1847. Married in this village, on the evening of the 17th inst., by Rev. James Abell, Mr. George Benedict, of Verona, Oneida Co., to Miss Sarah dau. of John I. Walrath, Esq, of this place.

MD - February 24, 1847. Married in this village , on the morning of the 24th inst., at the Hotel of H. Judd, by Rev. James Abell,. Mr. William H. Palmer, of Bridgewater, Oneida Co., to Miss Minerva Randall, of Perryville.

MD - February 24, 1847. Married in Fenner, on the 16th inst., by Rev. J. B. Pixley, Mr. Harvey L. Keeler to Miss Lauraette Allen, all of Fenner.

MD - February 24, 1847. Married in Syracuse, on the 10th inst., by Rev. Henry Gregory, Dr. Erastus Fitch, of Lee Centre, Oneida Co., to Miss Cornelia Lundegreen of the former place.

MD - February 24, 1847. Died in Dubuque City, Iowa Territory, on the 28th of Dec., 1846, Mrs. Rhoda Rowell, formerly of this place, aged 58 years.

MD - March 3, 1847. Erastus Harrison, of Richland, Oswego Co., was frozen to death while in a state of intoxication on the night of the 21st ult.

MD - March 3, 1847. On Sunday last, Mr. John Stowel, of Quality Hill attempted suicide - cause unknown. He has since died.

MD - March 10, 1847. Dr. Dan Foote of South New Berlin, Chenango Co., was charged with killing his wife by ill treatment. He was arrested in Warren, PA.

MD - March 10, 1847. On Tuesday last, a young man named Brown, residing in the town of Nelson, had both bones of one leg broken while engaged in a wrestling match.

MD - March 10, 1847. A young man, named A. P. McIntrye, came to Rensselaerville to the home of John Clark. He was in feeble health and died last Friday. From letters in his possession, it is supposed he had relatives in Madison Co.

MD - March 10, 1847. Married in this village, on the 25th ult., by Rev. O. Hesler, Mr. William Daniels to Miss Harriett C. Freeman, all of this town.

MD - March 10, 1847. Married on the 17th ult., by Rev. A. J. Crandall, Mr. Reuben Tuttle, to Miss Mary A. Monk, all of Cazenovia.

MD - March 10, 1847. At Bridgeport on the 25th ult., by Elder William Shapcott, Mr. Newton Palmer to Miss Diantha Carter.

MD - March 10, 1847. Died at his residence in Lenox on the 5th ult., Samuel Glidden, Esq., in his 56th year.

MD - March 10, 1847. Died in Lenox on the morning of the 19th ult., Mrs. Hannah Cranson, wife of Nathan Cranson, aged 55 yrs.

MD - March 10, 1847. Died suddenly in Lenox on the 11th ult., James, son of Simeon P. and Sarah New, aged 2 years and 3 months.

MD - March 17, 1847. Married in New York City, on the 10th ult., by Rev. Dr. Alexander, Mr. Thomas Farmer, of Boston, to Miss Henrietta C. Brown, dau. of Allen Brown, formerly of Albany.

MD - March 17, 1847. Died in Fenner, on the 12th inst., Ephraim Ballard, aged 50 yrs.

MD - March 17, 1847. Died in New Milford, PA, on the morning of the 5th, Mr. Allison Pratt, age 27 yrs., youngest son of Matthew Pratt, Esq., formerly of Pratts Hollow, Madison Co.

MD - March 24, 1847. Died, Mr. Ballou, a resident of Boonville, Oneida Co., fell from a sleigh. He had been drinking freely of the ardent and died in a state of intoxication.

MD - March 24, 1847. Mr Isaac Cole, of Otisco, Onondaga Co. was killed last Tuesday by the bursting of a buzz-saw. He was 43 years of age.

MD - March 24, 1847. Married in Cazenovia, on the 16th inst., by Rev. L. A. Eddy, Rev. O. Hesler to Miss Mary Porter, both of Chittenango.

MD - March 24, 1847. Died in Frankfort, Herkimer Co., on the morning of the 18th inst., Rev. Benjamin Harvey, aged 111 yrs. A Revolutionary Soldier.

MD - March 24, 1847. Died in Albany, on the morning of the 11th inst., of typhus fever, Mr. David Schuyler in the 37th year of his age.

MD - March 31, 1847. Died in this town on the morning of the 27th inst., Sophia White, daughter of J. Whipple, Esq., age 17 years., 5 months.

MD - April 7, 1847. Married at Oneida Depot, on the evening of the 24th inst., by J. Cooper, Esq., Mr. John Walden, to Miss Hannah Groat, both of Lenox.

MD - April 7, 1847. Died in this town on the 17th ult., of Consumption, Mr. Lewis Phillips, aged 36 yrs. He left a widow and two children.

MD - April 21, 1847. Died at his residence in this town, on the 11th inst., Mr. Joseph Adams, aged 78 yrs. One of the earliest settlers of the town.

MD - April 28, 1847. Died in this village on the 23rd inst., Louisa, dau. of Elisha Graves, of Cicero, aged 16 yrs.

MD - April 28, 1847. Died in the village of Canaseraga, on the 18th inst., of Typhoid Pneumonia, Mr. James Colter, age 45 yrs. He left seven orphaned children.

MD - May 5, 1747. From the Syracuse Journal, "Miss Sarah Marshall, of Syracuse, age 22 yrs., committed suicide, by taking poison."

MD - May 5, 1847. A young lady, about 20 yrs. of age, Almira Reed, on Wed., evening, last, fell into the mill pond on Wood Creek, at Rome, Oneida Co., and was drowned.

MD - May 12, 1847. Married in Nelson, on the 28th ult., by Rev. M. Harrington, Nathaniel Foote, Esq., of Morrisville, to Miss Olivia M. Knox of Nelson.

MD - May 12, 1847. Died in Ashtabula, OH, on the 6th ult., of disease of the heart, Mrs. Margaret J., wife of Mr. James Burton, and dau. of William Johnson, aged about 30 yrs.

MD - May 19, 1847. Married at Wampsville, on the 13th inst., by Rev. W. H. Cooper, Mr. Lyman Avery, dau. of William Spencer, Esq., all of that place.

MD - May 19, 1847. Died in this town on the 17th inst., Mr. George Stormes, aged 23 yrs.

MD - May 19, 1847. Mr. Ambrose Smith, of Eaton, is building a large woolen factory about 2 1/2 miles from Eaton village.

MD - May 19, 1847. Died the wife of Sheldon P. Clark, of Oswego, she was found dead in her bed on the morning of the 2nd inst.

MD - May 19, 1847. Died on Wed. last, (May 12th), a son of Mr. John Marsden, of Georgetown, age about 12 or 13 years, was killed by falling a tree.

MD - May 19, 1847. Died in the same day (May 12), a young man, some 17 or 18 years old, named Chares Hackley, was instantly killed in Cazenovia, by the bursting of a small cannon, which was being fired by some lads in honor of the victory of Cerro Gordo.

MD - May 26, 1847. Married in Nelson, on the 16th inst., by Rev. William Clarke, Mr. Charles (?) to Miss Jane M. Bumpus.

MD - May 26, 1847. Died at Ithaca, Tompkins Co., on the 21st ult., Hon. John Knowles, formerly of this village, in his 78th yr.

MD - June 2, 1847. Died in this village, on the 23rd ult., of Consumption, Miss Irene Sanger, in her 18th yr.

MD - June 2, 1847. From the *Rome Sentinel*: "On the morning of the 23rd ult., William West, was drowned in the Mohawk River, below the dam of Linch's Flour Mill."

MD - June 9, 1847. The wife of Rev. J. Rider, of Nuneaton, near Coventry, Canada, lately gave birth to four children, who are all living. About ten months since, she had three, all who lived.

MD - June 16. 1847. Died in this town, on the 9th inst., after a confinement of six years to a bed of suffering, Mary, wife of Henry Rightmyer, Esq., in her 87th year.

MD - June 16, 1847. Died at his residence in the town of Fenner, on the 12th inst., Mr. William Hathaway, an old respectable inhabitant, aged 76 yrs.

MD - June 30, 1847. Married at Fayetteville, on the 20th inst., by Rev. Mr. Wright, Mr. Leonard Goff, merchant of Perryville, to Miss Sarah Beeman, of Canaseraga.

MD - June 30, 1847. Married in Vernon on the 8th inst., by Rev. Henry Emmons, Mr. Everett Case to Miss Eva, dau. of Mr. E. Wilson, all of that place.

MD - June 30, 1847. Married in this town, on the 15th inst., by P. Valkenburgh, Esq., Mr. Hubbard Reals to Miss Margarette Feasenmyer.

MD - July 7, 1847. Married on the 23rd ult., by Rev. William Clark, Mr. Joseph W. Slocum, of Nelson, to Miss Elvira Griggs, all of Cazenovia.

MD - July 7, 1847. Married at [New ?] Woodstock on the 23rd inst., by Rev. Daniel Putnam, Mr. David Bedford, of Norwich, NY, to Miss Clara Walker, of the former place.

MD - July 7, 1847. Died in Cazenovia, on the 23rd ult., Mr. Robert B. Morton, a native of Scotland, aged about 30 years.

MD - July 14, 1847. Married at Holland Patent, Oneida Co., NY, July 8th, by Rev. J. F. Scoville, Rev. Lewis Benedict, of Rockton, IL, to Miss Martha D., dau. of the late Asa Taylor, Esq., of Holland Patent.

MD - July 21, 1847. Married at the Cazenovia House, on the 7th inst., by Rev. William Clarke, Mr. J. Henry Wright and Miss Julia C. Powers, both of Pompey.

MD - July 21, 1847. Married by the same (Rev. William Clarke), on the 11th inst., Mr. Henry C. Pease and Miss Sarah W. Earles, both of Cazenovia.

MD - July 28, 1847. Married in Norwich, Chenango Co., on the 4th inst., by Rev. C. T. Johnson, Mr. S. S. Bloom of Utica, to Miss Mary T. Lamb, of the former place.

MD - July 28, 1847. Died in this village, on Friday, the 23rd inst., of Consumption, William Brown, aged 24 yrs.

MD - Aaugust 4, 1847. Died at his residence, in the city of Rochester, on the 11th inst., Ralph Whipple, formerly of Cazenovia, aged 36 yrs.

MD - August 11, 1847. Married on the 28th ult., by Rev. E. J. Gillett, Mr. J. Lincklaen Darling, of Syracuse, to Miss A. Augusta, dau. of Mr. O. Shapely, of Cazenovia.

MD - August 11, 1847. Died in Nelson, on Fri., the 30th ult., Caroline M., only daughter of Dr. O. Mead, in the 31st year of her age.

MD - August 11, 1847. Died in Cazenovia, on the 2nd inst., Mr. Peries Bradford, aged 71 years.

MD - August 11, 1847. Died in Madison, on the 25th ult., Jacob Lamb, age 71 yrs.

MD - August 18, 1847. Married in Canastota, on the 16th inst., by Rev. C. G. Lee, Mr. Addison G. Williams, of Syracuse to Miss Lavina C., dau. of Judge Roberts, of the former place.

MD - August 18, 1847. Died at his residence in this town, on the 1st ult.., Ebenezer Calkings, Esq., aged 83 yrs. He was one of the earliest settlers and first Post Master in the town of Sullivan. [Probably Canaseraga P. O. cmh]

MD - August 25, 1847. Died in Fenner on the 10th inst., after a short but severe attack of scarlet fever, Scott W., only son of the late Abram G. Lansing, in his 3rd year.

MD - August 25, 1847. Died in Cazenovia, on the morning of the 18th inst., Lois, wife of Henry Brightman, Esq., in the 48th year of her age.

MD - August 25, 1847. On the 18th inst., a human skeleton was found 1 1/2 miles northwest of Oneida Depot, believed to have been there from two to three years. A copper coin was also found, with the initials "C. R". The skeleton was evidently male, about 6 ft. or more in height, a perfect set of teeth except for one double tooth from the right under jaw, denoting a younger man. The remains were buried at Oneida Depot.

MD - September 1, 1847. John Runkle, recently from the town of Westmoreland, Oneida Co., was murdered, Wednesday night last, in Utica, by his wife and daughter, it is supposed. The daughter is about 12 years old.

MD - September 1, 1847. Married in Manlius, on the 1st inst., by Rev. S. N. Gridley, Mr. William Vosburgh, to Miss Sarah F. Hitchcock, both of Cazenovia.

MD - September 1, 1847. Died in Lenox, on Sunday evening, the 15th ult., Wells Griggs, age 18 yrs.

MD - September 1, 1847. Also died on Thursday evening, the 19th ult., Mrs. Flora Griggs, aged 47 yrs. "Weep not, orphan sister."

MD September 22, 1847. Married in Verona, on the 16th inst., by Rev. Mr. Stickney, Mr. Gilbert Johnson, to Miss Emily T. Sage, both of Verona.

MD - September 22, 1847. Died in this town, on the 19th inst., Mr. Jacob Becker, age 56 yrs.

MD - September 22, 1847. Died at Perryville, on the 16th inst., Mr. Peter P. Ehle, aged 68 yrs.

MD - September 22, 1847. Died in this town, on the 20th inst., Mr. Harrison Hodge, aged 23 yrs.

MD - September 22, 1847. Died at Harrisville, OH, on the 3rd inst., David L. Brainerd, aged 27 yrs., only surviving son of Rev. Israel Brainerd, of Vernon, Oneida Co., NY

MD - September 29, 1847. Russell Cady was convicted of the murder of George Manwarring, Jr., on Friday last, Sept.16th, at the Chenango Court of Oyer and Terminer, sitting in Norwich.

MD - September 29, 1847. On the morning of the 20th inst., the trial of Daniel Foote for the murder of his wife in New South Berlin was commenced and the trial of Nancy Cady, mother of Russell Cady was expected to take place Tuesday.

MD - September 29, 1847. Married in this village on the 21st inst., by Rev. L. E. Swan, Mr. Maurice Humphrey, of Camillus, Onondaga Co., to Miss Hannah Mariah Holmes, of this village.

MD - September 29, 1847. Married at Bridgeport, on the 27th inst., by Rev. James Abell, Mr. Isaac Colyer of Cicero, Onondaga Co., to Miss Rachel W. Tripp, of Duanesburgh, Schenectady Co., NY.

MD - 29 September, 1847. Died in New Woodstock, on the 21st inst., Mrs. Sarah, wife of Rev. John Peck, aged 63 years.

MD - September 29, 1847. Died in Madison, on the 9th inst., Mr. Jacob Albert, aged 68 yrs.

MD - September 29, 1847. Died in Lebanon, on the 14th inst., Mr. Benjamin Livingston, aged 77 years.

MD - October 6, 1847. Married in this village, on the 3rd inst., by David Severance, Esq., Mr. James Coonrod, to Miss Amelia A. Lansing, all of this place.

MD - October 6, 1847. Died in this village on the 30th ult., Captain Peter H. Ehle, aged 96 yrs., a soldier of the Revolution.

MD - October 13, 1847. Died on the afternoon of Saturday last, Mr. James Vroman, a resident in the northern part of this town was stabbed in the abdomen by one Freeborn T. Burton, also a resident of this vicinity.

MD - October 13, 1847. The State of Arkansas invites emigrants to take lands which have been forfeited for taxes and no payment will be required.

MD - October 13, 1847. Married in this village, on the 7th inst., by Rev. James Abell, Mr. John Cheeseman, of Auburn, to Miss Mary Ann Chapman, of this place.

MD - October 13, 1847. Married in Rome, on the 5th inst., by Rev. F. H. Stanton, Mr. Sidney A. Powers, of Summit Co., OH, to Mary Jane, dau. of John Myers, of the former place.

MD - October 13, 1847. Married in Canastota, on the 6th inst., by Rev. W. Stickney, Mr. Peter Webler [Webber?], of Cazenovia, to Miss Adelia Walrath, of this town.

MD - October 13, 1847. Died in this town, on the 11th inst., an infant son of A. P. and Orluna Dewey, aged 3 weeks, 5 days.

MD - October 13, 1847. Default: Aaron Brower and Margaret, his wife to David Dominick, mortgagee, 205 1/3 acres more or less, part of Lot #26. Conveyed to Aaron Brower by William H. Redfield and wife, and Henry H. Ratnour and wife, by deed dated 10 September 1830.

MD - October 20, 1847. Married at the house of W. Benjamin, in Eaton village, on the 6th inst., by Rev O. Brown, Mr. Byron Poole and Miss Delilah Carpenter, both of Nelson.

MD - October 20, 1847. Died in Cazenovia on the 4th inst., Linus M. Peck, A. M., in the 29th year of his age and at the house of Mr. A. Abbott, in that town, on Wednesday morning, the 6th inst., Rev. Philetus Peck, A. M., in his 38th year.

MD - October 27, 1847. Married in this village on the morning of the 26th inst., by Rev. James Abell, Lorenzo D. Dana, to Lucy A., dau. of Robert Sanford, all of this place.

MD - October 27, 1847. Died in Utica, on the 19th inst., Kellogg Hurlbert aged 64 years.

MD - November 3, 1847. Married in Madison, on the 20th ult., by Rev. Mr. Platt, Mr. Solomon Henderson to Miss Emily A. White, all of Madison.

MD - November 3, 1847. Married on the 21st [ult.] by Rev. O. Brown, Mr. William Simmons, to Miss Matilda Ann Roe, both of Eaton.

MD - November 3, 1847. Died at his residence in this town, on the lst inst., Mr. Caleb Marshall, aged 79 yrs.

MD - November 3, 1847. Died in Clockville, NY, 20 October, 1847, Martha Adelaide, only daughter of Nelson and Mary Devendorf, aged 7 years.

MD - November 10, 1847. Married at Mt. Pleasant, IA, on the 11th ult., by J. T. Morton, Esq., (height 6' 3"), Silas G. Weeks, Esq., of Warren Co., IL (height 6' 4") to Mrs, Mary Robb, of Mt. Pleasant (height 6"1").

MD - November 10, 1847. Died at New Boston, in this town, on the 5th inst., Stephen Shute, aged 61 yrs.

MD - November 17, 1847. Married in Pulaski, Oswego Co., on the 9th inst., by Rev. W. I. Crane, Mr. C. W. Smart, of Hamilton, to Miss Jane Barrett, of the former place.

MD - November 17, 1847. Died at Sullivan, on the 10th inst., Seth Starr, Esq., aged 57 years; resident of this town over 25 years. Left a widow and fatherless daughters.

MD - November 17th, 1847. A little boy of 12 years, named Alanson Benedict, at Syracuse, on Friday morning, was run over by a train.

MD - November 24, 1847. Died in Canaseraga, on the 19th inst., Mr. William Brown, of this village, age 54 yrs., 6 mos.

MD - December 15, 1847. Died in this village on the 1st inst., Walter, infant son of Peter and Hannah Groesbeck, age 2 yrs. 2 mos.

MD - December 15, 1847. Died in this village, on the 13th inst., Gilbert Wessel, infant son of Peter and Loania VanValkenburgh, age 9 mos.

MD - December 22, 1847. Married at Matthew's Mills, on the 12th inst., by Rev. L. E. Swan, Mr. Nathan D. Allen and Miss Julia A. Little, both of that place

MD - December 22, 1847. Married at New Boston, on the 15th inst., by the same (Rev. L. E. Swan), Mr. George C. Crandall, of New London, Oneida Co., and Miss Martha A. Shute, of the former place.

MD - December 22, 1847. Died in this town, on the 23rd ult., Mr. Derrick Adams, aged 67 yrs.

MD - December 22, 1847. Died in Utica, on the 10th inst., Sarah, wife of Mr. David Shover, aged 29 yrs., formerly of this village.

MD - December 29, 1847. Married in Fenner, on the 22nd inst., by Rev. Mr. Weber, Mr. Orrin Britt, of Perryville, to Miss Jane Woodworth, of the former place.

MD - December 29, 1847. Died in this village, on the 24th inst., of Scarletina, Febra, an infant son of Mr. Harry Smith, age 7 mos... and on the 28th inst., of the same disease, Caroline, youngest daughter of Mr. Smith, age 2 yrs. 8 mos.

MD - January 5, 1848. Married in this village, on the 26th ult., by Rev. L. E. Swan, Mr. Robert Roberts, of Verona, and Miss Caroline M. Nash, of Fenner.

MD - January 5, 1848. Married in Cazenovia, on the 21st ult., by Rev. William Clarke, Mr. Andrew Lighthall, of Eaton, to Miss Lodema Morse, of Cazenovia.

MD - January 5, 1848. Died in Fenner, on the 26th ult., Maria Louisa, 2nd dau. of the late William Clough, aged 16 yrs.

MD - January 5, 1848. Married at Mapesville, WI, on the 17th ult., by E. P. Mapes, Esq., Mr. Anson G. Kelogg [sic], and Miss Juliette, dau. of Mr. Leman Lathrop, of Ceresco.

MD - January 5, 1848. Died at Oneida Lake, on Wed., the 5th inst., Miss Eleanor L., dau. of Eliphas Chapman, age 19 yrs.
[Was this actually the issue of January 12th?]

MD - January 19, 1848. Married in Canastota, on the 13th inst., by Rev. F. T. Drake, Mr. Albert J. Phillips and Miss Laura Jane Menzee, all of Canastota.

MD - January 19, 1848. Married in this village, on the 12th inst., by D. Severance, Esq., Mr. Thomas James and Mrs. Ann Maige, of this village.

MD - January 19, 1848. Married in Perryville, on the 12th inst., by Rev. W. Webber, Mr. J. E.. Didama and Miss E. A. Britt, all of Perryville.

MD - January 19, 1948. Died in Cazenovia, on the 9th inst., Mrs. Cornelia, wife of Mr. William H. Haight, and daughter of Enos Cushing.

MD - January 19, 1848. On Monday this week, William M. Fox, of Cazenovia, son of William Fox, age 16 yrs., drowned while skating on Cazenovia Lake.

MD - January 26, 1848. Married in Smithfield, on the 18th inst., by Rev. Asa Rand, Mr. Thomas A. Brown, of Stockbridge, to Miss Sophronia A. Bliss, of the former place.

MD - January 26, 1848. Married in Fayetteville, on the 23rd inst., Mr. John Bettinger to Miss Sarah Richards, all of this town.

MD - February 2, 1848. From the *Saratoga Sentinel*: Mrs. Rachel Vandermaker, 20 years old and married only three weeks, cut her throat with a razor on the 29th ult.

MD - February 9, 1848. Married at Wampsville, on the 29th ult., Mr. Reuben Smithson, to Miss Betsey Adams, all of Canaseraga.

MD - February 9, 1848. Died at the residence of her father, after a short but painful sickness, Ruth, dau. of Capt. Asa and Atlanta Cady, in her 16th year.

MD - Feb. 9, 1848: Died at Canastota, Jan. 29, ult., Joseph Henry, 3rd son of Daniel and Jane Crouse, age 5 yrs. 1 mo. 26 days.

MD - February 9, 1848. Died in this village, on the 26th ult., Edward J., son of Thomas and Olive A. French, age 2 yrs. 9 mos.

MD - February 23, 1848. Married at New Boston, on the 10th inst., by Rev. L. E. Swan, Mr. Henry V. Hull and Miss Mary E. Gardiner, all of the above place. By the same, at the same time and place, Mr. John Greenway and Miss Nancy A. Hull of Syracuse.

CHITTENANGO PHENIX

Published on Wednesdays. J. P. Olmstead, Editor

CP - December 13, 1848. Married in this village on the 3rd inst., by Rev. Mr. Abell, Mr. Robert Bruce Frederick and Miss Catharine Moore, all of this place.

CP - December 13, 1848. Married in this village on the 7th inst., by Rev. Mr. Abell, Mr. William Vaneppes, and Miss Clarinda Bolles, both of Perryville.

CP - December 13, 1848. Died in this village on the morning of the 26th September, Mrs. Hulda, wife of Joseph Sanger, Esq., in the 52nd year of her age. [A poem follows addressed to her children in Albany.]

CP - December 20, 1848. Married in Lenox, on the 14th inst., by Rev. A. A. Grayley, Mr. Martin Clark, late of Alabama, and Miss Caroline M., daughter of I. G. Cropsey, Esq., of the former place.

CP - December 27, 1848. Married in this village, on the 26th inst., by Rev. L. E. Swan, Mr. George T. Perry, Jr., of New York and Miss Anna H. Wells of this place.

CP - January 17, 1859. Died in Kirkville, Onondaga Co., on the 15th inst., Mrs. Tabathy, wife of Robert Cummings, aged 73 years and 7 months.

CP - January 24, 1849. Married in Madison, on the 11th inst., by Rev. Mr. Hartshorn, Mr. William L. Coolidge, and Miss Maranda E. Coffin, both of that place.

CP - January 24, 1849. Married on the 14th inst., by Rev. Mr. Clarke, Mr. Horace Hills, and Miss Oriann Stannard, both of Cazenovia.

CP - January 24, 1949. Married at Kirkland, on the 20th inst., by Rev. Mr. Raymond, Mr. Charles N. Griffin, and Miss Huldah Jane Stone, all of that place.

CP - January 24, 1849. Died in Bolivar, the 20th inst., Mr. George Siver, aged 60 yrs.

CP - February 7, 1849. Died on the lst inst., of apoplexy, at his residence in this village, Dr. Samuel Kennedy, aged 59 yrs. He resided and practiced medicine here for more than 30 years.

CP - February 7, 1849. Married in this village, on the lst inst., by Rev. L. F. Swan, Mr. Marcus L. Planck, and Miss Mary Ann Jones, all of this place.

CP - February 7, 1849. Married in Sullivan, the 24th ult., by Rev. Washington Stickney, Mr. Josiah P. Brown, of Boston, MA and Miss Amelia E., eldest dau. of Edwin Lewis, Esq., of Sullivan.

CP - February 7, 1849. Married in Sullivan, the 24th ult., by Rev. Mr. Strong, Royal Sweet, M. D. and Margaret Haywood only daughter of Thomas Haywood, all of Kirkville.

CP - February 7, 1849. Died in this village, on the 6th inst., Col. Chauncey Hatch, aged about 60 yrs.

CP - February 7, 1849. Sailing from New York for California, Messrs. Richard C. Walrath and John W. Schuyler

CP - February 14, 1849. Married at the Eagle Tavern in Utica, on the 8th inst., by John Parsons, Esq., Frederick Dodge, and Sarah Mayhew, both of New Hartford.

CP - February 14, 1849. Died in Leonardsville, Madison Co., on the 4th inst., Mr. Nathan B. Rodgers, undersherriff of Madison Co., aged about 25 years.

CP - February 14, 1849. Died at Butternuts, Otsego Co., on Friday last., John Cox Morris, aged 67 yrs. Mr. Morris was a son of the late Gen. Lewis Morris, and the uncle of Mrs. Hamilton Fish and Mr. John A. Collier.

CP - February 28, 1849. Married in this village, on the 25th inst., by Rev. L. E. Swan, Mr. Seymour Holbrook and Miss Maria, daughter of Mr. Tobias Brown, all of this town.

CP - February 28, 1849. Died in this village, on Wed., the 21st inst., Miss Jane M. Leavitt, daughter of John B. and Eunice R. Leavitt, aged 17 yrs. and 5 mos.

CP - February 28, 1849. Died in Rochester on the 21st inst., at the residence of R. M. Dalzell, while on a visit to her friends, after a short and painful illness, Mrs. Nancy, wife of Oliver Jewell, of Cazenovia, NY, aged 52 yrs.

CP - March 7, 1849. Married in this village, on the lst inst., by Rev. J. Abell, Mr. Joseph H. Walrath, and Miss Elizabeth Walrath, all of this place.

CP - March 14, 1849. Died in Canastota, on the 5th inst., Mary Elizabeth, youngest daughter of Asa D. and Ally Van Hooser, aged 19 yrs. 1 mos. and 5 days.

CP- March 21, 1849 (Wed.).. Married in Perryville, the 8th inst., by Rev. A. W. Bruce, Stephen Freeman, Esq. and Miss Rachel Brooks.

CP - March 21, 1849.. Died in Canaseraga, on the 12th inst., at the residence of C. E. P. Severance, Miss Jane Wilds, of Chenango Co., aged 17 yrs.

CP - March 28, 1849. Married on the 15th (?) inst., at the Lincklaen House in Cazenovia by the Rev. William Clarke, Mr. Nolton Barber, and Miss Emily Marshall, both of Fenner.

CP - March 28, 1849. Married in Lenox, March 6th, by Rev. Mr. Butler, Mr. Norris House and Miss Leonora Lovejoy.

CP - March 28, 1849. Married in Delphi, on the 13th inst., by Rev. Mr. Douglas, Mr. Spencer Smith, and Miss Minerva Hamlin, both of Nelson.

CP - March 28, 1849. Married at the Farmer's Exchange, Syracuse, on the 13th inst. by Rev. W. Newell, Mr. Cacchus Larrabee, of Cazenovia, to Miss Louisa McMullen, of Sullivan.

CP - March 28, 1849. Died in Perryville, on the 25th inst., Miss Emily Britt, aged about 23 years.

CP - March 28, 1849. Died on the 25th inst., a son of Mr. Daniel Fulfort, aged about one year.

CP - April 4, 1849. Married in Binghamton, on the 8th ult., by the Rev. Dr. Paddock, Ebenezer Geer, Esq., of Oneida Co., and Miss Harriet Ann Pardee, late of Earlville, Madison co.

CP - April 11, 1849. Married in New York City, the 24th ult., by the editor of the *Mirror of the Times*, his son, Thomas D. Wallace and Elizabeth [dau. of?] S. E. Hammond, Esq., all of that city.

CP - April 11, 1849. Married in Manlius on March 22nd, by Rev. E. J. Gillett, Mr. --- Avery and Miss Emeline Gillett, both of Manlius.

CP - April 11, 1849. Married in Cazenovia, March 29th, by Rev. E. J. Gillett, Mr. Joseph Davis and Miss Abigail Shapley, all of that place.

CP - April 11, 1849. Married in Cazenovia on the 1st inst., by Rev. D. Holmes, Mr. A. S. Ball and Miss R. A. Tuttle, all of the place.

CP - April 11, 1849. Died in this town, the 6th inst., a dau. of Coonrod Crater, aged 1 year.

CP - April 18, 1849. Married in this village, on Mon., the 16th inst., by Rev. James Abell, Mr. A. C. Sandford, of the firm of Matteson and Sandford, Proprietor and Publisher of the *Ontario Messenger*, Canadaigua, and Miss Eunice Whipple, daughter of Jeremiah Whipple, Esq. of this place.

CP - April 18, 1849. Married in Perryville, on Sunday, the 8th inst., by Rev. C. Blakeslee, Mr. Sergeant Hall and Miss Betsey Hall, all of that place.

CP - April 18, 1849. Married in Canaseraga, the 4th inst., by Rev. A. W. Bruce, Mr. Lorenzo F. Gooden, of Henrietta, Monroe Co., and Miss Margaret A, 2nd daughter of Eben Hazeltine, Esq., of the former place.

CP - May 5, 1849. Died on the 5th of the month, of consumption, Dr. James P. Kennedy, son of Dr. Samuel Kennedy, in the 23rd year of his age, beloved and lamented by the community in which he lived.

CP - May 16, 1849. Married on the 12th inst., at French & Severance's Hotel, in this village, by Rev. James Abell, Mr. Jason Brooks, of Skaneateles, and Miss Abigail Potter, of Cazenovia.

CP - May 23, 1849. Married in this village, the 16th inst., by Rev. James Abell, Mr. John H. Walrath and Miss Julia Yates, all of this town.

CP - June 6, 1849. Died in this village, the 1st inst., a son of Allen J. Burlingame, aged 10 mos.

CP - June 6, 1849. Died in this town, the 2nd inst., John, son of Richard and Harriet Truax, aged 2 yrs. and 4 mos.

CP - June 13, 1849. Married in this village, the 12th inst., by Rev. L. E. Swan, Mr. E. T. Frederick, amd Miss Amanda Roach, all of the village.

CP - June 13, 1849.. Married in DeKalb St. Lawrence Co., the 21st ult., by Rev. M. Nichols, Rev. A. A. Graley, of Lenox and Miss Margaret A., daughter of G. H. Dies of the former place.

CP - June 13, 1849. Died in Utica, the 7th inst., suddenly, Almena D., wife of Charles H. Hopkins, formerly of this village.

CP - June 20, 1849. Died in this village, on the 15th inst., Sarah Francis, daughter of L. E. Swan, aged 3 years and 12 days.

CP - June 27, 1849. Died at Black Rock Dam, Erie Co., NY, on the 10th inst., Elizabeth, daughter of John DeWitt, aged 5 years. On the 11th, Laney, wife of John DeWitt and daughter of Jacob Bellinger, aged 28 yrs.; on the 12th, John DeWitt, aged 30 yrs.; on the 17th, Catherine, daughter of Jacob Bellinger, aged 18 yrs. They were formerly residents of this village. Cholera was the cause of their deaths.

CP - July 4, 1849. Died on the 15th of June, at Ceresco, Fon-du-Lac, WI, of inflamation of the brain, Horace B. Kellogg, aged 20 years, son of Walter Kellogg, late resident of this town, after an illness of three days.

CP - July 11, 1849. Married in this village, the 4th inst. by Rev. James Abell, Mr. James R. Mills and Miss Margaret Phelps, both of Lenox.

CP - July 11, 1849. Married in this village, the 5th inst., by Rev. A. W. Bruce, Mr. Marshall Brosseau and Miss Sophia, eldest daughter of A. S. Nichols, Esq.

CP - July 11, 1849. Married in Syracuse, the 4th inst., by Rev. Dr. Adams, Mr. H. P. Hodge, of Cazenovia, and Miss Betsey Ransom, of Fenner.

CP - July 11, 1849. Died in this village, the 8th inst., Mr. Henry Smith, aged 47 years.

CP - July 11, 1849. Died in Kirkville, the 27th ult., Mrs. Marion B., wife of Alexander F. Plato, and eldest daughter of Thomas Blanchard of DeWitt.

CP - July 11, 1849. Died in New York City, the 7th inst., on board the Lake Boat, *John Bates* of this place, Capt. Ira Gilman, of Kirkville, aged about 32 years.

CP - July 18. 1849. Died in New York at 5 o'clock p.m.,Thursday of the prevailing epidemic [cholera], Arthur Young Greely only son of Horace and Mary Y. C. Greeley, age 13 years 3 mos. and 20 days.

CP - July 25, 1849. Died in this town, the 16th inst., Col. Zebulon Douglass, aged about 80 years.

CP - July 25, 1849. Died at Cherry Valley, on the 18th inst., of cholera, Sarah, wife of Rev. G. S. Boardman, after an illness of 13 hours.

CP - August 8, 1849. Married in this village, the 26th ult., by Rev. L. E. Swan, Mr. Julius S. Webber of Rochester, and Miss Mary A. Williams of Cazenovia.

CP - August 22, 1849. Died at his residence in Canastota, on the 19th inst., Hon. Sylvester Beecher, in the 69th year of his age.

CP - August 22, 1849. Died at Bolivar, the 13th inst., Mrs. ___ Stone, wife of Elisha P. Stone.

CP - August 22, 1849. Married in this village, the 18th inst., by Rev. L. E. Swan, Mr. Elisha P. Stone and Miss Jane Devolve, both of Bolivar.

CP - August 29, 1849. Died at New Hamburgh, Dutchess Co., on Sat., the 25th inst., of cholera, Mr. Franklin Frederick, formerly of this village, aged 27 yrs.

CP - August 29, 1849. Died at Schenectady, on Sunday the 26th inst., of cholera, the Rev., J. Austin Yates, D. D., son of the late Rev. Andrew Yates, D. D., formerly of this place. For many years he was one of the Professors at the Union College, but had recently been installed Pastor of the Reformed Dutch Church in Jersey City. He was born May 1, 1801.

CP - August 29, 1849. Died in this village on the 21st inst., Eugene, son of Perry O. and Mary Jane Weaver, aged 3 mos. and 12 days.

CP - September 5, 1849. Married at Morrisville, August 26th, by Rev. Roswell Thompson, Esq, of Morrisville, Mr. Thomas M. Macomber, of Hamilton to Miss Abigail Elizabeth Jones of Eaton.

CP - September 5, 1849. Died in this town on the 2nd inst., Mrs ---, wife of Mr. Elijah Anguish, aged ---yrs.

CP - September 12, 1849. Married in Perryvile, on the 4th inst., by Rev. A. W Bruce, John Richardson, Esq., to Miss L. D. Ransom, both of Perryville.

CP - September 12, 1849. Married at the Cazenovia House, August 22nd, by Rev. William Clarke, Mr. George W. Stanton, of Cazenovia and Miss Julia A. Patterson, of Madison.[This same announcement appeared in the September 26 issue of the same newspaper.]

CP - September 12, 1849. Married at Eaton Centre, on the 1st inst., by Roswell Thompson, Esq., Mr. John Howe, to Mrs. Esther Haight, of Eaton.

CP - September 12, 1849. Died in this village on the 7th inst., a son of Mr. Andrew Walrath, aged 9 weeks.

CP - September 12, 1849. Died in Marshall, Oneida Co., on the 25th ult., in the 74th year of his age, Mr. Roger Brooks, formerly and for many years a resident of Nelson, in this county.

CP - September 19, 1849. Married at the Cazenovia House, on the 6th inst., by Rev. Daniel Putnam, Mr. Morgan L. Smith, of Milford, Oakland Co., MI and Miss Mary E. Darrow, of Eaton.

CP - September 19, 1849. Married the 4th inst., by Rev. S. W. Raymond, of Kirkland Jerome B. Wilcox, to Susan M. Shepherd, both of New Hartford.

CP - September 19, 1849. Married by the same on the 5th inst., in Kirkland, Hon. Julius White of Milwaukee to C. C. Shackelford, of Madison Wi.

CP - September 19, 1849. Died in this village on the 17th inst., Mr. Henry I. Walrath, in his 62nd year.

CP - September 26, 1849. Married in Schoharie, Sept. 17th, by Rev. Ransford Wells, S. Hosack Mix, Editor of the *Schoharie Patriot*, to Miss Margaret Elizabeth, eldest daughter of Perry G. Gardiner, Esq., of New York

CP - September 26, 1849. Married at Wellsboro, PA, July 30th, by Rev. Mr. Winton, Mr. B.A. Batley, of Albion, PA, to Miss Jane L. Hart, of Eaton.

CP - September 26, 1849. Married on the 5th inst., by Rev. Dr. Adams of Syracuse, I. Newton Messinger, to Miss Frances Elizabeth, only dau. of William E. Fisher, Esq., all of Canastota.

CP - September 26, 1849. Married in Augusta, the 20th inst., by Rev. Mr. Ainsworth, Mr. Clark Bailey, of Brookfield, to Miss Orissa J. Cole, of the former place.

CP - September 26, 1849. Married in Potossi, WI, on the 23rd ult., by Rev. E. C. Jones, Mr. David Atwood, editor of the *Madison (WI) Express*, to Miss Mary Ann Poe, of the former place.

CP - September 26, 1849. Died in the village of Oran, Onondaga Co., very suddenly on the 25th inst., Mrs ___, Wife of Rev. A. Bruce of Canaseraga, aged about 30 years.

CP - September 26, 1849. Died near Morrisville, on the 11th inst., Mrs. Fanny Wilber, wife of Ahiman[?] Wilber, aged 50 years.

CP - September 26, 1849. Died in Lenox on the 18th ult., Marcus R. Hammond, aged 30 years, son of William and Matilda Hammond, of Peterboro.

CP - October 3, 1849. Died in this village, on the morning of the 29th inst., of consumption, Mrs. Sara Brown, age ---, leaving one son, the last of a numerous family to mourn her loss. Mrs Brown has had a life of peculiar trial, having within the last three years buried three interesting daughters, her husband, and one son, all of the same insidious disease.

CP - October 10, 1849. Married in Cazenovia, September 27, by Rev. William Clarke, Mr. F. Henry Gilbert, and Miss Mary T., daughter of Walter Clough, Esq.

CP - October 10, 1849. A notice in this issue of the wedding - in Dutch - of Nicolaus DeWitt, of Rotterdam and Katrina Elizabet Nellius, [of?] VanArnhem on October 4, 1849

CP - October 10, 1849. Died in this village, on the 8th inst., Mrs. Robert Hazzard, aged about 70 years.

CP - October 10, 1849. Died in Ceresco, Fond du Lac, WI, Mr. Walter Kellogg, formerly of this town.

CP: October 10, 1849. Died at Buffalo, on the 2nd inst., Paul Coburn, formerly of Utica.

CP - October 17, 1849. Married in Utica, the 4th inst., by Rev. W. H. Spencer, Mr. Almon C. Messinger to Miss A. J. Benjamin, both of Oneida Lake.

CP - October 17, 1849. Married in Haywood Co., TN, on the morning of September 7th, Mr. James S. W. Caldwell to Miss Edmonia Virginia, only child of Major Edmund Richmond and on the same day, the parents of this young couple, Major Edmund Richmond married Mrs. Lydia E. Caldwell, sister of the late ex-president, James K. Polk.

CP - October 17, 1849. Married at the City Hotel, in this city, on the 10th inst., by Rev. William H. Spencer, H. W. Dana, Esq., and Miss Elizabeth A. Dana [sic], both of Kirkland.

CP - October 17, 1849. Married at Governeur, St. Lawrence Co., NY, on September 16th, by Rev. G. Swan, Edward A. Tew, of Brookfield, Madison Co., NY, late graduate of Hamilton College, to Miss Hetty, dau. of Mr. John Crocker, of Clinton, [Oneida Co., NY]. [Hamilton College is located in Clinton, NY.]

CP - October 17, 1849. Married in Fulton, by Rev. T. R. Townsend, Richard K. Sanford, Principal of the Middlebury Academy, Wyoming Co [NY], to Miss Lucy A. Carrier, late teacher in the Willoughby Female Seminary in Ohio, dau., of Asabel B. Carrier, Esq., of Volney.

CP - October 17, 1849. Died in Gouvernour, September 29th, of typhus fever, Edward A. Tew, of Brookfield, NY, aged 23 years.

CP - October 24, 1849: Died in this town, on the 22nd inst., Avery, youngest son of Mr. John Groves, aged about 12 years.

CP - October 31, 1849. Married in Stockbridge, on the 18th inst., by Rev. Daniel Holmes, Mr. Henry Coolidge, Editor of the *Madison County Whig* and Miss A. Almene Horton, of Stockbridge.

CP - October 31, 1849. Married in Cazenovia, on the 21st inst., Mr. Ebenezer Pennock, of Bolivar, and Miss Ann Coats, of Fayetteville.

CP - October 31, 1849. Married in Sackville, WI, the 16th inst., Mr. J. H. Tibbitts, formerly of this village and Miss L. Topliff, only daughter of Elibius Topliff, formerly of Fayetteville.

CP - Oct 31, 1849. Died this morning, a daughter of Mr. Philip Smith, aged 3 years.

CP - November 7, 1849. Married at Harmony Hall, in this village on the 1st inst., by the Rev. L. E. Swan, Mr. Mirrick Rice of Aurelius, Cayuga Co., and Miss Sally Maria Butler, of Butternuts, Otsego Co.; married at the same time and place and by the same, Mr. David Loucks of Pouentine [sic], Herkimer Co., to Miss Electa Youngs, of Sullivan. [Note: No town or village of the name Pouentine could be located by the Editor in French's *Gazeteer of New York* (1860).]

CP - November 14, 1849. Married at Chittenango, on the 4th inst., by Rev. Mr. Colgrove [Methodist], Mr. Lester Volatine, of Syracuse, to Miss Jane Maria Waterbury, of Chittenango.

CP - November 14, 1849. Married on the 7th inst., at the Church of the Ascension, New York City, by the Rev. Francis Vinton, D. D., August Belmont to Caroline Slidell, daughter of Commodore M. C. Perry, U. S. Navy.

CP - November 14, 1849. Married in Boston, the 6th inst., by Rev. Dr. Peabody, Hon. Robert C. Winthrop to Mrs. Laura Derby Wells.

CP - November 14, 1849. Died in Montezuma, on the 3rd inst., David Dodge, age 32 years, 12 days, father of Ossian E. Dodge, the Vocalist.

CP - November 21 , 1849. Died in Cazenovia, on the 6th inst., Mrs. Catherine Childs, widow of the late Perry G. Childs, Esq., aged 60 yrs. She was the daughter of General Benjamin Ledyard, one of the earlist settlers of Cayuga Co. and sister of Gen. Ledyard of Cazenovia.

CP - November 28, 1849. Died in Lenox, the 15th inst., of consumption, Mr. William Bond, aged 32 yrs.

CP - November 28, 1849. Died in Morrisville, the 17th inst., Amanda, wife of Maj. Allen Smith.

CP - December 5, 1849. Married in New York on the 18th inst., Miss Cornelia Scott, daughter of Gen. Scott, to Major H. L. Scott, aide-de-camp to the Commander-in-Chief, at the city residence of the General in 8th street.

CP - December 19, 1849. Married in Sullivan on the 12th inst., by Rev. E. L. Swan, Mr. Benjamin Yarton [Yorton?] and Miss Sally Ann Harter.

CP - December 19, 1849. Also by the same [as above], on the 15th inst., in this village, Mr. Henry Daharsh and Miss Erena Adelaide Arnold, all of the town of Sullivan. [According to the cemetery stone in Oneida, the marriage took place on the 19th of Dec. Ed.]

CP - December 19, 1849: Married in Nelson, October 31st, by Rev. J. J. Teeple, Mr. Abijah B. Lindsley, and Miss Lucia M. Cutler, both of that town.

CP - December 19, 1849. Died in Morrisville, Saturday the lst inst., Mr. Harrison C. Bicknell, in the 42nd year of his age.

CP - December 19, 1849. Died in Morrisville, Monday morning, the 3rd inst., Mrs. Charlotte Dexter, aged 66 yrs.

CP - December 19, 1849. Died in Morrisville, Saturday, the 8th inst., Miss Elizabeth Williams, daughter of Mr. Elijah Williams, aged 22 years.

CP - December 26, 1849. Married in Schroeppel, Oswego Co., at the residence of A. Becker, by Rev. H. Warner, Mr. Henry Becker of Clay to Miss Esther Rhodes of Schroeppel. The Bridgroom was 80 yrs old, the bride was 74 and the Reverend was 71 yrs old.

CP - December 26, 1849. Died in Canastota on the 23rd inst., Mrs. ---widow of Hon. Sylvester Beecher, aged 66 yrs.

CP - December 26, 1849. Died in New York the 15th inst., Rev. John Peck, in the 69th year of his age. Funeral at the Oliver Street Baptist Church. His body was taken to Cazenovia [for burial]. He was born in Stanford, Dutchess Co., September 11, 1781. About the year 1796 when he was 15 years of age, his father removed to Norwich, Chenango Co. He was licensed to preach at 21 years of age; married at about age 23. In 1804 moved to Cazenovia. He was ordained Pastor of the Baptist Church in Cazenovia and resigned November 1834.

CP - January 2, 1850. Married in this village on the 1st inst., by Rev. James Abell, Mr. Henry Eggabroad and Miss Elmira Stone, all of this village.

CP - January 2, 1850. Married on the 28th inst. [ult.?] by Rev. L. Bowdish, Mr. Robert B. Avery to Miss Augusta M. Lansing of Perryville.

CP - January 2, 1850. Married in Syracuse, on the 1st inst., Mr. J. M. Shute and Miss Marion Nichols, daughter of A. S. Nichols, all of this town.

CP - January 2, 1850. Died at Clockville on the 20th inst., Mr. Austin J. Seeber, aged 29 years.

CP - January 9, 1850. Married in Rome, on the 1st inst., by Rev. H. C. Volgell, Mr. Ezariah Young and Miss Ada Carl, both of this town.

CP - January 9, 1850. Died in Canaseraga, on the 30th inst. [ult.?], Mary Elizabeth, daughter of Dr. William Oakes, aged 2 yrs. and 4 mos.

CP - January 16, 1850. Married in this village on the 9th inst., by Rev. L. E. Swan, Mr. John O. French and Miss Nancy Bellinger, all of this town.

CP - January 16, 1850. Married in this town, on the 15th inst., by Rev. James Abell, Mr. James Bell of Amsterdam, NY and Miss Martha Sophia, daughter of Capt. Asa Cady of this town.

CP - January 16, 1850. Married in Utica on the 7th inst., by John Parsons, Esq., Harvey Seward of Syracuse and Mercy M. Fling of Solsville, Madison Co.

CP - January 23, 1850. Married at William G. Burr's, Cazenovia, by Rev. William Clark, Mr. Ashley Pratt of Pompey and Miss Caroline Thompson, of Cazenovia.

CP - January 16, 1850. Married by the same [as above], on the 9th inst., Mr. Silas G. Reeeve of Newark, Tioga Co., and Miss Sarah Tucker, of Cazenovia.

CP - January 23, 1850. Died at Eaton on the 13th inst., Mrs. Zipporah, relict of Constant Avery, aged 77 yrs.

CP - January 23, 1850. Died in Hamilton, Mrs. Betsey, widow of Deacon Samuel Payne, aged 86 yrs.

CP - January 30, 1850. Married in Kirkland, Oneida Co, on the 24th inst., by Rev. S. W. Raymond, Mr. H. G. Trembley, publisher of the *Christian Cultivator*, McGrawville, NY, and Miss Jane Carothers, of the former place.

CP - January 30, 1850. Married in New York on the 24th inst., by the Rev. Dr. Hutton, William H. H. Prall, Grand Secretary, Grand Lodge of Northern New York to Martha Vorhees, all of New York City.

CP - January 30, 1850. Died in Morrisville, on the 17th inst., Amariah Williams, aged 74 yrs.

CP - January 30, 1850. Died at New Haven CT, on Friday, the 18th inst., Mrs. Harriet Stillman, wife of Prof. Stillman of Yates College, and daughter of Gov. Turnbull.

CP - February 6, 1850. Married in Hamilton on the 23rd inst., by Rev. George W. Eaton, D. D., Mr. Theodore R. Burchard, to Miss Emeline, only daughter of Jeremiah Green, M. D., all of that village.

CP - February 13, 1850. Died in Morrisville, on the 1st inst., Mr. James B. Thompson, aged 45 years.

CP - February 13, 1850. Died in Nelson on the 13th ult. Mrs. Sara Dexter, aged 95 years, 9 months and 3 days.

CP - February 13, 1850. Married in this town by Rev. James Abell. Rev. A. M. Beebe of Jordan, Cayuga Co. [sic] [actually in Onondaga Co. Ed], and Miss Catherine Jane Hall, of Sullivan.

CP - February 13, 1850. Married in Mentz, Cayuga Co, on the 5th inst., by Rev. H. C. Hall, Mr. C. L. Frederick, of Syracuse to Miss Sophia R. Paddock, of the former place.

CP - February 13, 1850. Born on the 6th inst., to the wife of Mr. John Bates, a daughter.

CP - February 27, 1850. Married in Cazenovia on the 15th inst., by Rev. William Clark, Mr. Chester H. Porter of Sandy Creek, Oswego Co. and Miss Mary Ann Stewart of Cazenovia.

CP - February 27, 1850. Married on the 12th inst., By Rev. D. Holmes, Mr. Ira Wright of Pompey to Miss Olive Webb, of Cazenovia.

CP - February 27, 1850. Married in Morrisville, Thursday morning last, by Rev. Charles Blakslee, Mr. William M. Fairbanks to Harriet S. Stephens.

CP - February 27, 1850. Died in DeRuyter, on the 14th inst., Mrs. Harriet Allen, wife of Henry Allen.

CP - March 6, 1850. Married in Fayetteville on the 21st inst., by Rev. David Pise [Pease?], Mr. Jason W. Allen of Cazenovia and Miss Sarah Holbrook, of Chittenango.

CP: March 6, 1850. Married on the 19th inst., at the Lincklaen House by Rev. Daniel Homes, Mr. Sumner Gill to Miss Lovina Brigham, both of Smithfield.

CP - March 6, 1850. Died in this village on the 5th inst., a child of Mr. Seymour Holbrook.

CP - March 6, 1850. Died in this town on the 28th inst., Amanda, daughter of Peter Robinson, aged about 50 years.

CP - March 6, 1850. Died in this town on the 2nd inst., Mrs. Sally Ann, wife of Rev. Calvin Flint, aged 43 years.

CP - March 13, 1850. Married February 21st by Rev. Charles Blakesleee, Mr. William Burns of Durhamville to Lucinda Holbrook of Eaton

CP : March 13, 1850. Married March 6, by the same, Mr. Harvey Matteson of Nelson to Miss Amanda Duel, of the same place.

CP - March 13, 1850. Married at Peterboro, February 18th, by Rev. George Hall, Mr. William A. Brown to Miss Sarah H. Blair, all of the same place.

CP - March 13, 1850. Died in this town on the 11th inst., Mr. Milton Leach, aged about 55 years.

CP - March 20, 1850. Born on the 26th of December, a daughter, Julia Gardner, to his Excellency John Tyler, ex-president of the U. S., at his residence, Sherwood Forest, Charles Co., Virginia.

CP - March 20, 1850. Married in Martinsburg, Lewis Co.,[NY], on the 12th inst., Mr. W. C. Johnson and Miss Julia A. Cadwell, all of that place.

CP - March 20, 1850. Died in Madison, on the 6th inst., Abby, wife of Samuel Brownell, Esq., age 57 years.

CP - March 20, 1850. Died in Camden, Oneida Co., NY, on the 8th of February, the Rev. Truman Gillett, aged about 70 years.

CP - March 27, 1850. Died in Robertson Co., TX, on the 21st ult., Mr. George Tobey, formerly of this village.

CP - March 27, 1850. Died in New Boston, on the 17th inst., by scalding, a son of Solomon and Esther Clark, aged 2 years and 5 months.

CP - March 27, 1850. Died at Adrian, MI, Feb. 10th, Mr. Perkins Bartlett, formerly of the town of Eaton.

CP - April 3, 1850. Married in this village on the 21st inst., [ult?], by Rev. L. E. Swan, Mr. George Washington Riley and Miss Olive Holmes.

CP - April 10, 1850. Died at his residence in this town, on Friday the 5th inst., Johannes C. Yung, aged 88 years. Mr. Yung was one of the first settlers of this town and remarable for his honesty and industry.

CP - April 10, 1850. Died in Morrisville, on the 28th inst. [ult.?], Mr. Jefferson Cross, aged 46 years.

CP - April 10, 1850. Died in Eaton, on the 31st ult., Mrs. Betsey, wife of George Maxwell.

CP - April 10, 1850. We regret to learn the Rev. J. W. Adams of Syracuse, died on Tuesday at Glen Haven, near Skaneateles. He was an able and prominent Presbyterian clergyman.

CP - April 17, 1850. Married in this village the 14th inst., by Rev. L. E. Swan, Mr. D. R. Nichols of Fenner and Miss Helen L. Routnour of Lenox.

CP - April 17, 1850. Married in New Hamburgh, Dutchess Co., on the 15th inst., by Rev. F. S. Williams, Mr. A. J. Wells, of this place and Miss Frances A. Brower of the former place.

CP - April 17, 1850. Married in Camillus, on the 10th inst., by Rev. Mr. Harmon, Mr. E. R. Harmon and Miss Helen S. Land, all of that place.

CP - April 17, 1850. Died in this village, on the 10th inst., Frances E., daughter of Mr. John Carter, aged 1 year 9 months.

CP - April 14, 1850. Married in Cazenovia, on the 17th inst., Mr. Jacob Clinton Dana and Miss Harriet, daughter of Mr. M. Moulter, all of that place.

CP - April 24, 1850. Died in Rochester, Racine Co., WI, of consumption. Mr. Anson Willard, formerly a resident of this town.

CP - April 24, 1850. Died in Leroy, Genessee Co., on the 12th inst., Mrs. Ann, wife of Mr. Isaac Pixley, aged 47 years, formerly of Clinton, Oneida Co.

Cp - May 1, 1850. Married on the 28th ult., by Rev. E. L. Swan, Mr. Robert Ehle and Miss Mary Quackenbush, all of this village.

CP - May 1, 1850. Died in this village on the 27th ult., Mr. William W. Kennedy, aged 32 years.

CP - Ma;y 1, 1850. Died in Canseraga, on the 28th ult., Mr. Jacob Patrick, aged 86 years.

CP - May 8, 1850. Born, May 3rd, at Canaseraga, to the wife of John O. French, a daughter.

CP - May 8, 1850. Born, May 5th at Chittenango, to the wife of Charles C. P. Severance, a son.

CP - May 8, 1850. Married on the 2nd inst., at the residence of Mr. William Spencer, in this town, by Rev. Mr. Holmes, Mr. Thomas Spencer and Miss Sarah M., youngest daughter of Rev. C. N. Flint of Clockville.

CP - May 8, 1850. Married on the 6th inst., at the residence of Deacon Albro Hall, by Rev. Mr. Abell, Mr. Silas Gates of LaFayette, Medina Co., OH, and Mrs. Mabel Lansing of Perryville.

CP - May 8, 1850. Died at Cazenovia on the 17th ult., William Shankland, aged 88 years, father of Judge Shanklin, of the Supreme Court of this state.

CP- May 15, 1850. Died on Tues. morning, May 14th, after a lingering and painful illness, Mr. David Kennedy, in the 56th year of his age. The deceased had been for upward of 30 years, a resident of this town...

CP - May 22, 1850. Married on the evening of the 19th inst., by Rev. Mr. Abell, Benjamin Dutcher, Esq., of Wisconsin to Nancy Popple of Cazenovia.

CP - May 22, 1850. Married on the 14th inst., by Rev. S. W. Raymond, Mr. John Green to Miss Eunice Stockwell, all of Kirkville.

CP - May 22, 1850. Married on the morning of the 15th inst., by the same, Mr. Orville Dodge, of Vernon and Mr. James Blackstone of Kirkland; the former to Miss Frances and the latter to Miss Kate Dean, daughters of the late John Dean of Westmoreland.

CP - May 22, 1850. Also on the evening of the same day, Mr. Alfred Baker of New Hartford to Miss Adaline Loomis of Westmoreland.

CP - May 22, 1850. Died in this town on the 15th inst., Mr. Edwin Lewis, aged ----.

CP - May 22, 1850. Died in Clinton, on the 19th inst., Dr. Dwight, Treasurer of Hamilton College, aged 73 years.

CP - May 24 (29?), 1850. Married in the city of New York, on Thursday, the 16th inst., Mr. Charles J. Pixley, of the village of Portchester to Agnes Woodhull, of the City of New York.

CP - May 24 (29?), 1850. Died in Bridgeport, on the 21st inst., Mr. James Wheat, aged 53 years.

CP - May 24 (29?), 1850. Died in Cazenovia, on the 19th inst., Mr. Cyrus Whitcomb, Sr., in the 73rd year of his age.

CP - May 24 (29?), 1850. Died at Oneida, on the 14th inst., Mrs. Cornelia, wife of Sand Higginbotham, aged 47 years.

CP - June 5, 1850. Married in Chittenango, June 2nd, by Rev. George Colegrove, Mr. James DePuy, to Miss C. L. House, all of this village.

CP - June 12, 1850. Married in Cazenovia, on the 4th inst., by Rev. William Clark, Mr. L. Prosser, and Miss Mary Hamblin, both of this town.

CP - June 12, 1850. Died at the residence of his son, in the city of Brooklyn, Mr. John Downer, in the 72nd year of his age. He was one of the first settlers and for a long time a resident of Peterboro, in this county.

CP - June 19, 1850. Born on the 15th, in this village to the wife of A. J. French, a son.

CP - June 19, 1850.. Born on the 14th, in Clinton, to the wife of Edward Stebbins, a daughter.

CP - June 19, 1850. Married in Fayetteville, the 14th inst., by Elder Wright, Mr. Stephen W. Dady and Miss Sophia Shaver, both of this village.

CP - June 19, 1850. Married on the 17th inst., by James A. H. Cornell, D. D., M. Edward Fitch Pratt, of New York, to Miss Irene Lawrence, daughter of Judge James R. Lawrence of Syracuse.

CP - June 19, 1850. Died at Pompey, Onondaga Co., Friday evening, very suddenly, Elder --- Dewey, aged 80 years.

CP - July 10, 1850. Married at Lenox, July 4th, by Esq. Thomas Lumis, Mr. R[obert] R. West, of Verona, to Miss Mary J. Beebee of Lenox.

CP - June 17, 1850. Died in this village on the 16th inst., Mary, wife of Mr. P. O. Weaver, and daughter of John Knowles, Esq., aged 28 years. Funeral today at 2 P. M. Funeral sermon on Sunday next at the Baptist church at 4 o'clock P. M. by Elder Wright

CP - July 24, 1850.. Died in this village on the 16th inst., of consumption, after a long and intense suffering, at the residence of her father, Mary Jane, wife of P. O. Weaver and only remaining daughter of John Knowles, Esq., in her 28th year.

CP - July 24, 1850. Died in this town, the 19th inst., Mary Elizabeth, widow of Johannes C. Young. [He died April 5th. Ed.]

CP - July 31, 1850. Born in this village, the 23rd inst., to the wife of Maj. Abel Wood, a son.

CP - July 31, 1850. Married in this village, the 29th inst., by Rev. George Colegrove, Mr. William Brown and Miss E. S. Coates, both of Fayetteville.

CP - July 31, 1850. Married in Fayetteville, this morning, the 31st inst., by Rev. Mr. Wright, Mr. James G. Reals and Catharine, daughter of Adam Grove, Esq., all of Fayetteville.

CP - July 31, 1850. Died in LeRoy, the 27th inst., Caroline Jenette, daughter of R. A. and Emily L. Law, of Grand Chute, WI, aged 9 months.

CP - August 7, 1850. Married in Syracuse, the 3rd inst., by P. H. Snow, D. D., Mr. Barton M. Hopkins, and Miss Margaret, daughter of the late Peter McDougall, all of that city.

CP - August 7, 1850. Died in Lenox, the 4th inst., George, son of Elanson Herrick, aged 4 years and 8 months.

CP - August 14, 1850. Married on the 31st of July, in Trinity Church, Fayetteville, by Rev. D. Pise, Mr. James G. Reals to Mrs. Catharine A. Grove Hadley, both of Fayetteville.

CP - August 14, 1850. Died in this town, the 8th inst., Mr. Frederick Platto, aged about 50 years.

CP - August 28, 1850. Born in this village, the 22nd inst., a daughter to Mr. William Velaskow.

CP - August 28, 1850. Married in Auburn, the 21st inst., Mr. Croly of this village, and Miss Celia, daughter of Mr. James Campbell of Perryville.

CP - August 28, 1850. Died in this town, the 23rd inst., a son of Mr. Isaac Bettinger, aged 10 years.

CP - September 4, 1850. Married in Hamilton, on the 26th inst., by Rev. G. W. Eaton, D. D., Rev. A. M. Hopper, a recent graduate from the Theological Department of Madison University, and Miss Lavantia, oldest daughter of Dr. B. Lewis, of Hamilton.

CP - September 4, 1850. Married on the 20th inst., by Rev. George S. Boardman, Kendrick N. Guiteau and Jane S. Childs, of Cazenovia.

CP - September 4, 1850. Died in Lenox, on the 28th ult., Mr. Obiel Blanchard, aged 48 years.

CP - September 4, 1850. Died in this village, on the 28th ult., infant son of H. T. Westcott.

CP - September 18, 1850. Born on the 11th to the wife of Mr. W. W. Daniels, a daughter.

CP - September 18, 1850. Born on the 9th, to the wife of Mr. Charles Cowden, a daughter.

CP - September 18, 1850. Born on the 7th to the wife of William H. Gale, a daughter.

CP - September 18, 1850. Born on the 6th, to the wife of Mr. Christopher DeWitt, a son.

CP - September 18, 1850. Married in Lenox, on the 30th ult., by Rev. Washington Stickney, Mr. George A. Ames, of Syracuse, to Miss Julia A. Palmer, of Lenox.

CP - September 18, 1850. Married in Cazenovia, on the 30th ult., by Rev. William Clarke, Mr. Caleb Abbott, and Mrs Mary Ann Brown, both of Nelson.

CP - September 18, 1850.: Died on the 12th inst., the youngest daughter of John and Sara A. Anguish, aged 6 years.

CP - September 18, 1850. Died at the Chittenango Railroad Station, on Wednesday last, Sept. 11th, Margaret, wife of the late Jonas Daniels, in the 53rd year of her age.

CP - September 25, 1850. Married in Norwich, on the 3rd ult., by A. J. Dana, Mr. Elisha S. French, of Binghamton to Miss Mary Van Benschoten, of Union.

CP - September 25, 1850. Married September 18th by Rev. William Clarke, Mr. William R. Nichols, of Cazenovia and Miss Lucy A. Judd, of Sullivan.

CP - September 25, 1850. Married in Madison, on the 10th inst., by the Rev. L. D. Davis, Mr. Harvey J. Taylor, and Miss Rebecca M. House, both of Madison.

CP - September 25, 1850. Died in this village, the 20th inst., Mrs. Sarah Holbrook, aged---.

CP - October 2, 1850. Died in this village, the 29th ult., of fever, Mr. Alex Seth Nichols, aged 56 years.

CP - October 9, 1850. Died at Cazenovia, this morning, Mrs. Evalina Donaldson, wife of Alexander Donaldson, Jr., aged 43 years.

CP - October 9, 1850. Married in Hamilton, on the 27th of April, last, by the Rev. J. Potter, Mr. Hiram R. Ackley, and Miss Julia A. Comstock.

CP - October 9, 1850. Died on the 21st ult., at Clinton, Oneida Co., Huldah Clark, wife of Dr. Seth Hastings.

CP - October 16, 1850. Married on Wed., the 9th inst. by the Rev. James Abell, Mr. Franklin W. Walrath, to Miss Lucretia J., daughter of Coonrod Crater, Esq., all of Sullivan.

CP - October 16, 1850. Married at Cazenovia, Wed. morning, October 9th, by Rev. William Clarke, Mr. Calvin B. Howe, of Brooklyn, to Miss Eliza Litchfield, daughter of the Hon. Elisha Litchfield, of Cazenovia.

CP - October 16, 1850. Died in this town, on the 15th inst., Orville, son of Ezra Bond, aged 15 yrs.

CP - October 16, 1850. Died in Clinton, the 4th inst., Alice, infant daughter of Edward and Lydia S. Stebbins, aged 4 mos.

CP - October 16, 1850. Died in Lenox, Sept, 18th, Fanny P. Allen, daughter of George Allen, aged 22 yrs.

CP - October 23, 1850. Married in New Woodstock, Oct. 14th by Rev. John Fulton, Mr. George Haight, to Miss Sarah M. Chandler, all of Cazenovia.

CP - October 23, 1850. Married in DeRuyter, Oct. 15th, by V. Bently, Esq., Harvey D. Williams, of Cazenovia and Celestia M. Rider, of the former place.

CP - October 23, 1850. Married in Earlville, August 21st, by Rev. L. S. Livermore, Mr. Amon C. Lyon, and Miss Evaline Sexton, all of the above place.

CP - October 30, 1850. Married in this town, the 24th inst., by Rev. E. L. Swan, Mr. Allen Davis and Miss Susan Cook, both of Sullivan.

CP - October 30, 1850. Married in Otego, Otsego Co., on the 8th inst., by Rev. William ---, Rector of Zion Church, Morris, Otsego Co., Mr. Charles Kellogg, of Sullivan and Miss Mary Amanda, daughter of -- of Otego.

CP - October 30, 1850. Married in Clinton, on the 10th (?) by the Rev. Mr. Pratt, Mr. Simmons, of Madison, to Miss Jane A. Plumbly, of Hamilton.

CP - October 30, 1850. Married in Cazenovia, October 14th, by the Rev. William Clarke, Mr. John Mann and Miss Lucy Ann Warren, both of Nelson.

CP - October 30, 1850. Married, by the same, October 17th, at the residence of Rev. J. Nickerson, Rev. George J. Johnson, of Burlington, IA, and Miss Maria L. Nickerson of Cazenovia.

CP - October 30, 1850. Married in Manlius, on the 20th inst., by Rev. John Smitzer, Mr. John Cox and Miss Rosanna E. Bentley, both of Cazenovia.

CP - October 30, 1850. Died in this village, the 24th inst., Flora, daughter of Jerry S. and Henrietta S. Harrington, aged 18 months.

CP - October 30, 1850. Died at Cazenovia, on the 23rd of October, Col. James Berthrong, aged 70 years.

CP - October 30, 1850. Died in Hamilton, on the 17th instant, Miss Jennie S. Osgood, aged 18 years.

CP - October 30, 1850. Died in Brookfield on Saturaday, the 12th inst., Mrs. Mary Ann Coon, aged 36 years.

CP - October 30, 1850. Died on the 12th ult., Mrs. Anne M. Burdick, aged 38 (or 88) years.

CP - October 30, 1850. Died on the 22nd ult., Mr. Henry C. Burdick, aged 44 years.

CP - Thurs., November 7, 1850. Married in Cazenovia, on the 31st ult., by Rev. Henry Bannister, Mr. Peter Like, of Owego, to Miss Camilla Dawson, daughter of Mr. A. Dawson, of Cazenovia.

CP - November 7, 1850. Married in Fenner, on the 22nd ult., by Rev. Mr. Anderson, Mr. F. A. Hyatt of Fenner and Miss E. M. Robinson, of Perryville.

CP - November 7, 1850. Married on the 30 inst. [ult?], by Rev. William Clarke, Mr. C. M. Benson, and Miss E. E. Lacy, both of Cazenovia.

CP - Wed., November 13, 1850. Married in this village, on the 7th inst., by Rev. L. E. Swan, Mr. Franklin A. Rouse, and Miss Jane E. Rice, both of Cazenovia.

CP - November 13, 1850. Married at Utica, the 16th ult., by Rev. Charles Wiley, Pastor of the Dutch Reformed Church, Mr. Charles H. Alexander, of Winchester, VT, and Miss Chiffonette L., 2nd daughter of Mr. S. W. Chubbuck, of Utica.

CP - November 13, 1850. Married at Hollisterville, Wayne Co., PA, the 17th ult., by the Rev. Mr. Mendenhall, Charles R. Hall, Civil Engineer, formerly of Lenox, NY, to Miss Ariann C. Hollister, of the former place.

CP - November 13, 1850. Married in Eaton on Tues., October 29th, by Rev. S. H. Norton, Rector of St. Thomas Church, Hamilton, William Henry Davis, Esq., of Cincinnati, OH, to Cathren O. Landon, daughter of Mr. John Landon, of Eaton.

CP - November 13, 1850. Married at Pompey Hill, on the 26th ult., by Rev. Mr. Hastings, Mr. J. R. Orvis of Hamilton, to Miss Lucy H. Heath of the former place.

CP - November 13, 1850. Died in Eaton, Monday morning, of consumption, Mr. Henry Haughton, aged 30 years.

CP - November 13, 1850. Died at Cazenovia, on the 1st inst., Elizabeth Leonard, wife of John Williams, Esq., aged 58 years.

CP - November 13, 1850. Died in Hamilton, 29th of Sept., Mr. Ezra Richards, aged 33 (or 83?) years.

CP - November 20, 1850. Married at the Elm-House, in Whitesboro, the 3rd inst., by Rev. W. A. Matson, Mr. Oney Talbot to Miss Margaret Hess, both of Oneida.

CP - November 20, 1850. Married at the Oneida Railroad-House, the 29th ult., by the Rev. James Nichols, Mr. John Cornelis to Miss Alishqueth Augustine, both descendants of the old Indian Chief, Skenandoah. [Chief of the Oneida tribe.]

CP - November 27, 1850. Married in this village, the 21st inst., by the Rev. L. E. Swan, Mr. Lyman March and Miss Harriet Howard, both of Madison.

CP - November 28, 1850. Married in Hamilton, Oct. 31st, by The Rev. G. W. Eaton, D. D., Mr. George Smith, and Miss Sarah A. Parker, of Hamilton.

CP - November 27, 1850. Married in Sangerfield, Nov. 7th, by Rev. G. W. Eaton, D. D., Mr. D. B. West of Hamilton, and Miss Eliza Mott, daughter of John Mott, Esq., of Sangerfield.

CP - December 4, 1850. Married on the 20th inst., [ult?], by Rev. H. L. Hammond, Mr. Benjamin Wilcox of Fairfield, Herkimer Co., to Miss Martha M. Brown of Eaton.

CP - December 4, 1850. Married at Clockville, the 21st ult. by Rev. Silas Spaulding, Col. Stephen Chapman to Miss Sally Forbes, all of that place.

CP - December 4, 1850. Married at Cazenovia, the 21st ult., by Rev. Francis Hawley, J. C. Pettibone, Jr., of Delta, Oneida Co., to Miss Mary Ann Hawley, of Cazenovia.

CP- December 4, 1850. Married at Utica, the 20th ult., by Rev. B. G. Paddock, Mr. Henry Brightman, of Cazenovia, to Mrs. A. T. Stafford, of Utica.

CP - December 11, 1850. Died in Madison, on the 3rd ult., Mr. Ichabod Manchester, aged 79 years.

CP - December 18, 1850. Married at the Sulphur Spring House, the 11th inst., by the Rev. L. E. Swan, Mr. George Ehle, and Miss Mary E., daughter of Mrs. Charles Cowden, all of this village.

CP - December 18, 1850. Died at Vernon, on Sunday, the 8th ult., Dr. Welcome Sayles, aged 74 years.

CP - December 18, 1850. Died in Syracuse, on the 9th inst., at the residence of W. C. Williams, Eleazer Silvester, aged 24 years.

CP - December 18, 1850. Died at Houston, TX, on the 6th of November, after an illness of four days, Mr. Henry C. VanNorthwick aged 25 years. He was a native of New Brunswick, NJ and came to this place when a mere lad with his mother, after her marriage to Job Wells, Esq., of this place.

CP - December 25, 1850. Married in Cazenovia, the 18th inst., by Rev. L. E. Swan, Mr. Loren W. Brown of Georgetown and Miss Elcena D. Prentess, of Cazenovia.

CP - December 25, 1850. Married on the 15th inst., by Rev. J. J. Teeple, Mr. Nicholas Coonrod and Miss Sarah F. Chappin, all of Morrisville.

CP - December 25, 1850. Married in Hamilton, on the 15th inst., by the Rev. Job Potter, Mr. Warren S. Pettis, of Homer, Cortland Co., and Miss Evelyn A. Nash of the former place.

CP - December 25, 1850: Died in Fenner, near Perryville, December 11th, Mrs. Jane Ehle, aged 36 years.

CP - December 25, 1850. Died at Philadelphia, 30th ult., Rev. Sereno E. Dwight, formerly President of Hamilton College [Clinton, NY.]

CP - January 1, 1851. Married in the Reformed Dutch Church last evening, by Rev. James Abell, Mr. Thomas H. French and Miss Francis M. Doolittle, all of this village.

CP - January 1, 1851. Married in Clockville this morning, Mr. M. D. Bailey of Hilsdale, Columbia Co., and Miss Mary J. Cady, of Clockville.

CP - January 1, 1851. Married in this town, the 26th ult., by Rev. L. E. Swan, Mr. Lemi B. Hemingway, of Dryden, Tompkins Co., and Miss Sylvia Stone of this town.

CP - January 1, 1851. Married in this town, the 26th ult., by the same, Mr. James C. Robie, of Perryville, and Miss Atlanta Case, of this town.

CP - January 15, 1851. Married this morning in Fayetteville, Mr. Uriel M. Toby of this town and Miss Mary Scoville of the former place.

CP - January 15, 1851. Married at the Park House, in Hamilton, January 1st, by the Rev. A. Sedgewick, Mr. Charles White, and Miss Wealthy Edgerton, both of Nelson.

CP - January 15, 1851. Married at the Cazenovia House, January 1st, by Rev. William Clarke, Mr. Albert Hill, and Miss Caroline Johnson, both of Manlius.

CP - January 15, 1851. Married December 30th, by Rev. William Clarke, Mr. Riley L. Nichols, of Fenner and Miss Emily O. Woodwin of Cazenovia.

CP - January 15, 1851. Married December 31st, by the same, Mr. William Winchell, and Miss Maria Kellogg, both of Cazenovia.

CP - January 15, 1851. Died in this town, on the 10th inst., Mrs. Oscar Roberts, aged about 23 years.

CP - January 15, 1851. Died in Lebanon, on the 25th ult., Mrs. Hannah Sharf, aged 76 years.

CP - January 22, 1851. Died in Cazenovia, on the 20th ult., after a short but distressing illness, Mr. Lydia Johnson, wife of Henry A. Johnson, in the 48th year of her age.

CP - January 9, 1851. Married in the Seventh Day Baptist Church, in Scott, Cortland Co., the 18th inst., by Rev. Mr. Maxon, Mr. John.M (?) Schuyer, of this town, and Miss M. Matilda Frisbie, of the former place.

CP - January 29, 1851. Married on the 16th inst., by Rev. George W. Eaton, D. D., Mr. John G. Saunders and Miss Pauline J. Hailing, both of Peterboro.

CP - January 29, 1851. Married on the 21st inst., by Rev. Mr. Bowdish, Mr. Joseph Critchley of Eaton, to Miss Caroline Gray of Smithfield.

CP - January 29, 1851. Died in Canastota, on the 13th inst., Mrs. Cornelia, wife of Hon. Thomas Barlow.

CP - February 5, 1851. Married in this village, on the 2nd inst., by Rev. George Colgrove, Mr. Gaylord Bateman to Miss Mary Ann Ackely, both of Sullivan.

CP - February 5, 1851. Married at Mechanicville in the town of Cazenovia, on Thursday, the 23rd ult., by the Rev. Henry Benson, Mr. Alphonso Hobert, of Homer and Miss Lucretia A. Billings, of the former place.

CP - February 5, 1851. Died in Cazenovia, on the 22nd ult., at the residence of her son, Luke May, Mrs. Sarah May, aged 95 years and five months.

CP - February 5, 1851. Died in Cazenovia, on the 22nd ult., Mrs. Lydia Thrall, wife of Lura Chandler, in the 49th year of her age.

CP - February 12, 1851. Married in this village, on the 10th inst., by Rev. James Abell, Russell L. Holbrook, Esq. of Morris, Otsego Co., and Miss Anna M. Leaveitt, of this village.

CP - February 12, 1851. Married in this village, on the 9th inst., by Rev. L. E. Swan, Mr. George W. Van Atwerp, and Miss Harriett E. Clay, of Cazenovia.

CP - February 26, 1851. Born in Rome, the 22nd inst., to the wife of Alfred Sandford, a daughter.

CP - February 26, 1851. Married in Lenox, the 20th inst., by Rev. A. A. Graley, Mr. T. W. Weedman, of this village and Miss Gertrude M. Hemstreet of Lenox.

CP - February 26, 1851. Died in this village, the 25th isnt., Abner Riddle, son of George E. and N. Marion Downer, aged 1 year 6 mos.

CP - March 5, 1851. Born in this village, the 27th ult., to the wife of James Walrath, a daughter.

CP - March 5, 1851. Married in Morrisville Feb. 19th, by Rev. L. Bowdish, Mr. James Woodin, of Cazenovia to Miss Sarah Nourse of Fenner.

CP - March 12, 1851. Married in Manlius, on the 5th inst., by Rev. Mr. Gay, Mr. Abram Scouten of Cazenovia and Miss Adaline Richman of the former place.

CP - March 19, 1851. Died in Racine, WI, March 1st, Elisha Raymond, Sr., aged 67 yrs. (He was from Onondaga Co. in 1835).

CP - March 26, 1851. Married in Manlius on the 13th inst., By Rev. L. E. Swan, Mr. William W. Heath of this town and Miss Sarah A. Cook, of the former place.

CP - March 26, 1851. Married in Clinton, on the 19th inst., by Rev. Mr. Cook, Mr. John Sandford and Miss Emily Blake, all of that place.

CP - March 26, 1851. Married in Brookfield, on the 9th inst., by A. M. Covey, Esq., William Green, Jr., and Miss Catharine Kenyon, both of Brookfield.

CP- March 26, 1851. Died in Eaton, on the 17th inst., Willard Dixon, son of Alfred and Martha Brown, in the 5th year of his age.

CP - March 26, 1851. Died at his residence in Sangerfield, Oneida Co., Feb. 26, 1851, George Washington Loomis, aged 51 yrs.

CP - March 26, 1851. Died in Cazenovia, March 5th, Mrs. Esther J. Munson, aged 21 years, wife of Mr. Charles Munson.

CP - April 2, 1851. Died in DeRuyter, the 22nd inst., Celestia M., wife of Harvey D. Williams, aged 23 yrs.

CP - April 9, 1851. Born in this town, the 5th inst., to the wife of Oliver Ehle, a son.

CP - April 9, 1851. Died in Perryville, the 27th ult., Mr. Arnold Ballou, aged 33 years.

CP - April 16, 1851. Born in Morrisville, on the 12th inst., to the wife of L. D. Dana, Esq., a daughter.

CP - April 16, 1851. Died in thes village on the 12th inst., Caroline M., wife of Doctor William Oakes, aged 23 years.

CP - April 16, 1851. Died in this town on the 15th inst., Robert Burnett, at the advanced age of of 91 years.

CP - April 23, 1851. Died in this village, at the residence of her daughter, Mrs. S. I. Brinkerhoff, on Monday, the 21st inst., suddenly, of apoplexy, Mrs. Rheua Skelding, in the 77th year of her age. The body was conveyed to the R.R. this morning...thence to be taken to New York and interred in Greenwood Cemetery.

CP - April 23, 1851. Died in Cazenovia, on the 19th inst., Maria, daughter of Horace and Maria Bacon, aged 18 years.

CP - April 30, 1851. Died in this town [Canaseraga], on the 29th inst., the wife of Edward Bradt, aged 60 years.

CP - May 7, 1851. Married in Cazenovia, NY, may 1st, by Rev. Mr. Boardman, Theophilus Fisk, Esq, of Philadelphia, to Miss Susan, second daughter of the late Hon. Justin Dwinelle, of the former place.

CP - May 7, 1851. Married in Syracuse, on the 2nd inst., Mr. Conrad Cress of this town and Mrs. Mary Bancien of the former place.

CP - May 14, 1851. Died in this town on the 6th inst., the wife of Deacon Thomas Fulford, aged 68 years.

CP - May 21, 1851. Married in this town on the 14th inst. by Rev. Elder Clark, Mr. Perry O. Weaver and Miss Sophronia Knowles, daughter of Mr. James Knowles, all of this town.

CP - May 21, 1851. Married in this town on the 18th inst., by Rev. George Colegrove, Mr. Thurston K. Wells and Miss Sarah A. Hall, all of this town.

CP - June 4, 1851. Married in East Bethany, Genesee Co., on the 2nd inst., by Rev. Mr. Young, Dr. J. C. Clark, of this village and Miss Martha M. Peck, of the former place.

CP - June 4, 1851. Died at Schenectady, NY, April 17th, Miss Ann Yates, aged 86 years, sister of the Rev. Andrew Yates.

CP - June 11, 1851. Died in Chili, IL, April 30, of consumption, Jane A., wife of Harrison Robbins lately of this town, aged 31 years.

CP - June 11, 1851. Died: Prof. Canfield, of the O. C. Seminary, Cazenovia, died on Monday last.

CP - July 2, 1851. Married in Stonington, CT, July 11th by the Rev. Erastus Miner, Joseph E. Morgan of Peterboro, to Mary S. Holmes of the former place.

CP - July 2, 1951. Married on the 21st of June, by Rev. J. J. Teeple, Mr. John Butler, and Henriette Griswold, all of Morrisville.

CP - July 2, 1851. Married on the 19th inst., by the Rev. G. S. Boardman, Mr. Robert D. Gillson of Rochester, and Miss Susan R. Jackson, daughter of Mr. Abraham Jackson of Cazenovia.

CP - July 2, 1851. Died at Madison, on the 20th day of June, inst., John Lucas, Esq., aged 71 years.

CP - July 16, 1851. Married in this town, Monday morning the 14th inst., by Rev. J. M. Austin, Rev. A. W. Bruce, of Jefferson Co., to Miss Elizabeth Denton of this town.

CP - July 16, 1851. Married in the village of Oneida Castle, on the 6th inst., by Rev. C. McHenry, Mr. Thomas Earll, of Lenox, to Miss Ann Elizabeth Stevens, of the former place.

CP - July 16, 1851. Died in this village on the 12th inst., James Brown, aged 19 years.

CP - July 23, 1851. Married in Bridgeport on the 10th inst., Mr. Nathan Sayles of this village to Miss----, daughter of Eli Jepson, Esq., of the former place.

CP - July 23, 1851. Died in this village on the 20th inst., an infant of Mr. John Vosburgh, aged 7 months.

CP - July 30, 1851. Married in Hamilton on the 31st inst., by Rev. Job Potter, Mr. Elias Sherman of Otselic and Miss Oresta Leonard, of Lebanon.

CP - July 30, 1851. Married in Cazenovia, on the 20th inst., by Rev. William Clarke, Mr. Michael Murphy of Manlius, and Miss Malinda Jewett, of Fenner.

CP - August 6, 1851. Married this Wednesday morning, by the Rev. James Abell, Mr. Francis G. Biggs and Miss Mary E. Fink, all of this village.

CP - August 13, 1851. Married in this town, the 6th inst., by Rev. L. E. Swan, Mr. Albertus Bassett and Miss Maria Hatter, both of this place.

CP - August 13, 1851. Married in Lenox, Madison Co., on the 3rd inst., by Rev. Charles Machin, Miss Adeline Morris of Lenox and Mr. W. S. Phelps pf Schenectady.

CP - August 13, 1851. Died in this town, on the 7th inst., Harriet, daughter of Peter Moulter, aged 19 years.

CP - August 20, 1851. Married in Cazenovia, on the 12th inst., by Rev. William Clarke, Mr. Philomen Dodge and Miss Mary Ann Wilcox, both of that village.

CP - August 20, 1851. Died in this town on the 16th inst., Mr. Daniel Hall, aged 73 years; one of the first settlers; had lived on the farm where he died 50 years.

CP - August 20, 1851. Died in Hamilton, on the 7th inst., Mrs. Deborah Wilcox, aged 88 years.

CP - August 20, 1851. Died in Eaton, on the 5th inst., Mrs. Mary Palmer, aged 65 years.

CP - August 20, 1851. Died at Lebanon, on the 11th inst., Amanda M., wife of Albert C. Owen, aged 27 years.

CP - August 20, 1851. Died at Eaton on the 8th inst., Mrs. Elizabeth Payson, aged 71 years.

CP - August 27, 1851. Married in Hannibal, Oswego Co., on the 16th inst., by Rev. J. T. Hewett, Mr. J. A. Place, Editor of the *Fulton Patriot*, to Miss Julia Lewis of Hannibal.

CP - August 27, 1851. Married at Erieville, on Sat., the 18th inst., by Rev. H. Tremain, Mr. William C. Tremain of Cincinnati, OH, and Miss Ann Eliza, daughter of Asa Raymond, Esq., of Erieville.

CP - August 27, 1851. Married at Glen Haven Watercure, on the 12th inst., by themselves, Mr. William L. Chaplin to Miss Theodocia Gilbert of that establishment.

CP - August 27, 1851. Died in this town, on the 35th [sic] inst., Dr. Royal B. Sweet, aged about 30 years.

CP - September 3, 1851. Married at the White Sulphur Springs, on Sunday, the 31st ult., by the Hon. Jarius French, Mr. Alfred R. Carter and Lovila Judd, all of this place.

CP - September 17th, 1851. Died in Hamilton, on the 6th inst., Velorus E. Russell, age 42 years.

CP - September 17, 1851. Died in Lebanon, on the 6th inst., Martha A. Skedmore, aged 23 years.

CP - September 24, 1851. Died in this village on the 19th inst., Mrs. Nancy, wife of David Riddle, aged 53 years.

CP - September 24, 1851. Died in this town, the 19th inst., Mr. Horatio Gates Douglass, aged 74 years.

CP - September 24, 1851. Died in this town, on the 15th inst., Charles Persons, aged 8 years.

CP - October 1, 1851. Married in this town by the Hon. Jairus French, Mr. James Youngs and Mariah Reels. At the same time by the same, Mr. James Johnson and Miss Mary Mage, all of Sullivan.

CP - October 8, 1851. Married on October 2nd, by the Rev. James Beathie at Elm Cottage, Saybrook, CT, the summer residence of her uncle, Oliver Cobb, Esq., Miss Caroline Fay, daughter of Henry H. Cobb, Esq., of Syracuse, to Mr. William H. Knoepfel, of New York.

CP - October 8, 1851. Married in this town, on Sunday last, by the Hon. Jarius French, Mr. Lyman Norton and Miss Phebe Schnell, of Sullivan.

CP - October 15, 1851. Married in Fenner, on the 8th inst., Mr. Vincent Cole to Miss Sarah Inman, both of that town.

CP - October 22, 1851. Married at the residence of her father, Mr. Joseph Harbottle, in this town, on Tues., the 21st inst., by Rev. James Abell, Thomas O. Bassett, of Manlius Center, to Miss Anna S. Harbottle.

CP - October 22, 1851. Married in Munnsville, Mon., the 13th inst., by Rev. T. L. Clark, W. H. Moore, of Pittsfield, Otsego Co., to Miss Sarah Temple, of Eaton, Madison Co.

CP - October 29, 1951. Died in Waterloo, the 26th inst.,Mr. Henry Vanwie, formerly a resident of this place, at the age of about 60 years.

CP - November 6, 1851. Married at Manlius Square , by Rev. L. E. Swan, Mr. James J. Walrath of the village, to Miss Mary, daughter of Mr. Grant Tuttle, of Chittenango Falls.

CP - November 6, 1851. Died in this town, on the 31st ult., Susan J., wife of Alexander S. Wager, aged 43 years.

CP - November 6, 1851. Died at the White Sulphur Springs, on the 30th inst., Capt. E. W. Buckbee, late of Auburn, aged 27 years.

CP - November 12, 1851, Wed. Married in this village, on the 26th ult., by Rev. J. J. Teeple, Mr. Anson Williams and Miss Delia Kelton, both of Manlius Square.

CP - November 12, 1851. Married on Sunday, the 9th inst., by Hon. Jarius French, Mr. Asa Bender, and Miss Louisa Daniels, both of this town.

121

· CP - November 12, 1851. Married in Lenox, Madison Co., October 16th, by Washington Stickney, Henry L. Burdick to Harriette P. Lewis, daughter of Young Lewis, Esq., of the former place.

CP - Novenber 12, 1851. Married at Grass Valley, CA, August 12th, by Judge Smith, Mr. Tench Fairchild, formerly of Cazenovia, NY and Miss Harriet Carpenter of San Francisco.

CP - November 12, 1851. Died in Fayetteville, on the 8th inst., Sarah, wife of Royal Nobles.

CP - November 12, 1851. Died in Cazenovia, on the 24th ult., Mr. Caleb S. Allen, aged 52 years.

CP - November 12, 1851. Died at Rockton, Herkimer Co., on the 5th inst., of Paralysis, Nathan P. Richmond, formerly of Stockbridge, this county, aged 41 years.

CP - November 19, 1851. Married at Munnsville, on the 9th inst., by Walter Simmons, Esq., Mr. John G. Sherman to Miss Mary E. Wyman, both of Eaton.

CP - November 19, 1851. Married in Canaseraga, on Sat. evening, the 15th ult., by E. Hazeltine, Esq., Mr. Daniel Fox to Miss Ellen Smith, both of New Boston.

CP - December 3, 1851. Married at Manlius, the 26th ult., by Rev. George Colgrove, Mr. Asahel L. Porter of this village to Miss Margaret A. Casler, of the former place.

CP - December 3, 1851. Died at Lakeport, on the 23rd ult., Miss Anna Cochran, aged about 64 years.

CP - December 17, 1851. Died in Fenner, on the lst inst., of typhus fever, Elijah, aged 25 years, and on the 3rd inst., Berkeley, aged 20 years, both sons of Oliver Cary of Fenner.

CP - December 17, 1851. Died in this town, this morning, of consumption, Silvenus Parazoo, aged about 17 years.

CP - December 24, 1851. Married in this town, the 23rd inst., by Rev. Mr. Bristol, of Cazenovia, Mr. Aaron S. Hyatt, jun., of Nelson, to Miss Sarah M. Knowles, daughter of James Knowles, of this town.

CP - December 24, 1851. Married in Morrisville, on Thursday morning, the 4th inst., by Rev. D. Blakeslee, Mr. H. D. Boyden, of Utica, to Miss Emily M. Blakeslee, daughter of the officiating clergyman.

CP - December 24, 1851. Died in this village, the 19th inst., of consumption, Hon. John G. Stowers, in the 60th year of his age. [Obituary in the Dec. 31st issue of same newspaper.]

CP - December 24, 1851. Died in Troy, the 19th inst., Clinton A., son of Augustus and Mary Frisbie, aged 4 years.

CP - December 31, 1851. Married in Lenox, on the 21st inst., by Rev. W. L. Palmer, Mr. N. P. Case of Hamilton, and Miss Malvina Case of Lenox.

CP - December 31, 1851. Married in Cazenovia, the 23rd inst., by Rev. D. W. Bristol, Mr. Henry A. Johnson, to Miss Zilpha M. Crocker, both of Cazenovia.

CP - December 31, 1851. Married on the 24th inst., by the same, Mr. Robert R. McDonald, to Miss Elizabeth M. Todd, both of Cazenovia.

CP - January 14, 1852. Married at the residence of the bride's father, Mr. Joseph Harbottle, on the 7th inst., by the Rev. James Abell, Mr. Richard R. Walrath to Miss Helen Harbottle, all of this town.

CP - January 14, 1852. Married at the house of O. Russell, of this village, on the 12th inst., by Rev. J. J. Temple, Mr Joel C. Lindsay of Lebanon, to Miss Marietta Cossett, of this town.

CP - January 21, 1852. Married in Canaseraga, on the 14th inst., by Rev. James Abell, David E. Owens of this village, to Caroline F. Beeman, daughter of Lemuel Beeman, of the former place.

CP - January 21, 1852. Married in Syracuse, the 6th inst., by Rev. J. A. Avery, Mr. Zina Bushnell, to Miss Harriet Larkin, both of this town.

CP - January 21, 1852. Married in Stockbridge, on the 7th inst., by Rev. Mr. Clark, Mr. John Mason Coburn to Miss Nancy Quackenbush, all of Stockbridge.

CP - January 28, 1852. Married at Bolivar, the 24th inst., by Jarius French, Esq., Mr. Harvey Bradley Hodge and Miss Louisa Seymour, both of Manlius.

CP - January 28, 1852. Died at Madison, on the 25th inst., Dr. B. F. Cleveland, aged 42 years.

CP - February 4, 1852. Married at the house of O. Russell, on the 23rd ult., by Rev. J. J. Teeple, Mr. Thomas W. Anderson of Eaton and Miss Lucy P. Bortle, of Lenox.

CP - February 4, 1852. Married in Wampsville, on the 22nd ult., Mr. Harvey J. Cobb and Miss Harriet H. Avery, both of Wampsville.

CP - February 4, 1852. Married in Oneida, January 27th by Rev. Mr. Terry, Mr. Silas Judd, 2nd of Perryvile and Miss Margaret Orr of Oneida.

CP - February 4, 1851. Died in Perryville, on the 28th ult., Hannah, widow of the late Peter Ehle, aged 73 years.

CP - February 11, 1852. Married in this village, the 4th inst., by Rev. J. J. Teeple, Mr. Henry H. Harter and Miss Esther B. Marks, all of this village.

CP - February 11, 1852. Married in Stockbridge, the 27th ult., Mr. E. Jesse Barber of Stockbridge and Miss Martha Bevens of Eaton.

CP - February 11, 1852. Married in Cazenovia, on the 19th ult., Mr. G. Thurston and Miss Laura A. Allen, both of that place.

CP - February 11, 1852. Died in Wilmington, Will Co., IL, on the 29th ult., Mr. Rodger Hazard, formerly of this place, aged 82 years.

CP - February 18, 1852. Married in Canastota, on the 11th inst., by the Rev. F. T. Drake, George A. Bradley and Miss Mary S. Richardson.

CP - February 18, 1852. Died in Chicago, IL, Dec. 31st, George Gulliver, formerly of this place, aged 60 yrs.

CP - February 25, 1852. Married in Fenner, on the 18th inst., by Rev. Mr. Anderson, Dr. Fisher Cushing and Miss Caroline H. Haight, all of that town.

CP - February 25, 1852. Died in this town, the 7th inst., Mr. John Crownhart, in the 80th year of his age.

CP - March 3, 1852. Died at Bolivar the 20th inst., Mr. David Pennock, aged 26 yrs.

CP - March 3, 1852. Died at Bolivar, the 29th ult., Andrew Justin, son of Jacob and Mary Chawgo, aged 4 years.

CP - March 10, 1852. Married in Stockbridge, on the 1st inst., by Rev. George A. Ames, Mr. Josiah P. Owen, of Oneida and Miss Mary L. Thompson, of the former place.

CP - March 10, 1852. Died in New York [City], on the 4th inst., Frederick H., youngest son of E. Henry and Sarah M. Cobb, aged 2 years, 10 days.

CP - March 10, 1852. Died in Stockbridge, on the 1st inst., Mrs. Rosana Adkins, aged 62 years.

CP - March 10, 1852. Died in Hamilton, on Friday, the 25th ult., Mrs. Matilda, wife of John Hargart. also on Wednesday, the 3rd inst. John Hargart, aged about 30 (or 50?) years.

CP - March 17, 1852. Married at Morrisville, the 4th inst., by Rev. J. J. Teeple, Mr. Ahiman Wilbur and Miss Harriet Thompson, both of Eaton.

CP - March 17, 1852. Died at the residence of E. Hazeltine, Esq., in Canaseraga, on the 9th inst., of inflamation of the lungs, Kate Maria, daughter of Lorenzo and Margaret A. Gooding of Henrietta, Monroe Co. NY.

CP - April 14, 1852. Married at Stockbridge, March 31st, by Rev. A. L. Crandall, Mr. John A. Foster to Miss Zoe Davidson, all of Stockbridge.

CP - April 14, 1852. Died in Morrisville, on Sunday, the 4th inst., Mrs. Almira Norton, wife of Edward Norton, one of the publishers of the *Madison Observer*, aged 28 yrs.

CP - April 14, 1852. [A] sad accident...on Monday last, a son of William H. Gale fell into a cistern at the residence of his father in this village and was drowned before his absence was discovered. He was a bright interesting child about aged 4 years.

CP - April 14, 1852. Died on Saturady last, while playing near the railroad at Canastota, the express train came up and struck a boy named Fowler, throwing him some distance and killing him instantly. He was a grandson of Deacon Fowler of Quality Hill, aged 13 years.

CP - April 21, 1852. Died on the 2nd inst., at Carthage, Jefferson Co., Sophia Affa, daughter of Carlos L. and Sophia R. Frederick, aged 8 months, 15 days.

CP - April 28, 1852. Married at East Hamilton, on the 7th inst., by the Rev. T. Potter, Mr. Reuben F. Throop to Miss Antoinette N. Sherman, eldest daughter of Mr. Hiram Sherman, formerly of Fenner.

CP - April 28, 1852. Died suddenly at Morrisville, on Sunday morning, the 18th inst., Mrs. Emily Stilwell, wife of Henry Stilwell, aged 44 years.

CP - May 5, 1852. Married in this village, on the 30th inst [sic], by J. French Esq., Mr. John McGarry and Miss Elizabeth Ransier.

CP - May 12, 1852. Married at the house of C. H. Abbott, of this village, on Sunday, the 9th inst., by Rev. James Abell, Mr. Milton Groat, of Canastota and Miss Elizabeth Orcutt, of this town.

CP - May 12, 1852. Died in Smithfield, April 10th, Mrs. Hannah, wife of Divan Berry, aged 79 years.

CP - May 19, 1852. Married on Wednesday morning, the 5th inst., by Rev. A. P. Smith of Cazenovia, Mr. J. B. (?) Richmond, of Buffalo to Miss Lurancy E. Green, 2nd daughter of Amos Green of Morrisville.

CP - May 19, 1852. Married in Syracuse, on the 13th inst., by Rev. Byron Sunderland, Mr. Alfred Cobb and Miss Mary M. Bickford, daughter of D. B. Bickford, Esq.

CP - May 19, 1852. Died in Madison on the 6th inst., Capt. Seth Blair, in the 92nd year of hs age.

CP - June 9, 1852. Died in Canastota, on the 29th ult., Mr. C. E. Hinman, aged 32 yrs.

CP - June 9, 1852. Died in this town, the 25th ult., Mr. John R. Peck, age 29 yrs.

CP - June 16, 1852. Married in Cazenovia, the 5th inst., by Rev. G. S. Boardman, Mr. George W. Nichols, of Oneida and Miss Aannah [Hannah?] Colman, of Manlius.

CP - June 16, 1852. Died at Manlius Center, last evening, Mr. Abram Crouse, youngest son of Mr. George Crouse of this village, aged about 23 years.

CP - June 16, 1852. Died in Schenectady, the 11th inst., Jeremiah Edward, son of Doct. Samuel Fuller of this village, in the 27th year of his age.

CP - June 23, 1852. Married in Fond du Lac, WI, at the residence of J. Q. Griffiths, by the Rev. L. C. Spafford, Mr. Andrew Laning of Ceresco to Miss Mary Jane Linsley, formerly of this place.

CP - June 23, 1852. Died in Nelson, June 1st, Mrs. Amelia Smith, relict of Deacon Nathan Smith, aged 75 yrs. Mrs. Smith was the first young lady that came to this town which was in 1793, while Nelson and Cazenovia comprised one township. She accompanied her sister, Mrs. Archibald Bates, whose husband was agent for Col. Lincklaen.

CP - June 30, 1852. Married in this village, this morning by the Rev. Mr. Atwell, Mr. Nelson Lower to Elizabeth Hood, both of this place.

CP - June 30, 1852. Married in Syracuse this morning, Mr. David Shaver to Miss Matilda E. Lower, both of this place.

CP - June 30, 1852. Married at Oneida Castle, June 21st, by Rev. Nelson Palmer, John Snow, Esq. of Canastota and Miss Elizabeth M. Eldridge of the former place,

CP - June 30, 1852. Died at sea after 3 days of illness, February 26th, James Fellows Summers, aged 18 years, youngest son of Rev. Charles Summers [Sommers] of New York.

CP - June 30, 1852. Died in this town, the 20th inst., Mrs. Betsey Robinson, aged 75 years.

CP - July 14, 1852. Married in Manlius, the 30th ult., by Rev. L. E. Swan, Mr. William Stewart of Cazenovia to Miss Mary Quackenbush of this village.

CP - July 14, 1852. Died in Lenox on the 5th inst., Mrs Myraetta Cloyes, wife of Mr. Zeba Cloyes, aged 32 years.

CP - July 14, 1852. An afflicted Family! Died in Lenox, Madison Co., on the 19th of March last, of typhoid fever, B. Franklin Lamb, age 36 years; also on the 8th of May last, Martin E. Lamb, son of Col. N. B. Lamb, aged 13 years; also on the 1st of July inst., of the same disease, Col. Nathan B. Lamb, aged 42 years.

CP - July 21, 1852. Married at the house of U. M. Toby in Fayetteville, on the 20th inst., by Elder Wright, Mr. William Marks to Miss Mary, daughter of John Shaver, both of this village.

CP - July 21, 1852. Married at the Church of the Epiphany, Washington DC, on Monday, the 5th inst., by the Rev. William J. Clark, S. Corning Judd, Esq., Jr. editor of the *Syracuse Star*, to Miss Lavina J. James, daughter of the late William James of Washington City.

CP - July 28, 1852. Died in this town on the 22nd inst., Col. John Brown, aged 52 years.

CP - August 4, 1852. Married in Toledo, OH, July 30, Mr. John B. Forrman, lately of Stockbridge and Miss Martha Gridley of Cazenovia.

CP - August 4, 1852. Married in Fenner, July 5, by the Rev. D. B. Collins, Mr. Lorin Gordon and Miss Mary Stafford, all of Fenner.

CP - August 4, 1852. Married in Fenner, July 28th by the same, Mr. John Stewart, of Cazenovia and Mrs. Lydia Baldwin of Canastota.

CP - August 4, 1852. Died in this village, on Sunday the 1st inst., Mrs. Anna Whiting, a Revolutionary pensioner, aged 91 years.

CP - August 11, 1852. Married in this town, the 8th inst., by Hon. J. French, Mr. Elijah Thompson and Miss Rachael Kelts.

CP - August 11, 1852. Died in this town, the 5th inst., Philip Wager, Esq., in the 84th year of his age. One of the oldest inhabitants of this town.

CP - August 18, 1852. Married in Stockbridge, August 8th, by J. M. Foreman, Esq., Mr. James Ottaway, of Vernon and Miss Eliza Castle, of the former place.

CP - August 25, 1852. Died in Hamilton on Sunday morning last, after a short by painful illness, Mr. Philemon Case, aged 36 years.

CP - August 25, 1852. Deaths From Cholera. Victims This Last Week: Mr. Harry C. Gardiner, formerly a respectable resident of this town; his son-in-law, Mr. Henry Hull; and his daughter, the wife of Mr. Hull. Mr. G. resided in Canastota; died Tues last, after two days of illness. [From *the Morrisville Observer*]

CP - September 1, 1852. Married in this village, August 20th, by Rev. James Abell, Mr. William J. Park and Miss Sarah McLure, both of Syracuse.

CP - September 8, 1852. Married at Lenox Furnace, August 31st, by Rev. W. H. Cooper, Mr. Warren Potter of Stockbridge, to Miss Jane Twining of Lenox. Also at the same time and place, and by the same, Mr. Solomon Quackenbush, of Stockbridge to Miss Mary L. Fox of Lenox Furnace.

CP - September 8, 1852. Died in this town, the 3rd inst., Mrs. Elizabeth H. Sage, wife of Col. Hezekiah Sage, age 58 years. [Eulogy published the following week.]

CP - September 8, 1852. Died in this village, the 4th inst., Mr. Laura G. Abell, wife of Rev. James Abell, aged 47 years. [Eulogy following week.]

CP - September 8, 1852. Died in this town on the 4th inst., Mrs. Isaac Wallace, aged 61 years.

CP - September 8, 1852. Died near Morrisville, on Tuesday last, Mr. Micajah Cloyes, one of the first settlers of that neighborhood, aged 76 years.

CP - September 22, 1852. Married in Fayetteville, on Thursday, the 16th inst., by Rev. Elder Wright, Mr. Henry R. Knowles to Betsey A. Huntley, both of this village.

CP - September 29, 1852. Married in New York, the 22nd inst., by the Rev. Spence H. Cone, Rev. Charles G. Sommers to Miss B. Seymour, all of that City.

CP - September 29, 1852. Married in Syracuse, the 22nd inst., by Rev. Mr. Mabie, P. C. Sampson, Jr., of New Haven CT, to Rebecca B., daughter of H. H. Cobb, of Syracuse.

CP - October 6, 1852. Married in Cazenovia, Thursday morning, the 30th ult., Mr. Charles M. Brown, of Green, Chenango Co., to Miss Charlotte D., daughter of M. Moulter, Esq., of Cazenovia.

CP - October 13, 1852. Married at Peterboro, Madison Co., September 21, by Rev. Mr. Remington, Mr. George Turner of Syracuse and Miss Abigail J. Clarke of Perryville.

CP - October 13, 1852. Married in Lenox, the 5th inst., by Rev. Mr. Graley, Mr. Clinton D. West. and Miss Jane Rouse, both of this place.

CP - October 13, 1852. Married at Chittenango, on the 6th inst., by Rev. J. J. Teeple, Mr. Hiram E. Isbell, of Eaton to Miss Juliette Stewart of Cortland.

CP - October 13, 1852. Married in Siloam, September 30th, by Rev. T. L. Clark, Mr. David Rawson of Stockbridge to Fidelia Nash of the former place.

CP - October 13, 1852. Died in this place [Canaseraga], the 11th inst., David Severance, Esq., age 70 years.

CP - October 13, 1852. Died in this town [New Boston], the 9th inst., George Clark, age 35 years.

CP - October 13, 1852. Died on the 3rd of September, at Belvidere, IL, Chauncy H. Cook, Esq., Aged 52 years, formerly of Lenox, Madison Co.

CP - October 13, 1852. A long obituary appears for J. W. Jenkins, Esq., of Vernon, aged 47 years.

CP - October 20, 1852. Died at his residence near Morrisville, on Wednesday, the 6th inst., after an illness of 24 hours from hemorrhage of the bowels, Colonel Uriah Leland, aged 59 years.

CP - October 27, 1852. Married on the 22nd inst., by the Rev. J. J. Teeple, Mr. Jacob Roggers and Miss Eliza Ash, both of this town.

CP - October 27, 1852. Died in Morrisville, the 18th inst., of consumption, Mt. George W. Ayer, of the late firm of Ayer & Phelps, merchants.

CP - October 27, 1852. Died in Fenner, September 14th, of dysentery, Helen Augusta, daughter of Avery and Laura Ann Maine, age 6 years and 8 months. [Announcement includes a long obituary. Ed.]

CP - November 10, 1852. Married in Lenox, on the 24th of October, by Rev. Charles Machin, Mr. William Pearson to Miss Sophronia Bettinger.

CP - November 10, 1852. Married in Oneida, on the 28th of October by Rev. N. Palmer, Mr. Aldin C. Ellis, of Verona to Miss Nancy A. Parkell of Oneida.

CP - November 10, 1852. Married at the Eagle Hotel in Hamilton on the 3rd inst., by Rev. Mr. Norton. Mr. George F. Chaphe of Morrisville to Miss Flavilla Stone of Nelson.

CP - November 17, 1852. Married in Chardon, OH, October 6th, Mr. James M. Comstock, formerly of this town, to Miss Martha Underwood, both of Chardon.

CP - November 17, 1852. Died at his residence in this town, on the 15th inst., Henry Rightmyer, aged 90 years. He was the last of the Revolutionary pensioners in this town. Funeral under Masonic Honors at his late residence. Sketch of his life to appear next week.

CP - November 25, 1852. George Moffit took poison. He was about 26 years old, son of Mrs. Fitch who lives in a dwelling on the farm of Albro Hall. He had previously lived in Onondaga Co. He died Monday morning refusing all medical attention.

CP - December 1, 1852. Married at Fayetteville, on the 24th inst. by Rev. L. N. Reid, Mr. Obadiah Garlock and Miss Ann Phillips, both of this town.

CP - December 1, 1852. Died at Pratts Hollow on Saturday morning last, after a lingering and painful illness, Edward Manchester, Esq., aged 38 years.

CP - December 8, 1852. Died in Springfield, IL, the 11th inst., Samuel M. S. Denton, formerly of this town in the 40th year of his age.

CP - December 8, 1852. Died in Morrisville, last Thursday night, Mr. Rufus Chapin, aged 38 years.

CP - December 15, 1852. Died in this village on the 11th inst., Mary, youngest daughter of Dr. I. T. Teller, aged 4 years and 10 months.

CP - December 15, 1852. Died in Stockbridge, on the 30th ult., Mrs. Nancy, wife of John Hadcock, aged 53 years.

CP - December 22, 1852. Married in Herkimer on the 8th inst., by Rev. S. S. Mead, Mr. Thomas L. James, publisher of the *Madison County Journal*, to Miss Emily I. Freeburn of the former place.

CP - December 22, 1852. Married at Hamilton, December 15, by Rev. Mr. Morton, D. Ira Baker, Esq., Counsellor-at-law, of New York, to Helen J., only daughter of Thomas C. Nye, of the former place.

CP - December 29, 1852. Married in this village, the 26th inst., Mr. John M. Saunders of Syracuse, and Miss Helen L. Hale, of this village.

CP - December 29, 1852. Married in Smithfield, on the 6th inst., by Rev. T. F. Petrie, Esq., Mr. Stephen Van Horn to Miss Catherine Huffman, daughter of the late Frederick Huffman.

CP - December 29, 1852. Married at the same time and place by the same, as above, Mr. William S. Bump to Miss Mary Ann Buyea.

CP - December 29, 1852. Died at Canastota, on the 27th inst., George B. Rowe, Esq., member of the Legislature from this county last winter.

CP - December 29, 1852. Died in this town, Mrs. Hessler, aged 101 years and 7 months. She was born and married in Englnd, came to the country during the Revolutionary War and at the time the English had possession of New York. She has been a member of the Presbyterian Church for 75 years.

CP - December 29, 1852. Drowned, a son of Mr. Joseph Nichols of Cazenovia, about 10 years of age. He broke through the ice.

CP - January 6, 1853. Married in Perryville, the 5th inst., Mr. Charles Mory of Ashtabula, OH, to Miss Flavilla, daughter of John Hill, Esq., of the former place.

CP - January 6, 1853. Married in Clockville, December 30th, by the Rev. J. W. Starkweather, Mrs. James Miner to Miss Emeline M. Forbes, both of Clockville.

CP - January 6, 1853. Married at Oneida Castle, on the 25th ult., by the Rev. Charles Machin, Mr. Jabez Adle, to Miss Elizabeth Gaut, both of Sullivan, Madison Co., NY.

CP - January 6, 1853. Died on Tuesday last, Mrs. __, mother of Col. George B. Rowe, aged 78 years.

CP - January 6, 1853. Died in Sullivan, Madison Co., NY, the 17th of December, 1852, Elura Dewey, 3rd wife of A. P. Dewey, in the 25th year of her age.

CP - January 19, 1853. Died in this town, the 13th inst., Marvin H., son of Hiram and Susan B. Young, aged 4 years and 16 days.

CP - January 19, 1853. Died in this village on the 13th inst., Mr. Hibbard Smith, aged about 50 years.

CP - January 27, 1853. Married at the parsonage, on the 26th inst. by the Rev. Mr. Atwill, Mr. Michael Cress and Miss Sarah Ann Western, both of Fenner.

CP - January 27, 1853. Married at the house of Mr. Levi Richardson in the town of Nelson, on the 13th inst. by Rev. G. Bridge, Mr. Morey M. Jones of Eaton to Miss Maria L. Richardson of Nelson.

CP - January 27, 1853. Died in Morrisville, on Saturday evening, the 15th inst., Albert S. Gaston, son of David Gaston, Esq., aged 39 years.

CP - February 2, 1853. Married in Rome, on the 1st inst., by Rev. L. D. Stebbins, Mr. Andrew Bort, of Clockville, to Miss Jane E. Elmer of Rome.

CP - February 2, 1853. Married in this town on the 20th inst., by Rev. Mr. Morse, Alonzo E. Swan, of Lenox, to Helen E. Whitman of Sullivan.

CP - February 9, 1853. Married at Perryvile, on the 30th ult., by Rev. T. B. Rockwell, Mr. P. J. Huyck of Lenox and Lucette A. Robinson of the former place.

CP - February 16, 1853. Married in Cazenovia, on the 14th inst., by Rev. L. E. Swan, Mr. John Martin, of Sullivan to Miss Gratia E. Stanley of Cazenova.

CP - February 16, 1853. Died at Fayetteville, the 11th inst., Mr. Jesse Worden, aged 71 years. Funeral conducted by the Order of Masons.

CP - February 23, 1853. Married in this town, this morning, Mr. Alexander S. Wager to Mrs.--- Major, both of this town.

CP - February 23, 1853. Married in Lenox, the 22nd inst., by Rev. William Shaver, Mr. Joshua C. Knowles of Sullivan to Miss Cornelia M. Bortle of the former place.

CP - March 5, 1853. Died in Florida, the 27th of January, Mr. Ira H. Gates of this place, aged 37 years.

DEMOCRATIC GAZETTE
Published by Walrath and Greenhow
Chittenango, New York

DG - March 26, 1853. Died on the 19th inst., at his residence in Fenner, of typhoid fever, Deacon Amos Covey, aged 73 yrs 7 mos. 19 days.

DG - March 26, 1853. Died at Clockville,, the 21st inst., of inflamation of the lungs, William, only son of William and Julia Ann Milliou, aged two years.

DG - March 26, 1853. Died in this town, the 7th inst., Captain William Bellinger, aged 55 years.

DG - March 26, 1853. Died in this town, the 14th inst., Jane, daughter of Mr. Lee Wells, aged 13 years.

DG - March 26, 1853. Died suddenly, while riding in his cutter near Fenner Hill, on the 15th inst., of heart disease, Dea. Joseph B. Plank, long a resident of this village, age 62 years.

DG - April 2, 1853. Married on the 25th ult., at Chittenango Falls, by Rev. George Matthews, Mr. James Chappell, to Miss Julia A. Dixon, all of that town.

DG - April 2, 1853. Died in Clockville, on Sunday, March 27th, of typhoid fever, Mr. Benjamin Bort, aged 38 years.

DG - April 9, 1853. Died by accident near the village of Perryville, Gordon Van Eps, son of Abraham Van Epes, Esq.. The wheel of his gig went into a rut throwing young VanEps against a tree so violently as to break his neck.

DG - April 9, 1853. Married in [New?] Woodstock, on the 31st ult., Jonathan Ransier, formerly of this place, to Elizabeth Verzell of that village.

DG - April 9, 1853. Married since our last, in this town, Joshua C. Warrick, to Miss Sarah A. Lawrence, of New Boston.

DG - April 9, 1853. Died in this village, on Thursday last, Elizabeth, daughter of Mr. Joseph Adams, aged 8 years.

DG - April 9, 1853.Died in this village yesterday, Mrs. Magdalene Walrath, aged 80 years.

DG - April 9, 1853. Died on the 12th ult., in this town, Sarah Catherine, daughter of Mr. Lee and Jane Wells, aged 12 years and 7 months.

DG - April 9, 1853. Died at Detroit, Wayne Co., MI, March 31, Mrs. Elizabeth, the consort of Gen. Lewis Cass, U. S. Senator for Michigan, a daughter of Dr. Joseph Spencer, of CT, who removed to Lansingburgh, NY in 1786, at which place she was born, September 27, 1788. [Additional details follow.]

DG - April 16, 1853. Married at Chittenango Falls, on Tuesday evening last, by Rev. T. J. Walson, William Sanderson, Esq., Attorney & Counsellor at law, to Miss Rhoda B. Humiston, daughter of Mr. Asa Humiston.

DG - April 23, 1853. Died in this village since our last, Mrs. Polly Adams, aged 79 years.

DG - April 30, 1853. Died at Lenox, Madison Co., on the 16th inst., of hemorrhage of the lungs, Harry W. Cotton, aged 33 years.

DG - April 30, 1853. Died at Morrisville, on the 25th inst., Harry Stilwell.

DG - May 7, 1853. Married on the 23rd ult., by Rev. L. A. Eddy, Mr. William Morey of Fenner to Emeline Lyon of the same place.

DG - May 7, 1853. Died at Sing Sing, May 1, Mary L. Ward, wife of Gen. Aaron Ward, age 55 years.

DG - May 14, 1853. Married at the Toby House in Cansatota, on Sunday, the 8th inst., by Maevin Keeney, Esq., Mr. Ezra Vandusen to Miss Amanda A. Moon, all of Lenox.

DG - May 14, 1853. Died at Savannah, GA, on the 2nd inst., of billious fever, Mrs. Jacob TenEyck. At the same place, of the same disease, on the 5th inst., Mr. Jacob TenEyck.

DG - May 21, 1853. Died at Cazenovia, on Tuesday, the 17th, at half past 10 o'clock, A. M., Mrs. Emily, wife of Henry S. Hitchcock aged 22 years.

DG - May 28, 1853. Died in Canastota, on the 11th, Mr. Eleazer Lewis, aged 80 years. The deceased was one of the oldest settlers in the town of Lenox, Madison Co..

DG - May 28, 1853. Died at Clockville, on the 13th inst., Mrs. Melinda Hathaway, aged 73 years.

DG - June 11, 1853. Married in Oswego, on the 24th ult., by Rev. Mr. Schuyler, Mr. Amasa Stowell and Miss Ellen Harrison, all of Oswego.

DG - June 11, 1853. Died in Granby, the 21st ult., Lovina, wife of Benjamin Lewis, aged 63 years.

DG - June 18, 1853. Married in this village on Tuesday, the 14th inst., by Rev. James E. Abell, Mr. Richard C. Walrath, and Miss Catharine Ehle.

DG - June 18, 1853. Married in this village, the 12th inst., by Jairus French, Esq., Mr. William K. Ingham and Miss Charity Daniels, both of Fenner.

DG - June 18, 1853. Died in this village on the 14th inst., Mr. Job Wells, aged 73 years.

DG - July 2, 1853. Married in Cazenovia on the 23rd ult., by Rev. George Burrett, Mr. O. L. Wilcox of Lenox and Miss Harriet Benson of the former place.

DG - July 2, 1853. Married at Syracuse on Thursday, the 23rd ult., Mr. Elihu Parry and Miss Julia Hammond, all of Chittenango.

DG - July 9, 1853. Married in this village on the 4th inst., by Rev. James Abell, Mr., Thomas Waller, of Frankfort (Canada West) to Miss Malvina Vosburgh of this place.

DG - July 9, 1853. Died in Clockville on the 5th inst., Mrs. Polly Walrath, aged 75 years.

DG - July 16, 1853. Died in Syracuse, on the 10th inst., Col. George Ehle, age 61 years.

DG - July 23, 1853. Died suddenly at the home of her son-in-law, D. G. Drummond, Esq., in the town of Lee, Oneida Co., on the 20th inst., Mrs. Martha Sexton, in the 59th year of her age, formerly a resident of this town.

DG - August 6, 1853. Died at Watertown, on the 21st ult., of consumption, Mrs. Susan Hoard, aged 44 years.

DG - August 20, 1853. Married at Lenox Furnace, the 7th inst., by S. H. Twining, Esq., Mr. Henry Thornton to Miss Harriet Adle.

DG - September 3, 1853. Married in this village, August 27th by the Rev. J. K. Browson, Mr. Daniel C. Allen of Delphi to Miss Caroline Hart of Pompey Center.

DG - September 3, 1853. Died in California, September 1st, Miss Sarah Parmelee, daughter of Moses Parmelee, formerly of this place.

DG - September 10, 1853. Married on the 30th ult., by Rev. L. E. Swan, Mr. Thomas Murphy of Fayetteville, and Miss Cornelia J. Andrews of Lenox.

DG - September 17, 1853. Married at Perryville on the 11th inst., by J. Hill, Esq., Mr. Moses Frank to Miss Mary Seymour, both of Canastota.

DG - September 17, 1853. Married in Edwardsville, St. Lawrence Co., on the 28th ult., Mr. Benjamin Harder and Miss Eunice C. Bellinger, both of Edwardsville.

DG - September 17, 1853. Died in this village on the 11th inst., of bowel complaint, Chauncey D., son of Mr. Chauncey H. Abbott, aged 2 years , 2 months.

DG - September 17, 1853. Died in Camden, Oneida Co., NY, on the 4th inst., Mr. Nelson F. Simmins, aged 58 years.

DG - September 24, 1853. Married in this village on the 13th inst., by Rev. I. K. Brownson, Mr. Owen Thomas of Ohio and Elnora Freeman of this place.

DG - October 1, 1853. Married in Chittenango, September 8th, by Rev. I. K. Brownson, Mr. Peter Rogers of Cazenovia to Miss Anna Ash of Lenox.

DG - October 1, 1853. Married at Jacksonville, Onondaga Co., on the 22nd inst., by Rev. Mr. Tuller, Mr. William Fink and Miss Sophia Tuller all of Jacksonville.

DG - October 15, 1853. Died in this village, October 9th, of consumption, Mrs. Betsey Page, aged 29 years.

DG - October 15, 1853. Died suddenly, while on a visit to her sister at Wolcott, Wayne Co.,September 24th, Mrs. Mary Ann, wife of Palmer Baldwin of Nelson, aged 29 years. [Long obituary follows.]

DG - October 22, 1853. Died in this village, October 16th, Emily Elizabeth, only daughter of Mariah Ann and Albertus Bassett, aged 1 year 5 months, 10 days.

DG - October 22, 1853. Died in this village on the 16th inst., of consumption, Henry Shaver, aged 17 years.

DG - October 22, 1853. Died in Clockville, Madison Co., October 12th of croup, Austin S., son of Randolph Webster, aged 4 years.

DG - October 29, 1853. Married in Syracuse, October 17, 1853, by Rev. Mr. Castle, Mr. David S. Capron of Phoenix to Miss Cornelia Lincoln of Chittenango.

DG - October 29, 1853. Married at Clockville, on the 12th inst., by Rev. William Parmer, Mr. Eli T. Covey of Utica to Miss Mary K. Walrath, daughter of J. L. Walrath, of the former place.

DG - November 8, 1853. Married at Perryville, on Thursday, November 3rd, by Rev. A. T. Matterson, Mr. Ziba Cloyes to Ellen Baldwin of Perryville.

[No papers published for the next few weeks, the press broke down.]

DG - December 3, 1853. Married at the residence of Nicholas Brown in Sullivan, on the 27th inst [ult?], by W. T. Abercrombie, Esq., Mr. Aaron Parker to Miss Elizabeth Blount.

DG - December 3, 1853. Married on the 30th inst. [ult.?], by Rev. James Abell, Mr. Jeremiah Wormuth and Lydia Holmes of Chittenango.

DG - December 3, 1853. Died at his residence in Fenner, November 7th, Aseph Humiston, aged 79 years. He was one of the early settlers of the town...lived at Chittenango Falls for 50 years.

DG - December 17, 1853. Died in this village, December 7th, Laura Frances, daughter of Ira and Laura Worden, aged 2 years.

DG - December 24, 1853. Married in Utica, on the 17th, by Rev. Mr. Fowler, Mr. Robert Bruce French and Miss Sarah Cobbett. They sailed for San Francisco on the 20th inst.

DG - December 24, 1853. Married at Bolivar, December 7th, by the Rev. I. K. Brownson, Mr. Benjamin Wadsworth of Arcadia, Wayne Co., and Miss Maria Dayharsh of Bolivar.

INDEX

The reader is advised to look under various spellings of a name as spellings have changed through the years and misspellings continue apace. Titles, such as Mr., Mrs., Dr. Rev., etc. have not been used in the index except when the first name was not given.

A ( ) following a page number indicates the number of references on the same page.

-- --

_____ Mary Amanda, 112
_____ Nancy, 34
_____ Rev. William, 112

-A-

ABBOTT
  A., 91
  C. H., 125
  Caleb, 110
  Chauncey D., 135
  Chauncey H., 135
ABEL J., 45, 52
ABELL
  Bruster, 82
  Elizabeth, 76
  J., 45, 51, 52, 55,
    58, 61, 67(2)
  Jabez, 76
  James, 46, 47, 48, 49,
    56, 57, 64, 67, 68,
    69(2), 71(3), 72,
    73(2), 76(2), 81, 83,
    84(2), 90(2), 91, 96,
    97(3), 103(2), 104,
    111, 115, 116, 119, 121,
    123(2), 125, 128(2),
    135, 136
  Laura G., 128
  Rev., 54, 74, 94(2),
    95, 107(2)
ABERCROMBIE
  W. T., 136
  William T., 24
ACKELY Mary Ann, 116
ACKLEY Hiram R., 111
ADAMS
  Betsey, 93
  C., 55
  Derrick, 92
  Electus, 67
  Elizabeth, 133
  Frederick, 82

George, 65
J. W., 57, 106
Joseph, 86, 133
Mary, 82
Polly, 133
Rev., 27, 98, 100
Vespasian, 61
ADKINS Rosana, 124
ADLE
  Harriet, 135
  Jabez, 131
AGELL James E., 134
AIKEN Rev., 18
AINSWORTH Rev., 100
ALBERT Jacob, 90
ALEXANDER
  Charles H., 113
  Rev., 85
ALLEN
  Caleb S., 122
  Daniel C., 135
  Earl, 75
  Fanny P., 111
  George, 111
  Hannah, 26
  Harriet, 105
  Henry, 105
  Jason W., 105
  John K., 47
  Laura A., 124
  Lauraette, 84
  Nathan D., 92
  R., 75
  Rev., 27, 29
AMES George A., 110, 124
ANDERSON
  Rev., 113, 124
  Thomas W., 123.
ANDREWS Cornelia, 135
ANGUISH
  Andrew, 68
  Elijah, 32, 99
  John, 19, 110
  Sara A., 110
ARKANSAS land in, 90
ARNOLD Erena Adelaide, 102

139

ASH
  Anna, 136
  Eliza, 129
ASHLEY George, 82
ATKINS Amos, 20
ATTWATER E. M., 29
ATWELL Rev., 31, 126
ATWILL Rev., 131
ATWOOD David, 100
AUGUSTINE Alishqueth, 113
AUSTIN
  J. M., 119
  Margaret, 35
  Susan, 37
AVERILL Chester, 38
AVERY, 96
  Abigail, 42
  Constant, 104
  Harriet H., 123
  J. A., 123
  Lyman, 86
  Oren S., 38
  Robert B., 103
  U. S., 20
  Zipporah, 104
AYER
  & Phelps, 129
  Mt. George W., 129
AYRES Maria, 30

-B-

BABCOCK
  B., 42
  Harry, 62
BACCHUS Rev., 27
BACON
  Horace, 118
  Maria, 118(2)
BAILEY
  Clark, 100
  M. D., 115
BAIN Mary Ann, 20
BAINBRIDGE S. M., 58, 67
BAKER
  Alfred, 108
  D. Ira, 130
  Elisha W., 67
  Jireh, 70
BALDWIN
  Abel S., 46
  Asa, 45
  Betsey, 19
  David, 59
  Ellen, 136
  Harriet, 19
  Lydia, 127
  Mary Ann, 136
  Palmer, 136
  Samuel, 57
BALL A. S., 96
BALLARD Ephriam, 85

BALLOU
  Arnold, 26, 117
  Mr., 85
BALTSLEY Sally, 30
BANCIEN Mary, 118
BANNISTER
  Charles B., 59
  Henry, 112
BARBER
  E. Jesse, 124
  Edward, 24
  Nolton, 95
BARLOW
  Cornelia, 116
  Thomas, 116
BARNARD
  Charles O., 39
  Pardon, 57, 60
  Phebe Ann, 63
  Rev., 15
  Wellington E., 57
BARNES
  Abby E., 64
  Appleton, 80
  J. R., 45
  Loania J., 29
  Z., 54(2)
BARNETT Ezra B., 79
BARNEY
  Sarah J., 38
  Throop, 38
BARR Laura A., 56
BARRETT
  H., 67
  Harvey, 51
  Helen, 67
  Jacob, 81
  Jane, 91
  Jane M., 56
  S. L., 24
BARRON
  Fletcher J., 60
  Mary, 60
BARROWS
  E. S., 32, 52
  Rev., 42, 47
BARTHOLOMEW Darwin, 55
BARTLETT
  Perkins, 106
  Ruth, 69
BARTON
  E. H., 23
  Samuel, 73
BASSETT
  Albertus, 119, 136
  Emily Elizabeth, 136
  Mariah Ann, 136
  Thomas O., 121
BATEMAN Gaylord, 116
BATES
  Archibald, 44, 126
  Cecelia A., 43

BATES, *continued*
  John, 43(2), 47, 48,
    105
  William, 40
BATLEY B. A., 99
BEACH Angeline, 29
BEATHIE James, 121
BECKER
  A., 103
  Henry, 103
  Jacob, 89
  Jane, 44
  Margaret, 62
BECKWITH
  Asahel, 30
  Barak, 74
  Elder, 31
BEDFORD David, 87
BEEBE
  A. M., 104
  Alathea, 63
  David, 41, 51, 74
  Eliza, 28
  Isaac, 28
  James, 63
  John, 29
  Lydia, 51
  Mary J., 109
  Sally, 25
  Sarah L., 63
  William, 18
BEECHER, 103
  Derias, 27
  Joseph S., 59(2)
  Laura, 42
  Matilda, 50
  Sylvester, 42, 59(2),
    98, 103
BEEMAN
  Caroline F., 123
  James, 49
  Lemuel, 123
  Sarah, 87
BELL
  James, 103
  Mary Ann, 49
BELLAMY
  A., 66
  Alfred, 35, 69, 82
  Edward Henry, 66
  Eliza A., 69
  Fanny Maria, 82
  J. & A., 35, 38
  Jonathan, 71
  Julius, 38, 71(2)
  Maria, 82
  Rev., 35, 42, 46
BELLENGER Laney, 41
BELLINGER
  Catherine, 97
  Eunice C., 135
  J., 21

  Jacob, 97
  Mary, 68
  Nancy, 103
  William, 132
BELMONT August, 102
BELMORE Joseph, 74
BENDER
  Asa, 121
  Silas, 37
BENEDICT
  Alanson, 91
  George, 84
  Isaac, 55
  Lewis, 88
BENJAMIN
  A. J., 100
  W., 91
BENSON
  C. M., 113
  Ethan, 32
  Harriet, 134
  Harry, 15
  Henry, 116
  Julia, 75
BENTLEY Rosanna E., 112
BENTLY V., 112
BERRY
  Divan, 125
  Hannah, 125
BERTHRONG
  James, 68, 112
  Jane Eliza, 68
BETSINGER
  Catherine, 73
  Nancy, 80
BETTINGER
  Anna, 34
  Eve, 18
  Isaac, 34, 110
  John, 93
  Nicholas, 32
  P., 83
  Sophronia, 129
BEVENS Martha, 124
BICAUYEA See also Buyea
  Adam, 49
BICKFORD
  D. B., 126
  Mary M., 126
BICKNELL
  Bennet, 61
  Harrison C., 102
BIGELOW Ely, 42
BIGGS Francis G., 119
BILLINGS Lucretia A., 116
BILLINGTON Eleanor, 34
BINGHAM Joseph, 22
BISHOP Alonzo, 32
BITELY Nancy, 42
BLACK Jared, 52
BLACKSTONE James, 108
BLACKWOOD Joseph, 25

BROWN, *continued*
  Grace, 58
  Henrietta C., 85
  Henry, 44
  Hiram, 29
  James, 119
  John, 127
  Jonas, 17
  Josiah P., 94
  L.Burdette, 32
  Loren W., 114
  Maria, 95
  Martha, 117
  Martha M., 114
  Mary Ann, 110
  Miranda, 59
  Nicholas, 136
  O., 83, 91(2)
  Oliva, 60
  Sara, 100
  Thomas A., 93
  Timothy, 42
  Tobias, 95
  Willard Dixon, 117
  William, 55, 88, 92,
    109
  William A., 105
  William H., 44
BROWNELL
  Abby, 106
  Mr., 25
  Samuel, 106
BROWNING
  Joanna D., 53
  John, 31
  Mary, 35
  Thirza, 54
BROWNSON I. K., 137
BROWSON
  I. K., 135(2)
  J. K., 135
BRUCE
  A., 100
  A. W., 95, 97, 98, 99,
    119
  Benjamin F., 25
  Joseph, 22
  Mrs., 100
  Nancy A., 22
BRUEN Mathias, 79
BRUSH Mills P., 31
BUCKBEE E. W., 121
BUCKLEY Philip, 34
BUDINGTON
  A., 29
  Elizabeth, 29
BULL
  Isaac, 21
  Jane E., 21
BUMP William S., 131
BUMPUS Jane M., 87

BUNNER
  Matilda H., 18
  Rudolph, 18
BURCHARD Theodore R., 104
BURDICK
  Anne M., 112
  Henry C., 112
  Henry L., 122
  Sanford, 48
BURETT George, 134
BURGHARDT Lambert, 65
BURLINGAME Allen J., 97
BURLINGHAME Ann, 24
BURN Henry B., 41
BURNETT Robert, 117
BURNS William, 105
BURR
  Calvin, 55
  William G., 104
BURROUGHS Alfred, 80
BURROWS E. S., 39
BURTON
  Charles, 63
  Freeborn T., 90
  Harriet, 41
  James, 86
  Margaret J., 86
  William, 41
BUSH H. B., 23
BUSHNEL
  J., 34
BUSHNELL
  Ira, 82
  Jesse, 33
  Mary, 82
  Zina, 123
BUTLER
  John, 118
  Maria, 44
  Rev., 96
  Sally Maria, 101
BUTTOLPH
  Edith, 59
  John, 59
BUTTON
  Harriet, 71
  Jehial, 36
  Louisa C., 45
  Mary A., 68
  William, 67
BUYEA See also Bicauyea
  Mary Ann, 131

-C-

CADWELL Julia A., 106
CADY
  Argalus, 25
  Asa, 23, 61, 93, 103
  Atlanta, 93
  Daniel, 57
  Daniel B., 18

CHUBBUCK, *continued*
  S. W., 113
CLARK, 76
  Asabel, 66
  Celina, 71
  Content, 49
  Deborah, 19
  Elder, 53
  Ephriam, 53
  Esther, 106
  George, 129
  H. C., 77
  Harry, 22
  J. C., 118
  J. V. H., 83
  John, 84
  Mariah, 40
  Martin, 94
  Mary, 39
  Norman, 71
  Oliver, 19, 27, 65,
    75, 79
  Rev., 50, 53, 118, 123
  Ruth, 64
  Sarah Helen, 83
  Sheldon P., 86
  Solomon, 106
  Sylvester, 80
  T. L., 121, 129
  Thomas, 64, 73
  Warren, 19
  William, 79, 87, 104,
    105, 108
  William J., 127
CLARKE
  Abigail J., 129
  Mary Anne, 78
  Norman, 71
  Rev., 68, 94
  Salina, 71
  William, 76, 78, 80,
    82, 87, 88(2), 92,
    95, 99, 100, 110,
    111(2), 112, 113,
    115(2), 119(2)
CLARY Joseph, 15
CLAY
  Hariett E., 116
  Mary, 80
CLEVELAND
  B. F., 123
  Grover, 73
  Rev., 67, 73
CLIGBEE David, 17
CLOCK Catharine, 83
CLOUGH
  Maria Louisa, 92
  Mary T., 100
  Walter, 100
  William, 92
CLOVER Benjamin F., 34
CLOYES

  Micajah, 128
  Myraetta, 127
  Zeba, 127
  Ziba, 136
CLUTE Geradus, 15
COAKLEY Cornelius, 28
COATES E. S., 109
COATS
  Ann, 101
  C., 54
COBB
  Alfred, 126
  Caroline Fay, 121
  E. Henry, 124
  Ebenezer, 60
  Frederick H., 124
  H. H., 128
  Harvey J., 123
  Henry H., 121
  Henry J., 46
  Henry S., 72
  Jerusha, 72
  Mary B., 46
  Oliver, 121
  Rebecca B., 128
  Sarah M., 124
COBBETT Sarah, 137
COBURN
  John Mason, 123
  Paul, 100
COCHRAN Anna, 122
COE Rev., 30
COFFIN
  Caleb, 26
  Jane Amelia, 26
  Maranda E., 94
COLE
  Albert, 15
  Isaac, 85
  Orissa J., 100
  Vincent, 121
COLEGROVE
  George, 108, 109, 118
COLFAX Ebenezer, 77
COLGROVE
  George, 116, 122
  Rev., 102
COLLIER
  Isaac, 21
  John, 44, 95
  Maria, 21
COLLINS D. B., 127
COLMAN Aannah ?, 126
COLTER James, 86
COLTON Melza, 33
COLVARD
  Asa, 16
  Clarine Amelia, 16
COLYER
  Isaac, 90
  Mary, 82
  Peter, 82

DEVOLVE
  Jane, 98
DEWEY
  A. P., 90, 131
  Elder, 109
  Elura, 131
  George, 69
  Henry, 37
  Margaretta, 20
  Mary Ann, 37, 38
  Orluna, 90
DEWING William H., 48
DEWITT
  Christopher, 38, 110
  Elizabeth, 97
  James, 24
  John, 15, 41, 97(2)
  Laney, 97
  M. A., 83
  Mrs., 15
  Nicolaus, 100
  William, 37
DEXTER
  Charlotte, 102
  Sara, 104
DICKERSON
  Charlotte, 17
  Thomas, 31
DICKINSON
  Rebecca, 25
  Thomas, 72
DIDAMA J. E., 93
DIES
  G. H., 97
  Margaret A., 97
DIKEMAN Czar, 58
DILLON Patrick, 17
DIMMICK K. H., 79
DIXON Julia A., 133
DOCKSTADER Leonard, 26
DODGE
  David, 102
  Frederick, 95
  Orville, 108
  Ossian E., 102
  Philomen, 119
DOMINICK David, 90
DONALDSON
  Alexander, Jr., 111
  Evalina, 111
DONALSON Alonzo, 70
DOOLITTLE
  E., 24
  Francis M., 115
  Franklin, 51
DORMAN Eunice, 19
DOTY Vashti, 34
DOUGLAS
  Nancy P., 18
  Rev., 96
  Zebulon, 18
DOUGLASS

Amelia, 70
Eliza, 32
Horatio Gates, 120
Jane, 76
John, 83
Polly G., 25
Zebulon, 25, 32, 98
DOWNER
  A. P., 47
  Abner P., 62, 66
  Abner Riddle, 116
  George E., 116
  Harriet L., 37
  John, 108
  N. Marion, 116
  Rachel, 62
DOXTADER
  Henry, 57
  Leonard, 53
  Mrs., 53
DOXTATOR Emeline, 35
DRAKE F. T., 93, 124
DREW James, 69
DRUMMOND D. G., 135
DRYER Matilda L., 53
DUEL Amanda, 105
DUNBAR Helen M., 83
DUNCAN John, 79
DUNHAM
  Albert T., 15
  Mary Ann, 15
  Samuel, 15
DUNN Richard, 62
DUNNING Rev., 73
DURFEE Frances M., 79
DURKEY Justus, 23
DUTCHER Benjamin, 107
DWIGHT
  A., 65
  Almon, 61
  Dr., 108
  Sereno E., 115
DWINELLE
  Justin, 118
  Susan, 118
DYGART James, 38

-E-

EARL Enoch W., 23
EARLES Sarah W., 88
EARLL Thomas, 119
EASTERBROOK
  James, 73
  Mary, 24
  Nicholas, 60
EASTWOOD Henrietta, 68
EATON
  Amos, 64
  G. W., 110, 114(2)
  George W., 104, 116
  Lucina, 18

EATON, *continued*
  Sophia, 31
EDDY
  John, 19
  L. A., 85, 134
EDGERTON
  Isaac H., 63
  Wealthy, 115
EDWARDS Aaron, 78
EGGABROAD Henry, 103
EGGLESTON
  Enos, 59
  Lydia M., 21
  Wilkerson, 29
EHLE
  Abram, 45
  Ann, 33
  Betsey, 55
  Catharine, 84, 134
  Catherine, 18, 73
  Charlotte, 47, 48
  David, 20, 50
  George, 29, 33, 47(2),
    48, 56, 114, 135
  Hannah, 124
  Henry, 25, 40, 59
  Hiram, 30, 68
  Irene, 29
  James C., 45
  Jane, 115
  John P., 50, 54
  Lany, 40
  Lucinda, 41
  Maria, 25
  Olive, 59
  Oliver, 117
  Peter, 124
  Peter H., 90
  Peter P., 68, 89
  Robert, 107
  Sophia, 56
EICKART John, 15
ELDRIDGE Elizabeth M., 126
ELLIS
  Aldin C., 129
  Eli A., 34
ELLISON Christopher, 26
ELMER Jane E., 132
ELMS
  Charlotte, 58
  Mr., 58
EMERY Betsey, 77
EMMONS Henry, 87
ENGLISH Jacob, 31
EVANS
  Jane, 17
  John, 28, 57
  S. C., 59
  Susan, 57
EVERSON John Charles, 26

FAIRBANKS William M., 105
FAIRBORN Delia, 44
FAIRCHILD Tench, 122
FAIRMAN Hamilton R., 25
FARGO Simon, 67
FARLEY Clarissa, 67
FARMER Thomas, 85
FARNHAM
  Catherine, 17
  Sarah, 69
FAY
  Almira, 22
  Jonas, 18, 33
  Mary J., 18
  Nahum, 22
FEASENMYER Margarette, 87
FELT
  Emmaline, 45
  Emmaline Elizabet, 45
  Norris, 45
FERAND Sally, 20
FINCH Alphus, Jr, 50
FINK
  Christian, 19
  Ichabod, 69
  Jacob, 50
  John, 22
  Josiah, 46
  Mary E., 119
  William, 136
FINNEY
  John, 76
  Sylvia, 76
FIPPEN Elder, 49
FISH Hamilton, 95
FISHER
  Frances Elizabeth, 100
  Samuel, 74
  William E., 100
FISK
  Theophilus, 118
  William E., 73
FITCH
  Erastus, 84
  Mrs., 130
FLARDING Dianthe, 17
FLEMING
  Harriet, 81
  John, 81
FLING Mercy M., 103
FLINT
  C. N., 107
  Calvin, 105
  Sally Ann, 105
  Sarah M., 107
FOAT Samuel, 44
FOLLET George, 24
FONDA
  Christopher Y., 24
  Harriet, 23

-G-

GALE William H., 62, 110, 125
GARDINER
  Harry C., 128
  Margaret Elizabet, 99
  Mary E., 93
  Perry G., 99
GARDNER
  Calcina P., 54
  Palmer, 73
GARLOCK
  Isaac, 64
  Nancy, 64
  Obadiah, 130
  William, 64
GARVEY Mara, 66
GASQUOINE S., 83
GASTON
  Albert S., 132
  David, 132
  Hervey, 81
  Martha, 81
  Ward L., 81
GATES
  Daniel, 40
  Ira H., 132
  Jeremiah, 35
  Judge, 44
  Silas, 107
GAUT Elizabeth, 131
GAY Rev., 117
GEER Ebenezer, 96
GIDLEY
  Anna Maria, 67
  Nicholas, 39
  Susanna, 60
GILBERT
  F. Henry, 100
  Harriet, 56
  Lucius, 34
  Samuel, 15
  Theodocia, 120
  William, 56
GILL Sumner, 105
GILLET E. J., 88, 96
GILLETT
  E. J., 96
  Emeline, 96
  Truman, 106
GILLSON Robert D., 119
GILMAN Ira, 98
GLIDDEN Samuel, 85
GOFF Leonard, 87
GOODELL Rev., 36
GOODEN Lorenzo F., 97
GOODING
  Kate Maria, 125
  Lorenzo, 125
  Margaret A., 125
GORDON Lorin, 127
GOULD James F., 39

GRALEY
  A. A., 77, 97, 116
  Rev., 129
GRANGER
  Elvira, 39
  Otis P., 39
GRANT
  Caroline, 21
  Ebenezer, 83
  George, 21, 83
  Oliver, 27
GRAVES
  Elisha, 86
  Louisa, 86
  Rebecca, 63
GRAY Caroline, 116
GRAYLEY A. A., 94
GREELY
  Arthur Young, 98
  Horace, 98
  Mary Y. C., 98
GREEN
  Amos, 126
  Emeline, 104
  Jeremiah, 104
  John, 107
  Lurancy E., 126
  Samuel F., 27
  Sarah, 65
  William, Jr., 117
GREENE
  Beriah, 71
  Rev., 57
GREENWAY John, 93
GREENWOOD
  George B., 66
  Henry, 74
GREGG Rev., 35, 39
GREGORY
  Henry, 84
  Rev., 62
GREGORY & BARTON, 23
GRENOLDS Stephen M., 20
GREY John, 21
GRIDLEY
  Marietta S., 65
  Martha, 127
  Rev., 38
  S. N., 89
GRIFFIN
  Charles N., 94
  Daniel, 37
GRIFFITHS J. Q., 126
GRIGGS
  Elvira, 87
  Flora, 89
  Ichabod, 72
  Wells, 89
GRINNELL
  Cornelia, 81
  Joseph, 81

GRISWOLD
  E. E., 71
  Henriette, 118
GROAT
  Hannah, 86
  Milton, 125
GROESBECK
  Hannah, 92
  Peter, 92
  Walter, 92
GROSVENOR
  Caroline M., 41
  E. O., 41
  Ebenezer O., 28
  Harriet, 28
  Mary Ann, 28
GROVE
  Adam, 109
  Catharine, 109
  John, 21
GROVER   George, 76
GROVES
  Avery, 101
  John, 101
GUILE   Mary Ann, 43
GUITEAU   Kendrick N., 110
GULLIVER   George, 124

-H-

HACKLEY
  Charles, 86
  George, 78
HADCOCK
  John, 130
  Nancy, 130
HADLEY
  Catharine A. Grov, 109
  Edward B., 51
  R. H., 67
HAGER   Ann, 40
HAIGHT
  Amy Maria, 36
  Caroline H., 124
  Charlotte, 58
  Cornelia, 93
  Esther, 99
  George, 111
  H., 57
  James Thompson, 63
  John W., 47, 63
  Julia A., 63
  Maria, 43
  Reuben, 17
  Sophie, 37
  William H., 93
HAILING   Pauline J., 116
HALE   Jane A., 83
HALL
  Adeline, 55, 75
  Albro, 55, 75, 84,
    107, 130

Asabel, 65
Belinda, 84
Betsey, 65, 96
Catherine Jane, 104
Charles R., 113
Chloe, 65
Daniel, 120
Elisha, 52
Eliza Ann, 25
George, 105
H. C., 104
Harvey W., 63
Helen Maria, 55
Hiram, 43
Mariam, 36
Nathaniel, 25
Sara A., 118
Sergeant, 96
HAMBLIN
  Harriet, 66
  Mary, 108
HAMILTON
  Elijah, 23
  Joseph, 78
HAMLET   Benjamin, 43
HAMLIN   Minerva, 96
HAMMOND
  Elizabeth, 96
  H. L., 114
  Julia, 134
  Marcus R., 100
  Matilda, 100
  S. E., 96
  William, 100
HANDY
  A., 61, 62, 63
  Rev., 62
HARBOTTLE
  Anna S., 121
  Helen, 123
  Joseph, 121, 123
HARDER   Benjamin, 135
HARGART
  John, 125
  Matilda, 125
HARMAN   Jane, 80
HARMON
  E. R., 106
  Rev., 106
HARPER   Samuel, 59
HARRINGTON
  Daniel B., 51
  Eliza, 24
  Flora, 112
  Henrietta S., 112
  J. S., 69
  Jerry S., 112
  John, 24
  M., 86
  Mr., 70
  Perez D., 57
  Rachel, 77

153

HITCHCOCK, *continued*
  Horace D., 44
  Sarah F., 89
HOARD Susan, 135
HOBERT Alphonso, 116
HODGE
  H. P., 98
  Harrison, 89
  Harvey Bradley, 123
HOES
  Catherine Anne, 34
  John C. F., 34, 35,
    37, 39, 79
  Louisa Antoinette, 79
  Lucy Maria, 79
  Peter I., 34
HOFFMAN Cornelius, 29
HOGER
  Anson, 27
  Harriet, 27
HOLBERT Allen, 77
HOLBROOK
  Charlotte, 58
  Lucinda, 105
  Russell L., 116
  Sarah, 105, 111
  Seymour, 95, 105
  Solomon C., 22
HOLLISTER
  Ariann C., 113
  Mary, 57
  Rev., 34
  Sarah M., 57
HOLMES
  D., 96, 105
  Daniel, 101
  Hannah, 30
  Hannah Mariah, 90
  Harriet, 66
  Ira, 28
  Jonas, 22
  Lewis L., 56
  Lydia, 136
  Mahala, 31
  Mary S., 118
  Milton, 41
  Olive, 106
  Rev., 107
  Richard, 48
  Ruhan, 18
  Seth, 59
  William, 28
HOMES
  Daniel, 105
  Eunice, 80
HOOD
  Benjamin L., 45
  Elizabeth, 126
  Henry, 36
  James, 84
  Jane, 71
  Mary Ann, 71

  William, 24
HOOKER Henry T., 46
HOPKINS
  Almena D., 97
  Barton M., 109
  Charles H., 97
  Esther, 35
HOPPER A. M., 110
HORNED Benjamin, 68
HORNER Sarah, 54
HORTON A. Almene, 101
HOTCHKISS
  A., 47
  Hannah, 79
  Henry, 79
  Susan E., 78
HOTEL
  Abel Wood's, 80
  Balch's, 69
  Cazenovia House, 88,
    99(2), 115
  City Hotel, 101
  Eagle Hotel, 130
  Eagle Tavern, 84, 95
  Elm-House, 113
  French & Severanc, 97
  H. Judd's, 84
  Judd's, 74
  Lincklaen House, 81,
    95, 105
  Oneida Railroad H, 113
  Park House, 115
  Sulphur Spring Ho, 114
  Toby House, 134
HOUGH
  J. T., 32
  James T., 30
  Rev., 33
HOUGHTAILING Jacob, 45
HOUGHTON Rev., 66
HOUSE
  C. L., 108
  Editha, 27
  Norris, 96
  Rebecca M., 111
  Rev., 37
HOUSTON
  Rev., 74
  T., 65, 66(2), 68(2),
    70(2), 72, 74
  Thomas, 63
HOVEY Horace M., 41
HOW
  David White, 48, 73
  Mary Anna, 73
HOWARD Harriet, 113
HOWE
  Calvin B., 111
  John, 99
  Rev., 77
HOWELL
  Jemima, 33

HOWELL, *continued*
  Mary, 28
  R., 28
HUBBARD
  M. Sanford, 73
  Martin A., 22
  Smedley, 22
HUBBELL   Cecelia, 43
HUFFMAN
  Catherine, 131
  Frederick, 131
HULBERT   Erastus, 51
HULL
  Henry, 128
  Henry V., 93
  Nancy A, 93
HUMISTON
  Asa, 133
  Aseph, 136
  Rhoda B., 133
HUMPHREY
  Mary, 80
  Maurice, 90
  Willis, 80
HUNT
  Benjamin F., 36
  Jonathan, 20
  Louisa, 15
  Montgomery, 40
HUNTINGTON
  E. A., 41(2), 42
  Horace F., 35
HUNTINTON E. A., 51
HUNTLEY   Betsey A., 128
HUNTLY   Esq., 41
HURD   Darwin E., 73
HURLBERT   Kellogg, 91
HUSTED   John N., 29
HUTCHINS
  Charles S., 42
  Eliza Ann, 50
  L., 50
HUTCHINSON   Amanda, 37
HUTTON   Rev., 104
HUYCK   P. J., 132
HYATT
  Aaron S., Jr., 122
  Clara, 54
  F. A., 113
  George W., 52
HYDE
  Oren, 41
  Orin, 43

-I-

INGHAM   William K., 134
INMAN   Sarah, 121
IRVING   Pierre P., 46
ISBELL   Hiram E., 129

-J-

JACKSON
  Abraham, 119
  Betsey, 29
  Susan R., 119
JAMES
  Lavina J., 127
  Thomas, 93
  Thomas L., 130
  William, 127
JENKINS
  Benjamin, 57
  J. W., 129
  J. Whipple, 33
  Timothy, 78
  Timothy Albert, 78
JENNINGS
  Moses, 69
  Mr., 68
JEPSON
  Eli, 119
  Miss, 119
JEROME
  Charles, 79
  George Henry, 79
JEWELL
  August G., 21
  Joseph H., 52
  Nancy, 95
  Oliver, 95
JEWETT   Malinda, 119
JOHNSON
  C. T., 88
  Caroline, 115
  Charles B., 77
  Christopher, 51
  Cordelia L., 83
  George J., 112
  Gilbert, 89
  Henry A., 116, 123
  James, 121
  Leonard, 66
  Lydia, 116
  W. C., 106
  William, 16, 18,
    22(2), 86
  Wm., 24
JONES
  Abigail Elizabeth, 99
  Ann, 54
  Charles, 54
  E. C., 100
  Edward, 31, 54
  Edward L., 50
  Elder, 52
  Isaac, 45
  Jonah, 46
  Mary Ann, 94
  Morey M., 132
  Rev., 27, 32
  Sarah, 31

JONES, *continued*
  William Tell, 53
JOY Celestia, 26
JUDD
  Harley, 77
  Lovila, 120
  Lucy A., 111
  Mabel, 21
  S. Corning, Jr., 127
  Silas, 49, 56
  Silas, 2nd, 124
JUDSON A., 78
JUNE Henry D., 24

-K-

KASLER Catharine, 73
KASSON William, 65
KAWHISS Peter, 46
KEELER
  Harvey L., 84
  Pamelia, 39
KEENE
  Louisa, 57
  Samuel A., 57
KEENEY Maevin, 134
KELLER Alvin, 59
KELLEY Luther, 64
KELLOGG
  Aaron, 54, 69
  Betsey Jane, 68
  Charles, 112
  Horace B., 97
  James, 28
  Maria, 115
  Walter, 97, 100
KELLUM C. B., 72
KELLY Polly, 67
KELOGG Anson G., 92
KELTON Delia, 121
KELTS Rachael, 127
KENDRICK
  Cordelia C., 81
  N., 78, 81
  Nathaniel, 81
KENEDY G. N., 76
KENNEDY
  Betsy, 16
  David, 107
  James P., 97
  Mary, 17
  Samuel, 94, 97
  William W., 73, 107
KENNEY Sarah Ann, 82
KENT
  James, 47
  Sarah Maria, 47
KENYON Catharine, 117
KILBORN Jesse, 49, 65
KILTS George, 83
KIMBALL John, 18
KINGSLEY Washington, 59

KINKAID Melinda, 76
KINNE James, 66
KIRKLAND
  Edward, 27
  General, 27
KNAPP Rev., 37
KNIGHT Rodolphus E., 30
KNOEPFEL William H., 121
KNOLAN Thomas, 18
KNOLLIN
  Rhoda, 24
  Richard, 24
KNOWLES
  Charles, 20, 21
  Henry R., 128
  Isaac, 17
  J., Jr., 53
  James, 53, 118, 122
  John, 31, 50(2), 52,
    82, 87, 109(3)
  John. Jr., 55
  Joshua C., 132
  Judge, 46
  Lucy, 52
  Mary A., 50
  Mary Jane, 55, 109
  Sally, 50
  Sarah F., 53
  Sarah M., 122
  Sophronia, 118
  Zevia, 53
KNOWLIN James, 18
KNOWLTON
  Caroline, 80
  Dean, 38
  Edmund, 80
  Esther A., 80
  William, 44
KNOX
  Harman, 60
  Olivia M., 86
  Rev., 68

-L-

LACY E. E., 113
LAIRD Elihu, 80
LAKE Delos, 83
LAMB
  B. Franklin, 127
  Jacob, 88
  Lovicy D., 65
  Martin, 80
  Martin E., 127
  Mary T., 88
  N. B., 65, 74, 127
  Nathan, 22
  Nathan B., 127
  Stephen G., 67
LAMPHERE Vaulkert, 79
LAND Helen S., 106
LANDERS Phebe, 51

157

MAY
  Luke, 116
  Sarah, 116
MAYHEW Sarah, 95
MAYO A. J., 29
MEAD
  Caroline M., 88
  John Wallace, 40
  O., 88
  S. S., 130
MEADE Myra, 34
MECOMBER
  B., 50
  Joseph C., 50
MEDCALF John, 42
MEEKER Lucien, 36
MENDENHALL Rev., 113
MENZEE Laura Jane, 93
MERRILL Henry A., 83
MESSINGER
  Almon C., 100
  I. Newton, 100
  John A., 27
METCALF
  Asenath, 72, 77
  John, 72, 77
  Sarah Ann, 72
  Sophia Jane, 77
MIERS John J., 24
MILLER
  Charles Dudley, 71
  Joseph, 26
  Lucy J., 63
  Martha, 40
MILLIOU
  Julia Ann, 132
  William, 132
MILLS
  Correll H., 42
  James R., 97
  Jane, 51
  Rebecca, 54
  Susan, 69
MINER
  Erastus, 118
  James, 131
MITCHEL Spencer, 53
MITCHELL
  Ann, 49
  David, 16
  John, 80
  Laura, 49
  Polly, 59
MIX S. Hosack, 99
MOFFIT George, 130
MONK
  Catherine, 82
  Mary A., 85
MONROE
  George I., 66
  Jesse, 36
  Jonas A., 80

  Melinda, 36
MONTAGUE
  O., 40
  Oreb, 30
MONTROSE John, Jr., 83
MOON Amanda A., 134
MOORE
  Betsey, 31
  Catharine, 94
  Franklin, 31
  Michael, 70
  W. H., 121
MOOT Daniel B., 18
MORANGE M., 48
MOREY
  Daniel S., 72
  William, 134
MORGAN
  Alfred B., 56
  Joseph E., 118
  Mary, 42
MORGEN Elder, 43
MORRELL
  Jane, 23
  L., 27
  Stephen, 27
MORRIS
  Adeline, 119
  John Cox, 95
  Lewis, 95
  Polly E., 48
MORRISON
  Alex, 75
  Elizabeth, 64
  William, Jr., 64
MORSE
  Abner, 39
  Edward P., 83
  Lodema, 92
  Rev., 132
  William, 72
MORTON
  J. T., 91
  Rev., 130
  Robert B., 87
MORY Charles, 131
MOSELY Vashti, 79
MOSS Mary, 17
MOTT
  Eliza, 114
  John, 114
MOULTER
  Charlotte D., 128
  David, 37
  Harriet, 107, 119
  Jacob, 24
  James, 41
  M., 107, 128
  Mary Ann, 24
  Peter, 119
  Serena, 37
MOWER Almira, 34

MOWERS Mrs., 75
MOYER
  Catharine, 30
  Daniel, 36
  Elijah, 68
MUNROE
  Elizabeth, 72
  Helen Elizabeth, 72
  Jonas A., 52, 72
  William, 53
MUNSON
  Charles, 117
  Esther J., 117

MURPHY
  Michael, 119
  Thomas, 135
MURRAY
  Allen, 56
  Archibald, 59
MYERS
  Clara Ann, 24
  John, 90
  Mary Jane, 81, 90
  Peter, 55
  William H., 20
MYRICK
  L., 28, 43
  Luther, 62, 70
  Thomas S., 64

-N-

NASH
  Caroline M., 92
  Evelyn A., 115
  Fidelia, 129
NEELY
  A., 39, 41
  Albert, 37
NELLIS
  Eliza, 18
  John I. D., 18
NELLIUS Katrina Elizabet, 100
NELLY A., 33
NELSON William, 23
NEW
  James, 85
  Sarah, 85
  Simeon P., 85
NEWELL W., 96
NICHOLAS A. S., 98
NICHOLS
  A. S., 103
  Alex Seth, 111
  D. R., 106
  George W., 126
  James, 73, 113
  Joseph, 131
  M., 97
  Marion, 103
  Riley L., 115

  Sophia, 98
  William R., 111
NICHOLSON Elder, 42
NICKERSON
  Amanda, 33
  J., 112
  Maria L., 112
NIFFEN Hannah, 63
NIMS
  A., 32
  Asa, 34
NINE Rev., 42

NOBLES
  Royal, 122
  Sarah, 122
NOLTON H., 82
NORRIS
  Abigail, 44
  Nancy, 46
NORTH
  F. L., 29
  Julia Ann, 48
NORTHRUP
  B., 21(3), 22, 30, 33
  Elizabeth M., 77
  Rev., 17, 19
NORTON
  Almira, 125
  Edward, 70, 125
  John N., 72
  Lyman, 121
  Orwin R., 49
  Rev., 130
  S. H., 113
NOTT Eliphalet, 66
NOURSE Sarah, 117
NOYES William, 66
NYE
  Helen J., 130
  Thomas C., 130

-O-

OAKES
  Caroline M., 117
  Mary Elizabeth, 103
  William, 103, 117
O'FARREL M., 59
O'FARRELL D. M. D., 59
OLCOTT
  Charlotte, 29
  Mary, 20
OLDS
  Ira M., 18
  Rev., 19
OLIN Eliza Ann, 63
OLIPHANT
  Eliza A., 35
  Esther R., 66
  R. W., 35, 66
  Robert W., 69, 71

ONEIDA Valley, 82
ONION
  Catherine, 49
  William, 64
ORCUTT Elizabeth, 125
ORR Margaret, 124
ORVIS J. R., 113
OSBORN Elizabeth, 37
OSGOOD Jennie S., 112
OSTERHOUT Sally, 45
OSTRANDER
  Caty Ann, 58
  Jacob, 35
OTIS John, 29
OTTAWAY James, 128
OVERHIZER
  Abigail, 74
  Conrad, 54, 55, 74
  James, 74
  Mary, 54
OWEN
  Albert C., 120
  Amanda M., 120
  Catherine, 46
  Josiah P., 124
OWENS
  Catherine, 26
  David, 26, 53
  David E., 123
  James W., 30
  Jane, 53

-P-

PACK Caleb, 40
PACKARD Catharine, 73
PACKER Emeline, 79
PADDOCK
  B., 25, 49
  B. G., 44, 114
  Elder, 37(2), 52
  Rev., 23, 96
  Sophia R., 104
  Z., 47, 48
PAGE Betsey, 136
PALMER
  A. H., 57
  Amelia, 60
  C. G., 16
  Elisha, 22
  Fidelia W., 57
  Harriet C., 61
  Henry, 23
  Henry D., 61
  Joshua J., 67
  Julia A., 110
  Lovice, 22
  Maria, 67
  Mary, 120
  Mary M., 56
  N., 129
  N. H., 60

Nelson, 126
Newton, 85
Sandford B., 56
W. L., 123
William H., 58, 84
PALMETER Lucia Maria, 52
PARAZOO Silvenus, 122
PARDEE Harriet Ann, 96
PARK
  Sarah, 77
  William J., 128
PARKELL Nancy A., 129
PARKER
  A., 51
  Aaron, 53, 136
  Sarah A., 114
PARKHURST Alice, 22
PARKILL George, 65
PARKS Thomas, 68
PARMALEE
  Charles, 48, 68
  G. R., 65
  George R., 40
  Homer W., 30
  Jane Hearsey, 65
  Moses, 30
PARMALEE & DUNHAM, 15
PARMELEE
  Charles, 43
  Charles Monroe, 26
  Harriet M., 77
  M., 26
  Martha A., 43
  Moses, 135
  Sarah, 135
PARMER William, 136
PARRY Elihu, 134
PARSONS John, 95, 103
PARTRIDGE Truman, 67
PATRICK
  Amos F., 15
  Jacob, 107
PATTEN John N., 81
PATTERSON Julia A., 99
PAYNE
  Betsey, 104
  Samuel, 104
PAYSON Elizabeth, 120
PEABODY
  Ann, 75
  Ephriam, 81
  Rev., 102
PEARCE Rev., 15
PEARSON William, 129
PEASE See also Pise
  Henry C., 88
  Rev., 64
PECK
  Betsey M., 66
  Deborah, 25
  Elder, 20
  Hannah, 39

PECK, *continued*
  James, 31, 63(2)
  John, 90, 103
  John R., 126
  Linus M., 81, 91
  Martha M., 118
  Philetus, 91
  Sarah, 90
PECKHAM James, 56
PENNOCK
  David, 124
  Ebenezer, 101
  Simeon, 25
PERKINS
  Fanny, 34
  William S., 41
PERRY
  Amanda H., 40
  Caroline Slidel, 102
  Cornelia B., 56
  Electa, 29
  Elizabeth G., 48
  George T., 32, 40, 42,
    48, 56
  George T., Jr., 94
  H., 17
  Henry, 17, 29
  Hiram, 82
  M. C., 102
  Melinda, 32
PERSONS
  Adelia Ann, 80
  Charles, 121
PETERS John, 76
PETRIE T. F., 131
PETTES John, 53
PETTIBONE J. C., Jr., 114
PETTIS Warren S., 115
PETTY Oliver C., 33
PHELPS
  Margaret, 97
  W. S., 119
PHILLIPS
  Albert J., 93
  Ann, 130
  Elmira C., 73
  Henry, 19
  Jonathan P., 73
  Lewis, 86
  Margaret, 27
  Nancy, 78
PICKUP John, 40
PIERSONS
  Anson, 74
  Clarissa, 74
  Josiah, 74
PINNEY Ann, 64
PISE
  D., 109
  David, 83, 105
PIXLEY
  Ann, 107

  Charles J., 108
  Isaac, 107
  J. B., 77, 84
PLACE J. A., 120
PLANCK Marcus L., 94
PLANK
  Harriet M., 81
  J. B., 81
  Joseph B., 133
PLATO
  Alexander F., 98
  Marian B., 98
PLATT Rev., 91
PLATTO Frederick, 110
PLUMB George, 82
PLUMBLY Jane A., 112
POE Mary Ann, 100
POLK James K., 101
POOLE Byron, 91
POPPLE Nancy, 107
PORTER
  Asahel L., 122
  Betsey, 58
  Chester H., 105
  Margaret, 31
  Mary, 85
  William, 60
POTTER
  Abigail, 97
  Emily, 22
  J., 111
  Job, 115, 119
  Rev., 66
  T., 125
  Warren, 128
POUND Jesse, 40
POWELL Rev., 27
POWERS
  Julia C., 88
  Sidney A., 90
POWESLAND George, 24
POWLSLAND Grace, 20
PRALL William H. H., 104
PRATT
  Allison, 85
  Angeline F., 73
  Ashley, 104
  Edward Fitch, 109
  Frederick, 73
  Matthew, 85
  Rev., 112
PRENTESS Elcina D., 114
PRENTICE Herman V., 56
PRICE David, 25
PRIEST
  Amanda, 34
  William, 16
PROD P. A., 20
PROSSER L., 108
PUTNAM
  Daniel, 87, 99
  Rev., 70

-Q-

QUACKENBUSH
Eliza, 22
Eliza Ann, 37
Henrietta, 72
Isaac, 43
Isaac Henry, 43
Mary, 107, 127
Mary A., 43
Nancy, 123
Polly, 24
Richard, 55
Solomon, 128
QUICK Maria, 83

-R-

R___ C___, 89
RAMSEY William, 20
RAND
Asa, 93
Rev., 76
William W., 73
RANDAL Elder, 49
RANDALL
B. F., 75
C. H., 83
Elizabeth, 34, 41
Jirah, 41
Lucy Maria, 39
Minerva, 84
Nicholas P., 37
Rev., 45
Roswell, 39
Warren, 73
RANISER Elizabeth, 125
RANSIER
Dolly, 23
John, 16
John J., 44
Jonathan, 133
Maria, 16
Rachel, 23
Wid., 67
RANSOM
Betsey, 98
E., 19
L. D., 99
RATNIER Eliza, 23
RATNOUR Henry H., 91
RAWSON David, 129
RAY
Gershom, 75
Lydia, 31
Polly, 36
William, 32
RAYMOND
Ann Eliza, 120
Asa, 120
Elisha, 117
Rev., 94

S. W., 99, 104, 107
REALS
Hubbard, 87
James G., 109(2)
REDDISH Helen A., 44
REDFIELD
Rev., 68
William H., 91
REED Almira, 86
REELS
James, 48
Mariah, 121
REEVE Silas G., 104
REID L. N., 130
REMINGTON Rev., 129
REYNOLDS
Elisha, 34
Ephriam R., 62
Margaret, 27
Richard, 27
RHODES Esther, 103
RIANT Elvira, 63
RICE
Eleazor, 37
Jane E., 113
Lydia, 73
Mandrack, 45
Maranda, 70
Mirrick, 101
Susan, 73
RICHARDS
Asenath, 42
Ezra, 113
Mary, 74
Sarah, 93
RICHARDSON
John, 99
Levi, 132
Maria L., 132
Mary S., 124
RICHIE George, 16
RICHMAN Adeline, 117
RICHMOND
Edmonia Virginia, 101
Edmund, 101(2)
J. B., 126
N., 60
Nathan P., 122
RIDDLE
Charlotte, 57
David, 120
Frances, 57
Henrietta, 69
Nancy, 120
Robert, 26, 57, 69
Sophia, 40
Thomas, 40
Thompson, 45
RIDER
Celestia M., 112
J., 87

SIVER
  David H., 76
  George, 94
SKANK Mary E., 56
SKEDMORE Martha A., 120
SKELDING Rheua, 118
SKELLINGER Mary A., 68
SKINNER
  Dolphus, 75
  Elder, 36
  H. C., 39
SLINGERLAND
  E., 29(2), 30
  Jacob, 34
  Rev., 26
  Sophia, 34
SLOAN Andrew S., 70
SLOCUM Joseph W., 87
SMART C. W., 91
SMITH
  A., 38
  A. P., 126
  Allen, 102
  Amanda, 102
  Ambrose, 86
  Amelia, 126
  Caroline, 92
  Catherine, 35
  David, 66
  Eleanor D., 33
  Elizabeth, 71
  Ellen, 122
  Febra, 92
  George, 114
  George C., 61
  Gerrit, 41, 71
  Harriet, 18
  Harry, 92
  Henry, 98
  Hibbard, 131
  John, 33
  John J., 21
  Judge, 122
  Lucretia, 18
  Lyman, 25
  Mary A., 33
  Morgan L., 99
  N. S., 18
  Nathan, 126
  Nathaniel S., 19
  Orrin, 39
  Peter, 41
  Philip, 101
  Rev., 15, 20, 22
  S. R., 33
  Spencer, 96
SMITHSON Reuben, 93
SMITZEL J., 53
SMITZEN Elder, 22
SMITZER
  Elder, 24
  John, 78, 81, 112

  Rev., 55(2)
SNELL
  Frederick I., 28
  Hannah, 28
  Josiah, 22, 58
  Mary Ann, 37
SNOW
  John, 126
  P. H., 109
SNYDER
  H., 23(2)
  H. S., 24
SOMMERS See also Summers
  C. G., 33, 49, 71, 73
  Charles G., 48, 81,
    128
  Sarah L., 71
SOPER
  Chauncey, 80
  George, 28
  Philo, 80
  Sidney N., 23
SOUTHWARD Thomas, 20
SPAFFORD L. C., 126
SPAULDING
  Adelia, 33
  Levi, 33
  Rev., 22
  Silas, 65, 114
SPENCER
  Charles A., 46
  Henry F., 28
  Israel S., 51, 54
  Joseph, 133
  Mary Jane, 54
  Thomas, 107
  W. H., 100
  William, 86, 107
  William H., 101
SPRAGUE
  Hannah B., 64
  Rev., 15
SPRING Susan, 36
STAFFORD
  A. T., 114
  Fidelia, 77
  Mary, 127
STALKER
  Alexander, 61
  Margaret, 61
STANDARD Erastus, 53
STANLEY
  Gratia E., 132
  L. H., 75
  Rev., 59, 72
STANNARD Oriann, 94
STANTON
  F. H., 90
  George W., 99
  Sidney, 34
STARKWEATHER J. W., 131

STARR
  Mary, 59
  Seth, 59, 72, 91
  William, 54
  William D., 72
STATE Bridge, 82
STEARNS Phebe, 22
STEBBINS
  Alice, 111
  Edward, 108, 111
  J. H., 78
  L. D., 132
  Lydia S., 111
STEELE George, 54
STEPHENS
  Harriet S., 105
  John, 24
STERLING George, 43
STERN
  Elijah, 29
  Sarah Antonett, 29
STERNE Curtis, 38
STEVENS
  Ann Elizabeth, 119
  William H., 79
STEVENSON Col., 79
STEWART
  A. B., 77
  John, 127
  Juliette, 129
  Mary Ann, 105
  William, 127
STICKNEY
  Rev., 89
  W., 82, 90
  Washington, 94, 110,
    122
STILLMAN
  Harriet, 104
  Prof., 104
STILLWELL
  Mary, 46
  S., 46
STILWELL
  Emily, 125
  Harry, 134
  Henry, 125
  Sarah Jane, 30
STOCKTON Rev., 15
STOCKWELL Eunice, 107
STODDARD Thaddeus, 42
STOKES
  Rev., 64
  Sarah, 15
STONE
  Elisha P., 98
  Elmira, 103
  Emerson, 76
  Flavilla, 130
  Huldah Jane, 94
  Lester, 39
  Mrs., 98

Sally, 45
Sarah, 55
Sylvia, 115
STORMES George, 86
STORMS
  Ann, 32
  Sylvanus, 41
STORRS Sarah P., 83
STORY Amos L., 56
STOWEL John, 84
STOWELL Amasa, 134
STOWERS John G., 123
STREETER Thomas S., 67
STRONG
  Rev., 95
  Thomas, 17
  William M., 43
STUART Nancy, 60
STUYVESANT John R., 53
SUITS
  Benjamin, 16, 50
  Joseph, 50
  Mary Ann, 50
SUMMERS See also Sommers
  Charles, 127
  James Fellows, 127
SUNDERLAND
  Byron, 126
  Phebe, 69
  Phoebe, 26
SUNDERLIN
  David, 54, 74, 75
  Mary, 52
  Sarah, 74
  Sarah Sophia, 74
SUTHERLAND
  Hannah, 23
  Jerusha, 35
  Louisa, 16
  Silas, 32
  Silas G., 36
SWAN
  Alonzo E., 132
  E. L., 102, 107
  G., 101
  L. E., 78, 81, 90,
    92(3), 93, 94, 95,
    97(2), 98(2), 101,
    103, 106(2), 112,
    113(2), 114(2), 115,
    116, 119, 121, 127,
    132, 135
  L. E., Sr., 117
  L. F., 94
  Sarah Frances, 97
SWEET
  Adelia, 78
  Mary Ann, 18
  Royal, 95
  Royal B., 120
SWEETLAND Joseph, 34

167

168

TUTTLE, *continued*
  Grant, 121
  John, 58
  Margaret, 58
  Mary, 121
  R. A., 96
  Reuben, 85
  Rev., 44, 54
TWINING
  Jane, 128
  S. H., 135
TWIST Alpheus, 80
TWOGOOD W. D., 83
TYGART Rev., 44
TYLER
  John, 105
  Julia Gardiner, 105

-U-

UNDERWOOD Martha, 130

-V-

VAIL Nathaniel, 39
VALKENBURGH P., 87
VAN ALSTINE
  Andrew W., 27
  Elizabeth Ann, 27
  Martin, 34
VAN ANTWERP George W., 116
VANARSDALE Cornelius, 77
VAN BENSCHOTEN Mary, 111
VANDERKAR Helen M., 65
VANDERMAKER Rachel, 93
VANDEWORKER Daniel, 37
VANDUSEN Ezra, 134
VAN EPES Abraham, 133
VAN EPS Gordon, 133
VANEPPES William, 94
VAN HOOSER
  Ally, 95
  Asa D., 95
  Mary Elizabeth, 95
VAN HORN
  Jane, 26
  Stephen, 131
VANNEST John G., 76
VAN NORTHWICK Abigail, 32
VANNORTHWICK Henry C., 114
VAN RENSSELEAR Rensselear, 57
VANSCHARCK
  Harriet, 82
  John, 82
VANSLYKE Albert, 63
VAN VALKENBURG
  P., 22
  Peter, 92
  Philena, 22
VANVALKENBURG
  Gilbert Wessel, 92
VAN VALKENBURGH Richard, 33

VANVALKENBURGH
  & Boardman, 52
  Harriet, 18
  Loania, 92
  P., 16, 38
  Richard Henry, 16
VAN VECHTEN
  J., 25
  Sara, 51
VANVETCHEN
  Anna E., 51
  Rev., 51(2)
VANVLECK
  Andrew, 17
  Harmanus, 17, 19, 49
  Mary, 17
VAN VOAST
  Anna, 24
  James, 24
VANVOLKENBURGH Peter, 29
VANWIE
  Charlotte, 68
  Diantha, 45
  Dolly, 52
  Henry, 52, 121
VANWINKLE Julia A., 78
VARICK Richard, 16
VELASKO William, 79
VELASKOW William, 110
VERZELL Elizabeth, 133
VIBBARD Edwin, 52
VINTON Francis, 102
VOLATINE Lester, 102
VOLGELL H. C., 103
VONSCHOULTZ Neils, 48
VORHEES Martha, 104
VOSBURGH
  John, 17, 49, 119
  Malvina, 135
  William, 89
VROMAN James, 90

-W-

WADSWORTH
  Benjamin, 137
  E. L., 54
WAGER
  Alexander S., 121, 132
  Joseph S., 63
  Philip, 63, 127
  Susan J., 121
WAIT J ., Jr., 50
WALDEN John, 86
WALKER Clara, 87
WALLACE
  Isaac, 128
  Thomas D., 96
WALLER Thomas, 135
WALRATH
  & Bellamy, 66
  Abraham, 17

169

WALRATH, *continued*
Adelia, 90
Andrew, 99
Catherine, 32, 70
Elizabeth, 95
F., 83
Franklin W., 111
Henry I., 99
J., 76
J. L., 136
James, 66, 117
James J., 121
John H., 97
John I., 34, 84
Joseph H., 95
Magdalene, 133
Marcus C., 72
Marion, 83
Mary Ann, 44
Mary K., 136
Polly, 135
Richard, 95
Richard C., 134
Richard R., 123
Sarah, 84
William, 83
WALSON   T. J., 133
WALTER
Adam, 28
Daniel, 23
Michael, 23
WALTS   Polly, 23
WARD
Aaron, 134
Diana, 76
Heman D., 79
Mary L., 134
Olive, 64
WARE
Newman, 22
Sylvester, 18
WARNER
Asahel, 15
Daniel, 63
H., 103
H. G., 15, 61, 63
Horatio Gates, 44
Isaac, 71
Judge, 42
Maranda, 34
Maria R., 71
Rebecca, 63
Sarah, 15
Sarah S., 58
WARREN
Celestia, 25
Fanny Jane, 52
James, 39, 49
Lucy Ann, 112
Mary, 70
Sarah, 60
Sylvia, 66

WARRICK   Joshua C., 133
WATERBURY   Jane Maria, 102
WATERMAN   P. Jane, 50
WATKINS
Anne Alida, 28
John D., 28
WATSON
J., 60, 80
Reuben, 49
Sylvanus, 37
WATTLES   Sally, 59
WEAVER
Eugene, 99
Mary, 109(2)
Mary Jane, 99
P. O., 109(2)
Perry C., 55
Perry O., 99, 118
Philo C., 61
WEBB
Amelia, 35
John P., 71
Olive, 105
Solomon, 56
WEBBER
Julius S., 98
W., 48
WEBBER?   Peter, 90
WEBER
Rev., 92
W., 93
WEBLER   Peter, 90
WEBSTER
Abraham, 16
Austin S., 136
Jane A., 79
Randolph, 136
WEED
Silas, 81
Susan, 81
WEEDMAN   T. W., 116
WEEKS
Mariet, 42
Silas G., 91
WELCH
Martha, 76
Nicholas, 76
WELLES   Anna H., 94
WELLINGTON   Eli, 15
WELLS
A. J., 106
Amanda M., 26
Damon, 43
David M., 38
Harriet C., 16
J., 58
Jane, 133(2)
Jane E., 15
Job, 16, 26, 32, 35,
38, 114, 134
Joseph V., 57

WINCHELL   William, 115
WINTHROP   Robert C., 102
WINTON   Rev., 99
WOLIVER   Joseph, 37
WOOD
  Abel, 80, 109
  Merilla, 38
  Rev., 38
  Rosannah, 23
WOODFORD   Sarah, 50
WOODHULL   Agnes, 108
WOODIN   James, 117
WOODWARD   Jerome B., 40
WOODWIN   Emily O., 115
WOODWORTH
  Benjamin, 66
  Franklin, 77
  Jane, 92
  Louisa M., 15
  Luther, 20
  Luther G., 37
WOOLAVER   James, 23
WOOLEN   factory, 86
WOOLEY   E. N., 41
WOOLSEY   Melancthon, 46
WOOSTER   Barclay, 70
WORDEN
  Antha, 75
  Betsey, 35
  Eliza, 23
  Ira, 75, 136
  Jesse, 132
  Laura, 136
  Laura Frances, 136
WORMUTH   Jeremiah, 136
WRIGHT
  Adelia E., 54
  Chauncey, 61
  Elder, 108, 109, 127
  Hannah, 61
  Ira, 105
  J. Henry, 88
  James, 30
  L., 64, 74
  Lydia A., 44
  Lyman, 67
  Rev., 67, 80, 87, 109,
    128
WYKOFF   Mrs., 76
WYLIE   Sarah, 69
WYMAN   Mary E., 122

-Y-

YARTON See also Yorton
  Benjamin, 102
YATES
  A., 24, 32, 53
  A. J., 30
  Andrew, 30, 98, 118
  Andrew J., 18
  Ann, 62, 118

  Catharine, 61
  Charles, 61
  D., 25
  Edward, 26
  Henrietta, 64(2)
  Henry, 61
  J. A., 64
  J. Austin, 98
  J. B., 62
  Jane, 67
  John Austin, 64
  John B., 38, 41
  John G., 41, 67, 83
  Joseph C., 28, 41
  Julia, 97
  Margaret Elizabet, 83
  Mary A., 53
  Mary E., 81
  Mary Elizabeth, 48
  Rev., 15, 17(2), 18,
    20(2), 23, 26, 29, 30
  Rev. A., 15(2)
  Robert G., 26
  V. N., 26
  William Austin, 30
YOUNG
  David, 49
  Elizabeth, 109(2)
  Ezariah, 103
  Hiram, 131
  Johannes, 109
  Joseph, 30
  Marvin H., 131
  Rev., 118
  Sarah Ann, 19
  Susan B., 131
YOUNGS
  Electa, 101
  James, 121
YUNG See also Young
  Johannes, 106

172

www.ingramcontent.com/pod-product-compliance
Lightning Source LLC
Chambersburg PA
CBHW070919270326
41927CB00011B/2644